How To Beat the High Cost of College

Books by Claire Cox

The New-Time Religion

The Upbeat Generation

Rainy Day Fun for Kids

How Women Can Make up to $1,000 a Week in Direct Selling

How to Beat the High Cost of College

Claire Cox

HOW TO BEAT THE HIGH COST OF COLLEGE

published by
Bernard Geis Associates
distributed by Random House

Library of Congress Catalog Card Number: 64–23305

Manufactured in the United States of America

First Printing

To Max

A WORD ABOUT THIS BOOK

How To Beat the High Cost of College fills a definite need in one interesting, easy-to-read volume. Claire Cox has written in a manner that keeps you reading. I like this book . . . you will too! Here's why:

How To Beat the High Cost of College completely informs the high school boy or girl, parent, teacher and counselor *where* and *how* to get financial aid to meet the ever-growing cost of a college education or advanced vocational training.

It discusses national scholarship organizations, various work-study plans, a wide variety of job opportunities on and off campus, several long-range savings and investment plans, the broad spectrum of loans (federal, state and commercial), armed forces and extension opportunities, the growing junior college movement (with its advantages and limitations), new "package" innovations being tested in various schools . . . and a great deal more.

This book is more than informational. It's motivating. It moves you to action. For you get ideas that you can apply in your everyday living, such as: how to raise funds for your favorite charity, how to finance a project of special interest to you, and how to receive the benefits of our credit system.

As President of the Chicago Boys Clubs and as a Director of Boys Clubs of America (clubs which service over six hundred thousand boys and several thousand girls), and as president of several corporations that employ thousands of persons, I have at last found *the* book which gives the information that will prevent any boy or girl from being deprived of a college education because of lack of funds.

This is the book I have been looking for. Perhaps you have been looking for it, too. For *How To Beat the High Cost of College* literally tells you what to do to help yourself or your child beat the soaring cost of a college education.

W. Clement Stone
President, Combined Insurance Company of America

TABLE OF CONTENTS

How To Beat the High Cost of College

1

THE COLLEGE COST
WHIRLPOOL

...sink or swim

College is *the* goal for millions of our young people. Whether this dream will be fulfilled or turn into nightmares of frustration is largely up to them and their families. Those who really want college, for themselves or their children, will manage somehow, either through their own ingenuity or with the growing variety of help that is being made available by the federal and state governments, by schools, by civic, fraternal, religious and private organizations, by business and industry, and by altruistically conceived national bodies. All those who think they have college in their future must face up to the fact, however, that in the last decade college enrollments—and costs—have more than doubled and are expected to increase another 100 per cent in the next few years, far outstripping the population explosion or inflationary trends in the economy.

The simple and frightening fact is that while college is becoming increasingly necessary in order to compete in the modern world, the cost of a higher education is skyrocketing beyond the average family's ability to pay.

In the whirlpool of college costs, the danger that is most likely to set you off balance is the misconception, nurtured by overly optimistic and often outright carelessly presented or irresponsible data, that scholarships abound and that financial aid goes begging for lack of interested, qualified applicants. The cold truth is that the race for the decreasing proportion of scholarships grows hotter every year, and that the criteria on which they are awarded has changed radically. The concept of a money award for the brainy student has been largely replaced by the realization that tens of thousands, ranging from the earnest average student to the brilliant, *must be helped to help themselves* if they are to gain the advantages of higher education.

This book is more than a list of scholarships. It is an attempt to map the *entire* field of financial aid for students, with chapters on national scholarship organizations, on work-study plans, on a wide variety of job opportunities on and off campus, on several long-range savings and investment plans, on the broad spectrum of loans (federal, state and commercial), on armed forces and extension opportunities, on the growing junior college movement (with its advantages and limitations), and on several "package" innovations being provided in some schools.

Never before has such a remarkable range of financial aid been made available. But these are not magic wands to provide a free ride. Rather, they are solid, practical, workable ways to meet what may be the most crucial and difficult expense of your life. The rewards of higher education are great in increased earning power, community leadership and the inner satisfaction of realizing one's potential for growth. But the obstacles are great, too, and the need for help—or at least guidance—is acute.

Perhaps the best way to launch a discussion of this enormous problem is to reduce it to the most common denominator—the individual. Let us consider the stories of Jane and Henry and how they were able to go to college.

A *tale of two students*

From the time she was a little girl, Jane and her parents counted on her going to Vassar some day. But Jane almost missed her dream education opportunity because her family had *counted* on it without *planning* for it, too.

The girl we are calling Jane grew up in well-to-do circumstances. Her father made $16,700 a year and the family lived well—too well, it turned out. Jane traveled during summers and when at home had the use of a car of her own (they were a three-car, one-mortgage, no-savings-account family) and did not have to work for spending money.

Because Jane was an unusually bright girl who always stood at the top of her class, her family assumed that she would win a scholarship to Vassar as a reward for her brilliance. When college time came, however, they received an unpleasant surprise. There was no question about Jane's being accepted for Vassar, but no scholarship was forthcoming and her father, despite his well-over-average income, had to face the painful truth that during his years of talk about sending his daughter to an expensive, prestige college, he had not saved enough to pay for even one semester there.

Jane's father did not know that *need* is a basic element in the awarding of scholarships these days. The college could not accept the family's plea of financial distress, which was solely a result of not planning ahead; they simply were not in the kind of straits that warranted help. There were too many other girls with fewer resources who were ahead of Jane on the list for a limited amount of scholarship money. Even low-cost college and government loans were earmarked for needy students.

However, Jane was offered a part-time job on campus to help pay her expenses and was told that because she could type, she probably would have no trouble getting a summer job. This still left a big gap in what was needed for a year at Vassar. Jane's father went out and borrowed the rest, some on his insurance policy and some through a bank loan at relatively high interest. He also made immediate plans to save enough money every month to pay for Jane's second year in college without borrowing. Jane's mother decided to help out, too, by going back to work in an office.

There are many families that find themselves in this position. But, fortunately, there also are a number that write their own happy endings well in advance, such as the parents of a boy we shall call Henry, who are far from well-to-do but who are much more prudent and resourceful than Jane's family.

From the day he was born, Henry's family also wanted him to go to college—but with a difference. They *planned* for his education. His father put away nickels and dimes left from his factory wages after the bills were paid. Whenever he could, the father moonlighted, working in part-time jobs in addition to his regular occupation. Henry's mother worked as a sales clerk and put nearly everything she earned into Henry's educational fund. As he grew older, the boy worked at odd jobs and saved, too. The family drove a second-hand car. They stayed home during vacations. Every cent not needed for essentials went in the bank and they, unlike Jane's family, managed without a mortgage and stayed out of debt.

When Henry was ready for college, he was accepted by the Midwestern school of his choice and lived on campus while earning a degree in physics. During summers he held well-paid jobs. He was able to complete college without borrowing a cent, applying for a scholarship or working during the school year. And he made the dean's list regularly.

It was all a result of planning ahead....

Misconceptions can be important, too

Both of these accounts point up the fact that there are misunderstandings about college financing, resulting from either misinformation or a lack of information. In Jane's case, she and her family assumed that scholarships were available to all of the brightest students. They did not know that one has to be in financial need to get a stipend in most schools, and that scholarships are pitifully scarce and often so inadequate that they are mere tokens. Henry's family also acted out of ignorance, for even though they managed to finance his education, he would have qualified for aid because their total income was below average. The standard formulas for determining need consider the total income and obligations of a family, and this one would have qualified easily for a scholarship for Henry, even though stipends and the companion jobs and loans that have become part of the college financial picture are available to a mere 25 per cent of all college undergraduates. At present about $35 million is available each year for freshman scholarships—an average of less than $25 per freshman expected to enroll in 1968.

Despite this, you will hear parents such as Jane's boast, "Oh, our child is so bright, she'll get a scholarship!" And then you will hear another father, equally hard-pressed to keep up with the Joneses in suburbia with the required quota of cars, deep freezes, TV sets, etc., saying: "If my kids are going to college, they'll just have to manage it for themselves. I can't afford it and do the things for them that I think are important right now."

Only about $200 million in scholarships of all kinds is awarded each year (frankly, no one knows the exact figure), while more than $600 million in loans was granted to students in the 1963–64 school year, and the amount is rising annually. Colleges paid students $100 million for term-time jobs in that year and summer work was at least as remunerative. The rest had to come from somewhere else— savings, insurance, loans to parents, investments, moonlighting fathers, working mothers and so on.

The fact that it is possible to get through college despite the high costs is a tribute to the student and to the family of the student who finally walks across a platform in cap and gown with a tightly rolled diploma in his hand.

It can be done, and it is done by millions, but. . .

It can be a nightmare

"Of course Bill is going to college! He is only 13 and college is *a long way off*, but we have known since he was born that he will go. A boy needs a higher education to get ahead these days!"

That was Bill's mother talking. She, like Jane's mother and father, is far from alone in nurturing the dream of having her children get a higher education. The parents of about 2,223,000 other youngsters who entered high school in the fall of 1964 also have decided that *their* children are going to college, for they know that a college degree soon will be as necessary to a successful career as a high school diploma was to theirs. It used to be said that *any man* could grow up to become President, regardless of how humble his beginnings. Now it is considered wise to be graduated from college before seeking even a minor elective post.

At this point, it seems reasonable to ask, "But what are the parents of these children doing about college, other than talking about it?" Precious little in too many cases, according to several recent surveys. An amazing number of parents do not seem to realize that their dreams, like that of Jane's father, are likely to turn into nightmares when college enrollment time comes. It is estimated that 70 per cent of the 3,175,000 youngsters who entered the ninth grade in 1964 have parents who want them to go to college. About half of these students actually will enroll in institutions of higher learning if present statistics are any guide. Of that number, about 890,000 have parents who will back up aspiration with action in the form of savings or investments. In other words, only about one-fourth of the parents who *want* their children to get degrees will *do* anything to make it financially possible! Even more surprising is the discovery, in a study made for the Ford Foundation, that half of those who actually do put aside money will save a *maximum* of $200 during their child's last high school year. That might be enough to buy books and cover a few incidentals during the freshman year.

The other half of this group of parents will save more than $200, and perhaps a few will put aside quite a bit, but in all likelihood only a small minority of family savings plans will provide enough for college financing.

Educators often hear parents and students blaming finances either for an inability to go to college or for the high dropout rate, and apparently this is an accepted *reason*, although not a very good *excuse*, for missing out on a higher education. The number who seek and get college degrees is considerable, of course. College has become "the thing," whether one has a degree from Harvard or a diploma from a small, obscure school. Many specialties require not one but two or three degrees. Employers are increasingly insisting on some college experience, whether academic subjects actually fit people for jobs or not. Junior college certificates are coming to replace high school diplomas as a minimum "must" for a job with a future. In 1900 only 4 per cent of the college-age population (18 to 21) was in college. By 1930 the figure was 12 per cent, and in 1962 it was 37 per cent. It is expected to reach the area of 50 per cent by 1970.

Estimated enrollment in institutions of higher learning in the fall of 1964 was nearly 4,800,000, more than double the 1950 figure, and the rolls are expected to double again by 1975. The cost of a college education has increased by 100 per cent in the last 10 years and will go up another 100 per cent in the next 10. The man who was graduated from a private college in 1940 paid a total educational bill averaging $5,000. At the same school in 1964, it cost his child $13,000.

The difficult aspect of the situation is that college costs are outstripping the increase in family income and the cost-of-living index. Until 1958 the upsurge in college costs generally trailed slightly behind rises in family income. Beginning that year, however, private school costs have outrun family income, while costs at the publicly supported schools have been catching up with it. Now they are about even.

In January, 1940, the Bureau of Labor Statistics' cost-of-living index was 59.5; at the beginning of 1957 it was 117.8. The cost of living had nearly doubled, but it had actually more than doubled in items of food, clothing, shelter and travel, all staples of the student budget. In the same period, tuition and fees increased 89 per cent in public colleges and 83 per cent in private colleges. An indication of how important college costs loom in the economy was given in 1964, when the Bureau of Labor Statistics announced that tuition would henceforth be included in computations leading to the monthly Consumer Price Index.

A few more statistics are needed for a fuller understanding of the college cost picture. Between 1962 and 1973, the government predicts, the gross national product will rise 63 per cent and average family income will increase about 50 per cent, from $6,000 to $9,300. But college costs will *double*. Why? Because of belated rises in faculty salaries, building programs, expanded curricula, additional staff members and increased services to students in the areas of health, vocational guidance and psychological counseling. Also, more people will stay in college longer, despite the persistent and rather high dropout rate.

The college and university population is soaring as a result of the population explosion as well as because of the insistence on college in order to "get ahead." A boom in junior college development has provided education beyond high school to many who would be academically unsuited for regular colleges. It has become possible, in fact, to earn a two-year college certificate qualifying one to be an auto mechanic or a secretary.

More than 25 per cent of all the people in the country are involved in some way with education, and more money is spent on schooling than on anything else except national defense. Estimates that a college degree enables a person to earn an average of $175,000 more in his lifetime than a high school diploma indicate that there can be a big return on the $6,000, or even $12,000 or $15,000, invested in four years of college. Nearly 20 per cent of all college men earn $10,000 or more a year; the figure for high school graduates is 3.7 per cent. College graduates earned 56 per cent more per capita on the average than high school graduates in 1956; in 1963 the figure was 65 per cent. Presumably the gap will continue to widen as more auto mechanics earn junior college certificates. There isn't a stock on the market that would have a yield even close to that of the money invested in a college education. Or, to put the matter another way, in many cases the cost of college represents a specific outlay surpassed in an individual's lifetime only by the purchase of a home.

Some educators argue there really is no "inflation" on the campus, that the costs of operating colleges and universities have simply been catching up with the facts of economic life. This, they maintain, is particularly true of faculty salaries, which have been unreasonably low and still are far from what they should be. It also is pointed out that no matter how much you pay to go to college, you are footing only a fraction of the total bill. For example, the total budget for higher education was about $4.3 billion in 1962. It is expected to reach at least $15 billion by 1980. This is the cost of operating more than 2,000 colleges and universities, of which the public, tax-assisted institutions make up about a third and enroll 60 per cent of the students. Nearly 700 of the total are two-year junior colleges, public and private.

College operating costs in the 1962–63 academic year were up 26 per cent from the year before, with total student fees producing about one-fifth of the cash needed. Voluntary support in the form of philanthropic gifts and endowments came to slightly more than $1 billion—and must double by 1970 to meet growing demands. All the rest came from the taxpayers—local, county, state and federal funds. This actually means built-in scholarships and grants-in-aid for every student in every school, regardless of tuition charges. But it also means that even the tuition-less schools are by no means free; *someone* has to pay for them.

Just paying the tuition fees that are required can be a hardship, or, at the very least, pose problems. There may be no institution, from Harvard to low-tuition state universities, where fewer than 40 per cent of the students do not work at some time to help pay their way—and this gets harder each year, because tuition increases have become regular events at some schools. New York University, for example, charged $5 a study unit in 1952. By 1964, the figure was $50. A student needed 32 units a year to graduate—or a total of $1,600 in tuition alone—during the 1964-65 year. Princeton, in the fall of 1964, raised its tuition for the seventh time since World War II. In May, 1947, the charge was $560 a year; by 1964 it was $1,770.

Generally speaking, the Eastern colleges are the most expensive and they attract most of the scholarship money. The Southern schools generally are the least costly, and the least well endowed. In the Midwest, tuition may be less but total costs can be more because of the stress on fraternities and sororities.

One ironical twist in the college cost picture is that parents in the lower income brackets, such as the family of Henry, generally have been found to be more likely to make better preparations for the financial strain of college than are families well in the five-figure bracket. This suggests that college financing can be arranged through planning no matter what the size of income (and provided there are no serious money-consuming illnesses or other family obligations). Yet, in the college stampede, many persons are thrown into panic or lost by the wayside.

But the dream can come true

Although many have complained to governmental and educational authorities that college threatens to price itself out of their lives, more seem to manage somehow. It is apparent that the motivation of the individual student and his family is important in determining who goes to college and stays there, regardless of the size of their income.

So much has been said and written about inflation on the campus in recent years that some parents have been inspired to act when there still was some precious time left. More planning ahead is done than a generation ago, and parents increasingly are becoming aware of avenues of help, thanks to wider publicity for aid sources, the establishment of sound college-loan programs and the development of high school counseling as a specialty. Also important are such movements as the National Merit Scholarship Corporation, which not only grants a large number of stipends but serves as a clearing house of talent information for colleges and universities to use in their search for the best students, and the Citizens' Scholarship Foundation of Fall River, Massachusetts, which is a grass-roots movement that raises money for scholarships based more on need than on academic excellence. You will learn more about these organizations in later chapters.

It has been estimated that it costs $14,000 for a family to put two children through four years in an average-priced, publicly supported institution as resident students. This does not include the Ivy League schools or graduate study. Educators generally appear to believe that, despite the fact that four years in college could cost $15,000 to $16,000 for one student and averaged around $7,000 to $10,000 in 1964–65, any young person who *really* wants a higher education will get it somehow and somewhere. Wanting an education—in other words, motivation—is widely regarded as the important ingredient. There are free junior colleges and low-cost state and municipal universities near the homes of enough ambitious young people to make college a possibility for them. The school you attend may not be the one of your choice, but it *is* a college, and perhaps even a good one. It is possible for those who have some money to go to less expensive schools than the ones listed as their first choices. Many good and expensive schools offer job-scholarship-loan packages.

There are all kinds of low-cost or no-cost alternatives—night school, correspondence courses, study via television, on-the-job training programs and service in the armed forces, which offer a wide variety of educational opportunities that will be described in later chapters. Perhaps one does not get all the extra status one wants by going to Somewhere Junior College instead of Princeton, or by learning accounting by mail instead of in lecture halls, but do not forget that although the 34th President of the United States, John F. Kennedy, went to prestigious, expensive and heavily endowed Harvard, his successor, Lyndon B. Johnson, attended a school little known outside his home state, Southwest Texas State College, where the tuition still is relatively low and the fewer than 60 scholarships awarded each year are valued at $25 to $150 each.

The current college boom got under way after World War II, when more than half the full-time students were veterans receiving financial aid through the G.I. Bill of Rights. That scholarship bonanza is no longer available to either the schools or the students, but the government does help out with loans and various educational opportunities as well as a scholarship program for orphans of some veterans. There is occasional talk of establishing a governmental scholarship program, although many educators are more than satisfied with the federal loan program, which is administered by the schools. All but about 400 of the 2,000 institutions of higher learning are participating in some way with one or more of the federal programs and all but a few institutions have some kind of financial aid programs of their own for undergraduates. The financial aid officer is, in fact, becoming as much of a fixture on college campuses as the dean.

Although the college cost situation has become a nightmare to many parents and students, it need not be, regardless of whether one has planned ahead or simply hoped for the best. In the chapters that follow, various ways and means of coping with educational finances will be described. Not every possible solution will be cited, of course, and only a few examples of some recommended measures will be offered. But it is hoped that a few seeds for thought—and action—will be sown. Perhaps there will be a measure of inspiration for those who can plan well ahead, as well as for those who must learn now and pay later. At least you should be assured that there are help and hope for the Janes and the Henrys who must cope with inflation on the campus.

2

YOUR PERSONAL PRICE TAG

...computing college costs

The scene was the United States House of Representatives. The speaker was Representative John W. Byrnes of Wisconsin. The topic was a stock investment that had increased a thousand per cent in only three years. Byrnes had bought shares in a company about six months after he had helped it obtain a favorable tax ruling. He had paid $2.50 a share for the stock in 1960. Now, three years later, it was worth $25 a share, and he was being criticized severely—so severely that he found it necessary to plead his case before his peers and to promise them that he would sell the stock, recover his original $2,300 and give the slightly more than $20,000 profit to a scholarship-granting organization in his home state.

Choking back tears, Byrnes explained that his stock purchase had been the only really profitable investment he had ever made. In two years his oldest boy would be ready for college, and the five other Byrnes children would follow him at almost yearly intervals.

"I confess that, with prudence, this investment would go a long way toward educating my children," he said, brushing his hand across his eyes.

This was a poignant scene that may well have touched the hearts of parents across America, many of whom, like Byrnes, want their children to go to college but do not have the funds to finance it. Within a month after he made his tearful speech, Byrnes was asked to be a favorite-son candidate for the Republican Presidential nomination in Wisconsin. Shortly after that, he carried out his promise and turned his stock profit over to a scholarship foundation.

Actually, Byrnes was overly optimistic when he said that $23,000 "would go a long way" toward financing college for his six children. His bill for four years each in an average-priced, tax-supported college would total at least $56,000, and probably more. Suppose that his children went to college exactly a year apart, beginning in 1965, and attended a four-year, publicly supported college costing $2,000 a year (the average) for room, board and other charges. The following chart shows what it would cost, taking into consideration the inevitable 5 per cent annual increase in college costs. (It does not include such items as clothing, transportation and other expenses.)

Number in School at Once	"John"	"Mary"	"George"	"Henry"	"Frank"	"James"	Amt.	Year
1	$2,000						$2,000	1965
2	2,100	2,100					4,200	1966
3	2,205	2,205	2,205				6,615	1967
4	2,315	2,315	2,315	2,315			9,260	1968
4		2,430	2,430	2,430	2,430		9,720	1969
4			2,551	2,551	2,551	2,551	10,204	1970
3				2,678	2,678	2,678	8,034	1971
2					2,812	2,812	5,624	1972
1						2,953	2,953	1973
TOTALS	$8,620	9,050	9,501	9,974	10,471	10,994	56,610	

The bill for this family's education would average nearly $6,300 a year for nine years. The last year of the last child would come to nearly 50 per cent more than the first year of the first child, and had Byrnes's program followed this pattern, the $23,000 he had hoped to use would have been enough to finance only about the first four years. For three successive years, Byrnes would have four children in college at the same time, with his peak year costing over $10,000. The total cost would be higher if the youngsters were spaced further apart in age, but the cost per year would be less. At a privately supported college, with an average expense of $2,500 a year in 1963–64, the grand total would be considerably higher.

Were Byrnes or any other parent to invest between $55,000 and $60,000 in the education of six children, it could mean as much as a million dollars in increased lifetime earnings if all were graduated from college. However, if this were a statistically representative family, only three or four would finish college. Two probably would drop out after the first year; on the other hand, two might go on to graduate school. At least one would qualify for some kind of scholarship and most, if not all, would find summer and part-time jobs to help pay the bills. The ones who finished college probably would also have obtained loans, either from their schools or from the state or federal government.

When it comes to college financing, a man in Byrnes's position may be just as needy as many persons with incomes much smaller than the $22,500 annual salary of a congressman. But can he prove it? To get any kind of scholarship help or a low-cost loan, one almost invariably must *prove* need. To do that, one must open his family's financial books and disclose his innermost secrets to the sources of potential aid.

If this becomes necessary, it is a wise idea to make some determination of your situation for yourself first. If you have children who are likely to go to college, whether it be in the next year or in 15 years, sit down today and find out where you stand.

Be your own auditor

Begin by writing four to six colleges and universities for their catalogues, materials on financial aid programs, cost estimates and application timetables. The colleges you list should offer a variety

WORK SHEET
College Costs and Financial Resources
(fill out a sheet for each college in which you are interested)

Name of College:

	1st year	2nd year	3rd year	4th year	TOTAL
Tuition					
General fees					
Books					
Equipment & supplies					
Laboratory fees					
Activity fee					
Other fees					
Room					
Board					
Recreation and entertainment					
Travel to and from home					
All other travel, for recreation, etc.					
Transportation in connection with actual school attendance					
Snacks					
Clothing					
Grooming					
Fraternity, sorority or club dues					
Health					
Laundry, dry cleaning, etc.					
Church, charity					
Other—TV, car, bicycle, record player, sports equipment, etc.					
GRAND TOTALS					

of cost figures. Start with the school your child is likely to want to attend or should attend regardless of expense; then include a less expensive school, but one that still is in the class of the first; then add a state university in your home state; then schools in several different parts of the country; then a college near enough to your home to make daily commutation feasible and, finally, a free school within commutation distance.

Using the suggestions on the following pages as guides, make out several sample computation sheets. When you have finished, consult the graph compiled by the College Scholarship Service indicating how much parents *should* contribute from income to the higher education of their children. This graph is based on both income and number of children.

In making computations you must consider the year in which your child is planning to go to college. Take this year's figures as supplied by each college and add 5 per cent a year (and remember that, except in rare instances, this increase continues while the student is in college).

Try to base your figures on the assumption that no outside help will be forthcoming. If your resources are not enough, then you may have no difficulty in proving need.

If your computations are accurate, you should find that the total for room, board, clothing and recreation makes up about two-thirds of the total for all the last 15 items on the list combined. As a guide, you may be interested in knowing that a government analysis of the costs of attending college gave a general range of $92 to $312 for clothing costs in the course of a school year, with the poorest spending a mere $5 and the richest more than $1,000. The two extremes were rare, however. Recreation costs generally ranged from $55 to $180.

Now fill out a family resources chart, totaling every source of income and funds available to you and your children. It should include the following assets:

Savings accounts
Stocks and other investments
Bonds
Insurance
Other cash assets of family and the student
Equity in home

Divide the total by four, then add:

Estimated summer earnings of student
Estimated school-year earnings of student
Earnings of either parent or both that can be applied to college fund

The grand total is what will be available each year for a full college course.

To determine still further where you stand, make a computation along these lines:

Name of college:
Annual expenses:
Cash available annually:
Amount available from current income for each year:

Total the figures for the last two items. If they are equal to or larger than the figure for annual expenses at the college, your financial plan is assured. If the sum is less than the amount needed, this book may guide you in obtaining the needed funds.

How much can you really afford?

Perhaps you feel that the amount of money needed is out of proportion to the family income. As a possible guide to you in your thinking, turn to the College Scholarship Service chart on Page 55, which, with certain qualifications, presents the *minimum* amount parents are expected to contribute from income for college when financial aid is provided. The table outlines the minimum that a successful candidate for student aid might be expected to pay. It may help you in your own computations in deciding whether you are justified in seeking funds outside the family.

Your computations should, of course, take into consideration that the cheapest way to go to college is to live at home and commute to a free or low-tuition, four-year, tax-supported school or attend a free two-year junior college. Next would be a state university in your home state. At the top is the private institution, where nearly half the total cost is made up of tuition and fees. Also to be considered in any computation is the cost of travel between home and school, figured on the basis of at least two round-trips a year and perhaps three. Find out about the living standards on the campus of your choice—how the students dress, what kind of transportation they use, recreational costs and so on. You will find that the habits and styles and therefore the costs vary between campuses and sections of the country.

You will be aware by now of the fact that tuition, fees, and room and board—the fixed costs—make up 40 to 60 per cent of what a student spends each year. The variable costs, such as books, supplies, dues, clothing, laundry, travel, recreation, entertainment and the like, constitute the rest.

Most of the living costs (room and board, clothing, laundry, cleaning and recreation) would have to be financed whether a person was in college or at home. They usually are accounted for in the family budget at a rate of about $50 a month per child.

Once you have put down all the figures you can think of and have determined where you believe you stand in the college financial picture, then make a plan, based on your income and resources and the resources of the student in your family. No matter how little you can manage, every cent you set aside in advance will ease the burden on you and your children that much more when it comes time for enrollment.

But do not give up if you find that you are doing all you can to plan for college and still will not have enough money. There are many alternatives open to you and your children for financing a higher education, including scholarships, a number of loan programs involving either parents or students or both, insurance programs and student job opportunities. All you need for reassurance is another look at those statistics on college attendance. It is growing every year and is rapidly approaching the five million mark. If all of these students—and their families—can find a way up the mountain of college costs, there is undoubtedly a route open to you.

For further information on college costs

Costs of Attending College, by Ernest V. Hollis and Associates, Department of Health, Education and Welfare, Washington, D.C. 20002.

Digest of Educational Statistics, Department of Health, Education and Welfare.

Economics of Higher Education, edited by Selma J. Mushkin, Department of Health, Education and Welfare.

Facing Facts about College Admissions, Prudential Insurance Company of America, Prudential Plaza, Newark, New Jersey.

Facing Facts about College Costs, Prudential.

Financial Aid to the Undergraduate, by Elmer D. West, American Council on Education, 1785 Massachusetts Avenue, N.W., Washington, D.C. 20036.

Higher Education, a magazine published by the Department of Health, Education and Welfare ($1.25 a year).

Higher Education, Basic Student Charges, 1962–63, Department of Health, Education and Welfare.

"How about College Financing? A Guide for Parents of College Bound Students," American School Counselor Association, 1605 New Hampshire Avenue, N.W., Washington, D.C. 20009.

How People Pay for College, by John B. Lansing, Thomas Lorimer and Chikashi Moriguchi, University of Michigan.

Journal of the Association of College Admissions Counselors, 610 Church Street, Evanston, Illinois ($2 a year).

Student Expenses and Sources of Income, 1960–61 Academic Year, University of Wisconsin.

Student Financial Aid and Institutional Purpose, College Entrance Examination Board, 475 Riverside Drive, New York, New York 10027.

Student Financial Aid in the United States: Administration and Resources, by Rexford G. Moon Jr., College Entrance Examination Board.

Queries may be addressed to:

College Entrance Examination Board.

College Scholarship Service, 475 Riverside Drive, New York, New York 10027.

Ford Foundation, 477 Madison Avenue, New York, New York 10022.

National Education Association, 1201 16th Street, N.W., Washington, D.C. 20006.

Office of Information, Department of Health, Education and Welfare, Washington, D.C. 20002.

3

THE TRUTH ABOUT
SCHOLARSHIPS

... and where to find them

No single source of college financial aid is more sought, less available and the cause of more heartache and disappointment than scholarships. Countless young people—and their families—have come to believe that there is a horn of plenty on every campus spilling out money for tuition, books, and room and board to any student with good grades and even to many who may be average but worthy. This is pure fantasy.

The truth is that there really are not very many scholarships in proportion to the total college population, and the ratio is falling every year. The money available simply is not keeping pace with the rise in the campus population, and unless the federal government steps in with a college scholarship program, the situation is almost certain to get worse as the number of students continues to soar.

As you will learn in the chapters that follow, there *are* some relatively large scholarship programs, but each reaches only a few thousand students at the most. Despite masterful attempts on the part of the College Scholarship Service (see Chapter 5) and the National Merit Scholarship Corporation (see Chapter 6) to systematize applications for grants and their allocation, there still is too much fragmentation. There are different criteria for proving financial need for each of the large programs, thus creating considerable confusion. The plain fact is that scholarships are publicized all out of proportion to their availability. Newspapers run sizable articles on "a major scholarship program," but what do they add up to? Perhaps 1,000 or 2,000 grants at the most, but more often only a handful, and not very large ones at that.

Although it is only sensible to seek scholarship money, a student should approach this source of aid realistically, knowing that his chances for a part-time job or a low-interest loan are much greater, or that if he gets help it will be in a "package" containing a loan and a job along with the small scholarship.

There are many misconceptions about scholarships, much too often nurtured by misleading information disseminated by some of those who are supposed to keep the public accurately informed. Possibly the biggest misconception about scholarships involves the number of grants actually available. Currently, only 10 to 20 per cent of the total cost of college, nationwide, is financed through scholarships—not including athletic grants, which usually are handled apart from regular aid programs. Because they are gifts, scholarships are the form of aid most sought after. Because of their scarcity, they are the most difficult to obtain. In 1961, for example, about $130 million of the approximately $200 million in scholarship assistance was controlled by colleges and universities. To do their job meaningfully, the schools needed at least $750 million. And while some individual grants have run to as much as $2,500 or $3,000 a year, most have been for less than $500 and a few honorary stipends have been for a mere $10.

Here are some other fancies and facts about scholarships:

Fancy: Scholarships are prizes awarded for academic excellence regardless of financial need.

Fact: While it is true that academic excellence usually figures in the allocation of scholarships, even the smartest person in the world will not get one, except in rare instances, unless he genuinely *needs* the money. And as we have indicated, there are many formulas for determining need, and the criteria for one may be different from those for another (see Pages 55, 75 and 92).

Fancy: Grants are so plentiful on nearly every campus that many go begging every year.

Fact: There is no evidence that any responsible academic authority can uncover to indicate that a substantial number of scholarships have ever gone begging. A relative handful of specialized grants may not be awarded from time to time, but there almost invariably are lists of alternate winners for most awards if the first person selected drops out of the running.

Fancy: There are many "full" scholarship grants that pay for all college expenses.

Fact: A full scholarship is virtually unheard of these days. A student is more likely to receive a scholarship *and* a loan *and* the offer of a job than to be handed a full cash grant. This kind of package aid has become standard on most campuses (see Chapter 12).

Fancy: Athletic scholarships are available far out of proportion to those for genuine scholars, who often are discriminated against while athletes are favored.

Fact: There are more myths than truths about athletic scholarships. While it is true that some schools provide generous help to stars of baseball, football, track and other sports, the ranks are thinning and the total is not really significant.

Now, before elaborating on these points, perhaps we should define some terms.

What is a scholarship?

For a full understanding of the award picture, one should know the definitions attached to the various kinds of aid. A *fellowship* is an outright grant, almost always for graduate work. A *scholarship* is a "no-strings" gift, but usually for undergraduate work. A *grant-in-*

aid is also outright, but most often for a specific postgraduate project, for financial emergencies or for athletic activities. Nearly all stipends are granted for one year, which means the student has to "sweat out" a new application every summer. Even most four-year grants are subject to annual review to make sure that the student's work is up to par and that he still needs money.

Institutional scholarship money is that controlled by the school; other scholarships, such as those awarded by fraternal and business organizations, are often controlled by the donors, who make their own rules, although frequently using need as well as other factors in determining their awards. These grants, of course, are taken into consideration by financial aid officers when institutional funds are allocated to deserving students. If, for example, a boy receives a $500 Elks Club award, that sum may be subtracted by the school from the total amount it plans to allocate to him.

History of scholarships

Although the merit-plus-need concept that is almost universally accepted by the colleges and universities is relatively new, there has been concern for the impecunious student from the earliest days of campus life in the United States. In many instances the poorer students were treated as charity cases until late in the 19th Century; today there is a more democratic approach.

The first recorded scholarship was established at Harvard College in 1643 by Lady Mowlson, the former Anne Radcliffe, for whom Radcliffe College is named. She gave a fund of £100, a substantial sum then, to provide a £15 annual scholarship. Since then, thousands of individuals, organizations, businesses and governmental agencies have donated money for scholarships.

Aid programs not involving scholarships have been introduced by colleges periodically. Some schools offered work programs early in the 19th Century to teach trades to the students and enable them to earn money at the same time. These doubtless were the forerunners of today's cooperative work-study programs (see Chapter 13).

Other measures were initiated for the needy. Yale, Emory, Brown and Princeton opened dining halls for poor boys. A bureau of "self-help" was established at Yale to serve as an employment agency for needy students. Princeton built a dormitory for the poor, and a condescending attitude toward poverty was perpetuated by Dartmouth in an insistence that all needy students who received help had to promise not to drink, smoke, dance or play billiards. Special allotments made available to the poor students on various campuses were tagged "charity funds" rather than scholarships. The general attitude was unpopular with the recipients of this largesse, but it was not until after the Civil War that the democratization of higher education in the United States began.

The Civil War gave the same kind of impetus to college education that World War II was to do. A new generation of American millionaries began donating money to colleges. The once-unpopular charity funds were renamed "scholarships," and they still bear that label.

Who qualifies for scholarships?

As has been pointed out, few such cash awards are *won* these days. For the most part they are allocated as financial aid to students who *need* money for college, and even though scholastic ability usually enters the picture, the student who receives the largest stipend is not necessarily the smartest. In fact, the brightest may not get anything except a medal, a certificate, a check for $10 or a pat on the back. Although parents usually feel that all academic achievement should be rewarded, and although they tend to regard anything other than cash as inappropriate, this feeling that the bright students should win a free ride is part of what could be regarded as "magic thinking" about college. The cold truth is that there is no magic way to solve the college financing problem.

However, the parents of the brilliant child should not feel affronted when their young genius does not receive recognition in the form of a scholarship, for the entire area of financial aid, including scholarships, has undergone a change, a result of exploding college enrollments and the pressure to assist greater numbers of students from less affluent families. Computations based on economic need have become necessary because of a change in aid sources. In the mid-1950's scholarships constituted the largest pool of student aid funds. By 1960 the amount of money students earned in jobs during the school year and summers edged past the known value of scholarships. The number of loans was smaller but the total value was greater. Between the falls of 1934 and 1959, tuition and fees rose 187 per cent in small public institutions and as much as 335 per cent in medium-size private schools; enrollment during that time increased by about 245 per cent in all types of colleges and universities.

As the number of students has grown, the percentage of scholarship recipients among them has fallen. The figures were about 14 per cent in 1955 and 11 per cent in 1959. Yet writers persist in turning out cheery articles, such as one published recently in a national periodical proclaiming that there is a *good chance for any student* who wants to go to college to win a scholarship, that persons with scholarship money are combing the nation for the best candidates. However, the author, as is almost invariably the case, cites figures in the hundreds, not the thousands or millions.

There are several major published lists of scholarships for which one may apply. Even the best ones are out of date as soon as they appear, and those that are not revised thoroughly and regularly are shamefully inaccurate. You will find some sources of scholarship information at the end of the next chapter, but the best way to find out about grants is to write to the college you hope to attend and ask for a list of the scholarships it controls and how to apply. Unless you plan to study at one of the schools offering a number of scholarships, you are likely to be surprised at how few and how small are those that are available.

This should not discourage a student from trying to obtain a scholarship; rather, it should *encourage* him to start planning ahead for the scholarship search. Even so, he should not be too disappointed if he does not get a stipend or if the one he does get is far smaller than he had hoped.

You doubtless have heard some father say that his child is going to college on a "full scholarship." In actual truth, he either does not know what he is talking about, is acknowledging that he cannot afford the education, has incorrectly presented his claim of need or simply is not being accurate. A "full scholarship" today—that is, a stipend covering tuition, room and board and all fees—is extremely rare. In these times of inflation on the campus, *some kind of need* may not be difficult to prove to financial aid officers, but a total subsidy would be made only if no other money was obtainable from any other source.

However, some students may be getting aid because their fathers did not plan ahead, which raises a rather sore point: The student whose family has sacrificed for college and can make the grade without help is often penalized for his thrift while a student in a family that did not make provision receives aid. College finance officers are concerned about what seems to be the inequity of rewarding failure on the part of some parents; at the same time, they believe that when an able student comes along, he should not have to suffer for his parents' shortcomings.

How available are scholarships?

As has been noted, the notion that scholarships are so plentiful that they often go begging is incorrect. Scholarships are not plentiful in comparison with the number of persons qualified for them. They are not available at every school, and schools that do have them may offer only a few, most of them small. Although there are a number of generous state scholarship programs—such as those in Illinois, California and New York, which tend to spread aid among many schools rather than just a few—only 50 institutions of higher learning, constituting less than 3 per cent of the total and enrolling fewer than 15 per cent of the full-time undergraduates, control about 35 per cent of all the cash available for scholarships awarded at the college level. The rest of the schools must rely on scholarships from independent sources, but these noncollege awards are not so numerous or so large as those controlled by schools. In fact, the trend is toward college control of all aid money. Also, the aid received from outside is often subtracted from what the college would provide, and the students who receive these independent stipends tend to go to the same colleges that control most of the academic wealth.

(Not taken into account here is the huge amount in hidden scholarships to *all* students provided through compulsory endowments by taxpayers to low-cost state and local universities and free junior colleges. This discussion must be limited to what are known popularly as scholarships, which are far from hidden—and which are often awarded with far more ostentation than seems warranted.)

What about "unusual" scholarships?

Perhaps the same people who think scholarships are there for the asking also are the ones who have been led to believe that many go begging. When a question about this was posed to experts in the Office of Education of the Department of Health, Education and Welfare and to college officials, the unanimous response was wonderment that such an idea could exist. Because of odd or unusual requirements or because some students are offered several stipends but can accept only one, reports persist that $30 million in scholarships goes begging every year. The information provided by college financial aid officers simply does not substantiate these reports.

There are, of course, a few rather unique stipends, such as one highly publicized scholarship at Yale providing that only persons named Leavenworth need apply. In some years Yale has found no qualified Leavenworth available for the grant, which comes to $900 a year. Bucknell University in Pennsylvania has been left a sizable sum for scholarships for students who do not use tobacco, narcotics and intoxicants and who do not participate in "strenuous athletic contests." Vassar, with $500,000 in scholarship funds, has a few old stipends with hard-to-fill requirements, such as the one for daughters of missionaries, which is used only periodically. Of the school's total, however, the most that has ever been passed up in a single year is $20,000. At the University of Southern California there is a long-standing endowment to aid a student of Oriental descent who plans to become a missionary. Because applicants are few, the income builds up during the periods between awards to an amount that is of real help.

There are a number of bequests that might be considered odd, but most of these are modest in size and exist mainly at the older schools. Fund-raisers now try to encourage persons with unusual bequest ideas to include the phrase "whenever possible," so that if the stipulation cannot be met, the financial aid officer can use his discretion. This does not mean that specific bequests are discouraged; it means only that the hard-to-meet stipulations are gradually being eliminated.

Various scholarship contests are staged with limiting regulations, such as that of the Josephite Fathers, who gave five $1,000 stipends to students at Roman Catholic schools in one year for the best essays dealing with ways to combat racial prejudice. Corporations, organizations and unions allocate grants to help finance education for the children of employees or members. Fifteen California Indians receive scholarships each year through a bequest of Long-Haired Willie Taggart, an Indian who left his property to the state for educational purposes. An Irish immigrant woman willed $450,000 to Princeton for scholarships for New Yorkers. These are considered legitimate and nonlimiting, as is the program of a Puerto Rican hotel that gives stipends to Cornell's School of Hotel Administration for residents of Puerto Rico or those with strong ties to the island who are fluent in English and Spanish and who want to work in hotels there. Four scholarships for $2,500 a year plus up to $1,000 for transportation are offered each fall. These are among the most generous grants awarded in any program.

As for duplication, there is hardly a scholarship granted for which there are not alternate recipients waiting if the first choice selects another award or drops out of the running. With college aid officers controlling most of the important scholarship money, the grants are parceled out methodically, sometimes with one student receiving two or three small stipends to eke out the aid he has been allocated and sometimes with several students sharing one larger sum. Careful account is kept of most scholarship awards allocated by colleges to ensure that no one will get more than his fair share or more than he really needs.

How about those athletic scholarships?

There may be no aspect of college financing more controversial than the athletic scholarship. One hears all sorts of reports about the dimensions of athletic aid—that it is far larger and more extensive than people generally are led to believe, that there are no academic requirements so long as a young man can run 90 yards to a touchdown, that athletics keeps some schools alive with big profits and so on. As much as one hears and reads on the subject, it is difficult to obtain exact information about athletic stipends. What seems to be the most reasonable estimate available at this time, based on computations of the College Scholarship Service and reports of individual schools, is that about 20 per cent of all scholarship aid allocated to *men* in college is a reward for athletic ability.

The National Collegiate Athletic Association has reported that 210 schools spent nearly $15 million on grants and loans to athletes in 1959 and $1.8 million in part-time jobs. They invested an additional $1.4 million just to send scouts out to recruit athletes, according to this report.

Some colleges and universities insist on using a need formula in awarding grants even to the best players, but others have dropped all pretense that the stipends are in any sense scholarships and have adopted grant-in-aid programs providing tuition, fees, books, supplies, and room and board without regard to whether the player needs the help or can make the grade academically.

It has become the practice in a few football conferences to put limits on the number of athletes who are allowed to receive grants in any one year. In the Southeastern Conference, where football is especially popular, a maximum of about 120 football and 20 basketball grants are permitted a school at one time. Big Ten schools in the Midwest usually limit to 80 the number of freshmen sports grants at each institution. In the Southwest the usual quota per school is 100 full grants in football and 20 in basketball.

Georgia Tech withdrew from the Southern Conference in 1964 to protest that organization's refusal to raise the limit on the number of basketball and football scholarships. In announcing Georgia Tech's decision, Bobby Dodd, the coach, issued a statement that "simple mathematics will show that such a figure would limit the recruitment of freshmen athletes to 30 per year if none left school before they graduated. Of course, we do lose a few each school year because of academic difficulties or for other reasons, but a careful survey of prospective student athletes and *a well-planned program of tutoring* for any that need it after their arrival has cut our losses to a figure much below that of most conference schools. This has resulted in limiting our recruiting program to the extent that we feel we cannot comply with the rule and field a respectable team. This is not fair to our school, our alumni, our players or anyone connected with the program." [Italics added.]

Grades are no object when it comes to the admission of qualified athletes to some schools; applicants at one college need present only high school diplomas. In the Southeastern Conference, on the other hand, all potential students, even football stars, must pass entrance examinations. Schools with the highest standards have tried to upgrade the others by setting uniform academic requirements for halfbacks and tiddlywinks players, but apparently this has not always been accepted by the less scholastically oriented institutions dependent on the generosity of old grads who like to yell themselves hoarse at football games.

The late A. Whitney Griswold, as president of Yale, denounced athletic grants-in-aid as a sign of an absence of a real sense of purpose in the American educational system. "For the most part," he said, "the traffic [in athletic scholarships] constitutes one of the greatest educational swindles ever perpetrated on American youth. Its aim is not the education of that youth, but the entertainment of its elders; not the welfare of the athlete, but the pleasure of the spectator." Moreover, he said, athletic scholarships cause confusion about educational values in the minds of students by prompting them to choose colleges for the agility of their athletes rather than the acuity of their academicians.

At Princeton, which, along with Rutgers University, launched intercollegiate football in 1869, the official policy calls for no subsidization of athletics. All financial aid to students is awarded by an official committee that does not include any member of the athletic department. It is possible for a football player to win a scholarship, but only on the same basis as all others are awarded—need and scholastic ability. Nor does football help finance other sports at Princeton; in fact, it operates at a loss.

When asked about athletic grants, college officials often become vague. In cases of schools that do have awards for athletes, some of them generous ones, the financial aid officer will carefully point out that they are not scholarships and that they are handled entirely by the athletic department. A Stanford University official answered a query about athletic awards by saying that "there are grants given to deserving athletes. There are scholarships designated for use by students entering many fields of study or extracurricular activities." The term "deserving athletes" was not defined.

The situation was described this way by an aid officer at the University of Southern California: "Athletic programs are not scholarships; they are grants-in-aid. Funds for these grants come from different sources than funds for scholarships. The criteria of selection are also different. I don't think they are of less importance, but there are more scholarships in proportion for academic purposes. A good many scholarships are for students in particular fields of study: music, science, engineering, speech, journalism and so forth."

There are no athletic scholarships at the University of California, but the Department of Intercollegiate Athletics awards grants-in-aid for which neither scholastic ability nor financial need is a requirement.

Dr. Herbert Smith, president of Willamette University in Salem, Oregon, has posed several questions about college athletic programs. He doubts that today's students have enough time to spare from their academic courses for the extensive training and practice sessions required in team sports. He also wonders whether athletics can continue to claim as large a share of the college budget as in the past in view of the rising costs of such important items as libraries and laboratories. But most significant, he asks whether the college athlete can compete with the professional, who threatens to end the reign of the gridiron hero as the Big Man on Campus.

Smith wants all monetary assistance provided for athletes to be controlled by the financial aid officer, not the athletic department. He calls also for awards to athletes based solely on the scholarship-need formula. His hopes may never be fulfilled, however, for the college that is heavily in the business of granting athletic awards probably is not interested in academic excellence. The brightest spot in the picture is the fact that only about 100 schools award 90 per cent of all athletic stipends.

There are individuals who defend athletic scholarships with the assertion that they have made college possible for men who would not otherwise have been able to qualify for financial aid or even to have made the grade through college. One such defender said that these grants had enabled an entire generation of sons of Pennsylvania coal miners to escape from lives of drudgery in the pits. Perhaps this is true, but it makes one wonder what college is all about when there is a double standard on some campuses, one for the muscle men and the other for the eggheads. Without implying anything against the sons of coal miners, one may validly question whether other even more deserving and more potentially valuable students have lost out because so much of the limited money available has gone into athletic scholarships. On the other hand, it can be argued that the money probably would not have been made available *except* for athletic purposes, because many alumni have no interest in academic excellence—an attitude that seems to be on the wane.

Although most athletes who receive stipends are sought after, and although the total provided for such aid has been exaggerated generally, a young man who has demonstrated athletic skill in high school would be foolish not to try to obtain this kind of assistance as long as it is available. The prospective college student who can handle a basketball or football and still nurture academic ambitions might start his search for an athletic stipend by consulting his high school coach, who is quite likely to be in touch with college officials. If nothing comes of that, the youth should deal directly with the college of his choice, sending an inquiry first to the student aid office and then to the athletic department. But his greatest chance lies in being discovered by a scout sent out by a school with a big-time team.

The changing scholarship picture

The ratio of athletic grants to the total number of students and to the total amount of money available has dropped, and presumably the sports stipends will continue to shrink in importance as the student population grows still larger. While the over-all scholarship-student ratio also is down, loans and jobs for all students have become more important. In 1934 they were so insignificant that government statisticians did not bother to record them. Now they figure as prominently as, and in some cases more prominently than, scholarships.

Here is another way to view the declining relative importance of stipends: The *average* college-controlled scholarship for the academic year 1959–60 was $340, while the average tuition charged by private colleges was $938; the average *combined* aid offer of scholarship, loan and job to a student in the 1962–63 academic year was $395 in publicly controlled, tax-supported colleges and $725 in private colleges, while tuition averaged more than twice that.

Although scholarships are too few to meet present needs, with many being mere tokens, they do provide a means of motivating students in secondary school. Even a token grant may give a student the encouragement he needs to go ahead with college plans, although they might involve going into debt. The stipend may be small, but the recognition tells him that he *is* college material.

Unfortunately, if a student does not merit a stipend in his first year in college, he is unlikely to be considered for one in later years unless his financial situation changes drastically for the worse. The fact that a student does not qualify for a scholarship need not keep him from going to college with the assistance of a loan and a job.

In all fairness to the bright students who do not qualify for scholarships because they do not need the money, the label "scholarship" should be dropped unless scholarship is actually being rewarded. The word should be supplanted by such labels as "stipend" or "gift"— or simply "financial aid." Let the brilliant but solvent student receive a medal or a certificate or some small cash token for his *scholarship*, while the recipient of genuine aid is given a cash benefit bearing another label. Publicize and honor the scholar and let the needy student quietly accept his grant.

For further information on scholarships

See notes at the end of the next chapter.

4

WHERE ARE THE JACKPOTS?

... some scholarship opportunities

The treasure hunt is on! The object of the search is cash, and the hunters are students hoping to help pay for college with money that is given to them in recognition of their talents. It has been made clear that far less "free" money is available than is popularly supposed, but it need not be so difficult to find the sources of whatever help *is* available, even though there are limitations on academic generosity.

There are many sources of information about scholarships. High school students should start their search by consulting their guidance counselors. Then they would be wise to invest $2 in a copy of the College Scholarship Service's *College Handbook* and $1.25 in the Department of Health, Education and Welfare publication *Financial Assistance for College Students: Undergraduate*. Their counselor, if he is serious about his work, should have a copy of A *Handbook for the Counselors of College Bound Students*, published by the Association of College Admissions Counselors and revised every year. This contains breakdowns of costs, aid opportunities and admissions requirements of some 500 schools. Any specific questions that remain unanswered involving aid at particular schools can usually be dealt with by correspondence with the schools themselves. You will find other sources of information in the following pages.

Scholarships classified

First, on the local level there are grants from parent-teacher associations, lodge chapters, churches, chambers of commerce, women's clubs and individual businessmen, and few of these are included in national scholarship lists. To learn about them, check the churches, clubs, unions and lodges and ask if they have scholarship programs and what one must do to qualify. An inkling of what may be available near home appeared in a report on financial aids to Antioch College students. One had received a scholarship from a supermarket; several others had them from their local high schools and PTA's. Teacher associations had granted modest stipends and so had a drive-in church, a woman's club, Kiwanis, Elks, Lions and two Italian-American groups. Included also were gifts from a number of foundations that offer aid apart from that controlled by the college.

There are three broad classifications of scholarships and therefore three broad areas in which to search for them: general, open to anyone; regional, for students from certain areas; and special, calling for persons of specific race, religion, career interest or the like. Keep these in mind when looking for a scholarship. Make a list of the well-known nationally administered programs. If your interest is science, you may find the financial answer in the Westinghouse Science Scholarship program, under which awards are presented in annual talent searches conducted by the Science Clubs of America. To qualify, one must take a special science aptitude test and submit high school records, personal data and a report on a personal scientific project. Forty finalists are selected from among senior high school students to attend a five-day Science Talent Institute in Washington, where *five* students win four-year, $7,500 scholarships and 35 others receive $250 grants. Some of the outstanding students who do not receive scholarships get awards from other sources as a result of their participation in this competition.

Some special grants

Other scholarships are worthy of investigation, although you should be forewarned that they are relatively few in number and are sought by large numbers of highly qualified students. At any rate, here are some of them:

National Honor Society Scholarships, which are awarded by the National Association of Secondary-School Principals of the National Education Association. Members of high school senior classes who belong to the society compete for scholarships totaling $13,500. In one year, nearly 90,000 students sought this rather modest jackpot by taking an extensive examination. Obviously only a fraction were winners. (More information is available from your high school principal or guidance counselor.)

Labor union stipends, which are numerous and usually available only to the children of members. The AFL-CIO and its affiliates helped more than 1,200 students with $700,000 in 1963–64. Twenty national and international unions have their own programs, and the AFL-CIO also participates in the National Merit Scholarship program (see Chapter 6). About one-third of all state AFL-CIO organizations and many city central bodies have programs. At least 300 local unions make some kinds of grants each year, with *one* stipend valued at $3,500.

After the death of William Green, president of the American Federation of Labor, in 1952, the federation gave $100,000 toward a memorial scholarship at Ohio State University, providing two undergraduate liberal arts grants a year, for a minimum of $800 each, and two graduate fellowships.

The AFL-CIO Education Department, in a guide for locals on how to set up a scholarship program, points out that the "inequality of opportunity for higher education not only erodes the democratic character of our society, but prevents many industrious and able young people from reaching their maximum educational potential and from making their maximum contribution to society." Legislation is urged to guarantee every able student a college education. Meanwhile, the giant of labor is providing what help it can.

American Legion scholarship aids, which include the annual publication of a booklet entitled *Need a Lift?,* 500,000 copies of which were distributed in 13 years. This document, obtainable from the American Legion Americanism Division in Indianapolis for 25 cents, is one of the more useful guides to specific educational opportunities. The Legion also has its well-known high school oratorical contest, in which secondary students compete annually for four national prizes, ranging from a $4,000 scholarship down to one for $500. This program reflects the overpublicizing of some college aid—only *four* prizes, totaling no more than $10,000, and 360,000 youngsters competing for them!

Church scholarships, which are provided by nearly every major denomination and some smaller ones, as well as by local congregations. ("Church" as used here refers to all religious institutions, Protestant, Roman Catholic and Jewish.) Most also offer low-interest loans. The gifts may be based on ability and need or may be awarded through competitions, such as one conducted by the Presbyterian Church in the United States (South) in an essay contest on "Why I plan to attend a church college." Eighteen stipends were awarded according to need, up to a maximum of $500 a year for each of four years.

Many religious organizations also sponsor colleges and universities, which usually provide an education at less cost than some other private schools. Church-connected scholarships are almost always restricted to members of the denominations involved and require recipients to attend church-connected schools.

There are specialized scholarships in the church category, too. For example, 45 students receive $200 Samuel Robinson Scholarships each year for reciting the 107 answers to the Westminster Shorter Catechism and writing a 2,000-word essay on a topic related to the catechism. To qualify one must be a lower classman at a college sponsored by the Presbyterian Church.

Business and industry programs, which usually figure in college financing through large grants made directly to schools for constructing buildings, buying equipment or paying salaries; through scholarships administered by the schools or an organization such as the National Merit Scholarship Corporation (see Chapter 6); or through direct awards to individuals. The largest commercial contribution is in the form of grants to the schools.

General Motors offers grants-in-aid totaling more than $5 million a year to about 1,600 students in more than 180 public and private institutions. These young people need have no direct association with G.M. *There is no need to apply to the company for one of the stipends, either,* for they are carefully administered by the schools themselves, which select the recipients and decide how much they should receive. G.M. limits its grants to a maximum of 10 at any one school in any year. They range in size from $200 to $2,000 annually, depending on need. In addition, G.M. matches each stipend with a grant to the college and makes still further amounts available to the United Negro College Fund and other worthy scholarship causes. The company places no restriction on the field of study. The scholarships are awarded for four years but are reviewed annually in terms of need and grades. All winners are expected to work during the summer and are encouraged to find part-time jobs during the school year, but they are not obliged to work for G.M. while in school or after graduation.

Ford has set up a continuing education program under which nearly 5,000 salaried employees are studying in college and 70 scholarships a year are granted to children of employees. Each of the latter grants consists of full tuition, a contribution toward living costs and an outright gift of $500 a year, which is about as close as one can come these days to a full scholarship. Ford also spends $50,000 a year to support stipends and other prizes for outstanding 4-H Club work.

Another industrial giant, the International Business Machines

Corporation, awards 50 annual four-year scholarships through national competitive examinations, with the grants ranging from $250 to $2,000 a year. Information about these is available either through guidance counselors or from the company itself.

Scholarship contests

Special talents are required of recipients of the corporate generosity of the Fisher Body Craftsman's Guild, which conducts an annual competition for young model car designers and builders. Two $5,000 scholarships are awarded each year, with a total of nearly $50,000 presented to about 20 youngsters. One boy, Ace Fogarty of Sarasota, Florida, assured his college career by placing in the Chevrolet All-American Soap-box Derby to win a $4,000 prize and then earning a $4,000 Craftsman's Guild award. This kind of jackpot is a rarity, however.

Other contests are sponsored by business and industry. The Western Tablet and Stationery Corporation, for example, gives scholarships of $500 to $5,000 for the best 100-word statements on "Why I want to go to college." Eastman Kodak presents photo awards ranging from $15 to $400. Columbia Pictures provides grants for drama students, while the Alfred P. Sloan Foundation spends more than $1 million a year on stipends. During the 1964–65 year there were 460 scholarships at 45 institutions ranging from the minimum of $200 awarded as an honor to deserving scholars with no financial need to tuition-plus-$600, which in the case of an expensive school such as Dartmouth amounted to $2,400 for the year. Sloan scholarships are awarded to men only. They are allocated by the schools included in the program. There is no limitation as to a student's major and the emphasis is on getting the most capable student. The foundation contributes an additional $650 per year to each participating school for each scholarship student. All or part of this may be added by the school to the Sloan scholarship grant. Lists of participating schools and application procedures are made available to every high school in the country every year. Students interested in seeking one of these grants should consult their high school counselors.

Procter & Gamble provides more than $1.2 million a year toward scholarships, *which again are awarded through the colleges,* and grants of varying sizes are provided, among others, by the Union Carbide Company, the Sears-Roebuck Foundation, the National Restaurant Association, the Radio Corporation of America and the Kroger Company.

To learn about a corporate scholarship, a student should check with his counselor, consult his local library's collection of volumes listing specific scholarships, talk with an official of his local Chamber of Commerce or get in touch with the college of his choice or the company itself. In most cases where scholarships are of significant value, he will find that they are controlled either by individual schools or by the National Merit Scholarship Corporation.

Government programs

The major exception to the general rule that the schools control the most important scholarships is the aid provided by government— mainly the states. There has been much criticism of Congress for its refusal to enact scholarship legislation providing for more and larger grants and for the repeated defeat of bills that would give tax relief to parents financing college. In some of the states, however, there are programs that are both generous and democratically administered.

New York, which appears to have the most liberal program of aid to individual college students, spent more than $50 million during the 1963–64 academic year to provide funds to more than 150,000 students. Thousands of young people receive state scholarships and incentive grants as well as the state-guaranteed loans (see Chapter 9). You might say that the state has its own package plan, for it provides some students with both grants and loans.

Scholar-incentive grants, introduced in New York in 1961, actually amount to a scholarship for every student. Sums ranging from $50 to $400 are given, with eligibility open to almost every bona fide resident attending an institution in the state. First, of course, one must pass the State Board of Regents college admissions test or some other recognized examination. Then the money goes to the school involved. Even students on probation during their college careers qualify for this award, and no one is required to prove need for the minimum stipend of $50. There have been many criticisms of the program, because it gives money to some students who have no need while some who could use more have to find funds elsewhere.

An unsurprising number of colleges raised their tuition fees after the program was adopted, thus in effect eliminating any financial benefits to students. The schools maintained that their prices would have gone up anyway, but the timing seemed to be more than coincidental.

Probably the most outstanding of the New York benefits is the long-standing Regents Scholarship Program, which provides four-year grants totaling well over $22 million to more than 50,000 students in colleges, universities and nursing schools.

So extensive is the total New York program that in one recent school year half of all the residents of the state in full-time higher education were receiving assistance from Albany in the form of scholarships, fellowships or incentive grants. These and thousands of others also had state-guaranteed loans, while a larger number of additional students were enrolled in low-cost or free tax-supported state and local schools.

The New York program has been described here in some detail because it is more generous than those of most states and has led the way for others. It also shows what can be done to open college doors to as many qualified students as possible. Further, it emphasizes the extent to which the taxpayer can become involved in stipends to students.

Among the other leading states in the area of college financing are Illinois, Kansas, Rhode Island, New Jersey, Massachusetts and

California. Probably no state spends more money on higher education over all than California, with $150 million in tax funds going to the low-fee University of California and its various branches and $100 million to the equally modestly priced state college system, with 17 campuses. The state has contributed millions toward the free junior colleges, which get most of their support from taxpayers in junior college districts. Very little of the state's investment comes back in the form of student payments, since even at the university the fees are so low they could be described as nominal. This contrasts with New York, where tax money not only goes to the schools directly but also may be funneled through the students, who in most cases pay much higher tuition and fees than in California.

If it were not for business and government the price tag on higher education would be prohibitive for most people. The direct contributions of taxpayers and corporations to the schools actually provide aid for all who are enrolled. The funds available for aid to individual students in the form of cash grants are the cream that tops the much more sizable liquid assets.

What about the average student?

In recent years it has become increasingly apparent that not all business and professional leaders were "straight A" students, and that persons attaining academic excellence are not the only ones who can benefit from higher education. Accordingly, there is a growing tendency to make scholarships available to the promising although not academically supreme students. More effort is being made to recognize the unusual "average" student, whether it be through the Yale method of regarding all students as excellent, through the special Harvard program designed to help the well-rounded C student or through special scholarship funds.

Harvard has several funds with preferences for students who are not brilliant and who do not exhibit extraordinary academic inclinations. One of the major efforts at Harvard in recent years, in fact, has been to seek out young men of promise who are not necessarily the most able academically.

The University of Chicago grants assistance to average as well as bright students; a $100,000 fund to provide full tuition for "average" students who display leadership has been established at Brandeis University. The Jessie Smith Noyes Foundation of New York distributes about $350,000 a year to colleges and universities for needy but average students, while the National Merit Scholarship program has started a series of experimental stipends for the less than brilliant undergraduates.

The Boys' Clubs of America offer scholarships for young men interested in receiving an education and training for professional careers in youth work. Special curricula have been established for club work at Arizona State, Ball State, George Williams, Indiana, New York University, Springfield College and Western Kentucky State College. Students with these stipends work part time in a Boys' Club and attend school full time. They receive up to $300 a year in grants-in-aid, plus earnings, and are required to work in a club for at least two years after finishing school. If for some reason a graduate does not carry out his obligation, he is asked to return all funds advanced.

An additional scholarship program for Boys' Club trainees is offered by W. Clement Stone, president of the Combined Insurance Company of America and of the Chicago Boys' Clubs. The Stone scholarships are coordinated and controlled by the Chicago clubs but are available to any member of the organization in the country who wishes to attend George Williams College in Chicago, which has one of the special training programs. Accompanying the stipend, which covers the cost of attending the college, is a job on the staff of a Chicago club. To qualify a young man must have been a member of either a club or a club staff for two years and must have been accepted by the college. Stone makes the awards for one year at a time, which means that they must be renewed each fall. Upon graduation, there is no requirement that a recipient work for the

Boys' Clubs, but Stone has expressed the hope that all will. In both Boys' Club training programs academic excellence is less important than a sincere interest in the special field.

In the two chapters that follow, you will see further evidence of an interest in fostering the academic career of the average student, and also of the culturally deprived young person, principally the Negro. In most cases, the recognition of average youngsters has come in the form of admitting C students who otherwise would be turned down, but increasingly, scholarship help is becoming available. Some of the top colleges and universities are actively searching for capable underprivileged students. They include Ivy League schools and their sister schools for women, such as Radcliffe and Wellesley.

In New York City, the Joseph L. Fisher Foundation Scholarships, each for $6,000 over a four-year period, are awarded to students with "good potential" whose grades are not high enough to win them acceptance to the free institutions in the city, where competition is keen. Winners of this stipend must exhibit a real desire to go to college and prove economic need. The first winners, named in 1963, were a Negro girl from an economically depressed home and a white boy who lived on the Lower East Side, a neighborhood of spectacular poverty.

Some schools that do not offer scholarships to average students have other benefits for them. At Princeton, the C student does not qualify for a cash gift, but he can take tuition loans of a maximum of $3,000 over four years and repayable within three years after leaving the university. The interest rate is 1 per cent during the undergraduate years and graduate school and 4 per cent thereafter.

Dr. Sharvey Umbeck, president of Knox College, in Galesburg, Illinois, says that the student whose ability is not quite high enough for scholarships must use loans and jobs and therefore make a greater personal sacrifice to get an education. Knox offers a deferred plan that enables the spreading of payments for four years of college over six or eight, and this is regarded as a benefit to average and excellent alike.

As has been pointed out, however, whether a student is average or receives straight A's, he must be able to prove he *needs* money before he can get help. Several formulas for determining individual need have been devised, the most important of which will be described in full in the following chapter.

For further information on scholarships

Refer to:

The College Handbook, College Entrance Examination Board, Box 176, Princeton, New Jersey 08540, or Box 1025, Berkeley, California 90027 ($2).

Financial Assistance for College Students: Undergraduate, Department of Health, Education and Welfare, Washington, D.C. 20002 ($1.25).

A Handbook for the Counselors of College Bound Students, Association of College Admissions Counselors, 610 Church Street, Evanston, Illinois (available through school counselors).

Need a Lift? a handbook published annually by The American Legion, Indianapolis, Indiana (25 cents). This guide to where to obtain scholarship information lists addresses of government, industrial, religious and other sources of help.

Write to:

AFL-CIO, 815 16th Street, N.W., Washington, D.C. 20006.

B'nai B'rith Vocational Services, 1640 Rhode Island Avenue, N.W., Washington, D.C. 20006.

Boys' Clubs of America, 771 First Avenue, New York, New York 10017.

Church organizations. If you are interested in finding out about stipends offered by religious groups, consult your local clergyman about where to write.

Individual colleges, which control most scholarship awards.

5

WHAT IS STUDENT NEED?

... the College Scholarship Service

The race to college began in earnest after World War II, in good part under the impetus of the G.I. Bill, which provided educational subsidies for millions of veterans. As the pressure for higher education increased, the colleges and universities began a race of their own —to attract the best students. Unfortunately for students as a whole, most of the scholarship money was concentrated—and still is—in a few schools, and these institutions lured the most promising students by offering financial help. Students who knew where to find the scholarship money simply applied to a number of these schools and then sat back and waited for the highest bid. One school would offer a scholarship, job and loan; another a scholarship and a job; still another just a scholarship. The situation became chaotic as a result, with a relatively few students getting most of the offers and many promising young people undoubtedly being lost by the wayside. The duplication of applications was so large that some schools found they had to accept far more freshmen than they could accommodate each year to make sure of having a full complement of beginning students.

How the service was started

In 1954 representatives of 95 schools got together to do something about the applications mess. All of them were members of the College Entrance Examination Board, founded half a century before to bring order to entrance procedures. From the meeting of the 95 came the formation of the College Scholarship Service as a branch of the C.E.E.B. Today more than 500 institutions, including junior colleges, participate in its program, and much—but not all—of the confusion over student aid has been eliminated or reduced through standardization of procedures by which scholarships, loans and jobs are applied for and allocated.

The rapid growth of the C.S.S. was stimulated by the National Defense Education Act's loan program (see Chapter 9), which actually forced colleges to get into the business of analyzing the financial needs of students. The federal program did two important things: It spread aid money across the country, to large and small and rich and poor colleges and universities alike, and it exploded an old theory that most students would not borrow for education. Many educators had become convinced that students would not borrow, despite the fact that a school as prominent as the Massachusetts Institute of Technology had been arranging student loans for years. Through the federal loan program, the educational community and just about everyone else learned they had been wrong about loans. Now they are finding out the same thing about jobs (see Chapter 11). These aids have revolutionized the college finance picture. With national programs such as that operated by the federal government, a standard formula for computing need is deemed both desirable and useful.

The organizers of the College Scholarship Service were primarily interested in finding a way to single out the students most deserving of the various kinds of financial aid and to award the aid as fairly, reasonably and uniformly as possible. Out of this came what is known as "the need analysis," the key factor in determining allocations.

Through this analysis, the student gets what he *needs* to go to school. If he cannot prove financial need, he gets no aid at schools using the C.S.S. formula, which include those controlling about 80 per cent of all the institutional scholarship money in the country. It is important to remember that the College Scholarship Service itself does not actually award scholarships.

At the heart of the Scholarship Service program is the Parents' Confidential Statement, a detailed report on the financial status of the family of a student seeking aid. Forms are distributed to every high school in the country for use by any student who wishes to have his family participate; they also are obtainable from the College Scholarship Service. The parents submit one copy of the completed form to the C.S.S. and retain a work sheet. The service reviews the form for completeness and errors and prepares an estimate of the amount the parents can reasonably afford for college expenses from income and assets, plus what the student can provide, and the financial requirements at each college to which the student is applying. An estimate and a copy of the confidential statement are sent to each college listed by the student and his family, at a charge of $3 for the first copy and $2 for each additional one. The colleges then use the figures to decide whether aid should be provided and how much it should be. Currently, about 150,000 families submit forms to the C.S.S. each year, and more than twice that number of estimates and copies of forms are sent to schools.

In addition, the Citizens' Scholarship Foundation of Fall River (see Chapter 7) and the National Merit Scholarship Corporation (see Chapter 6) have their own particular need formulas. This means that any student applying to them for assistance and through the C.S.S. as well must ask his parents to fill out three forms. Most data of this nature are filed through the C.S.S., the compilations of which often are used by other groups, but as you can see, there still is some duplication of effort that may in time be eliminated if these three major groups not only can agree on one uniform basic need formula but can find a way to enable applicants to file only one set of forms.

How the need analysis works

The policy of the College Scholarship Service is that "students should be selected for financial aid according to their previous academic achievements and their promise of success in college, but that the size of the awards should be determined by their financial need." In determining how much help a student needs, therefore, the service takes into account both income and assets. A family is expected to draw on current income as the primary source of funds for college expenses. The service provides a chart from which it is possible for a family to estimate how much it is expected to provide from income, according to the amount of income and the number of dependent children (see Page 55). In these computations, the estimates apply only to families with no unusual or complicating financial circumstances, with only one working parent, with no children now attending college or private school, and with no extraordinary expenses.

Rexford G. Moon Jr., director of the College Scholarship Service, explains that the figure their system produces is the "best estimate we can make of what the parent can pay per year for the particular individual who is applying for financial aid. In the event there are two children in college, it would be incorrect to divide this sum into two parts. In this case a new computation is required for each applicant to reflect the expenses faced by the family in providing educational support not only for the applicant but for another dependent. We expect, incidentally, that when a family has two children in college, its amount of support, though not necessarily double what it is for one child, will certainly be half again as much, and of course this will vary with the circumstances of the particular family. Remember, one of the basic precepts of our system is that families will at least contribute as much toward the child's support in college as they do toward the child's support at home. Therefore, if there are two children in college, there will be at least this amount available

PARENTS' ANNUAL CONTRIBUTION FROM NET INCOME

Number of dependent children

Net income (before federal tax)	1	2	3	4	5	6	7	8
$ 2,000	$ 90	$ —	$ —	$ —	$ —	$ —	$ —	$ —
2,500	140	90	—	—	—	—	—	—
3,000	200	130	110	90	—	—	—	—
3,500	280	190	150	120	100	—	—	—
4,000	350	250	190	160	140	110	—	—
4,500	440	320	240	210	180	150	120	100
5,000	530	390	300	250	220	190	160	140
5,500	630	470	360	310	260	240	210	190
6,000	730	550	430	370	310	290	270	240
6,500	840	640	510	420	370	340	320	310
7,000	950	720	590	500	430	410	390	370
7,500	1,070	830	670	580	570	470	450	440
8,000	1,190	930	750	660	660	540	520	510
8,500	1,320	1,040	850	740	740	620	590	580
9,000	1,450	1,160	950	830	830	700	670	660
9,500	1,600	1,270	1,050	920	920	780	760	740
10,000	1,730	1,390	1,170	1,020	1,030	870	840	830
10,500	1,880	1,530	1,280	1,130	1,130	970	940	930
11,000	2,030	1,660	1,400	1,230	1,230	1,070	1,030	1,020
11,500	2,180	1,780	1,530	1,350	1,340	1,160	1,130	1,120
12,000	2,320	1,930	1,650	1,470	1,460	1,280	1,240	1,230
12,500	2,480	2,070	1,780	1,600	1,580	1,380	1,350	1,340
13,000	2,650	2,210	1,910	1,720	1,710	1,510	1,460	1,450
13,500	2,820	2,370	2,060	1,850	1,830	1,630	1,580	1,570
14,000	2,990	2,510	2,190	1,980	1,960	1,740	1,700	1,690
14,500	3,160	2,680	2,320	2,120	2,110	1,880	1,830	1,810
15,000	3,340	2,840	2,470	2,260	2,110	2,010	1,960	1,940

Reprinted by permission from *Financing a College Education: A Guide for Counselors*, published in 1963 by the College Entrance Examination Board.

for each applicant plus some additional amount for each, representative of some proportion of the so-called disposable income of the family."

You will note that the chart lists net income before federal taxes. Under this computation, a family with a $2,000 income and one dependent child would be expected to contribute $90 a year from income to a child's education. (Contributions from assets are computed separately, as will be seen later in this chapter.) At the other end of the scale is the eight-child family with an income of $15,000 before taxes; it is expected to supply $1,940 a year for the education of one child. The so-called average family, with three children and a $6,000 income, would be expected to provide a minimum of $430 a year from income to send a child to college.

The same information, based on C.S.S. figures, is presented in simpler form by the National Merit Organization (see Chapter 6) as follows:

Family income	Expected contribution	Family income	Expected contribution	Family income	Expected contribution
$3,000	$180	$ 7,500	$1,009	$11,000	$1,706
4,000	360	8,000	1,108	12,000	1,940
5,000	540	8,500	1,207	13,000	2,174
6,000	720	9,000	1,306	15,000	2,642
6,500	811	9,500	1,405	17,000	3,305
7,000	910	10,000	1,504	20,000	3,988

This table is for a family with one child. The expected annual contribution is decreased by approximately $125–150 for each additional child (somewhat less at low incomes and somewhat more at high incomes).

Or the computation can be made from this scale:

If a family has:	then the normal expected annual contribution from net assets will be:
one child	1/40
two children	1/48
three children	1/56
four children	1/64
five children	1/72
six children	1/80

How assets are analyzed

Now, for assets. The College Scholarship Service formula involves totaling a family's liquid assets, such as cash, stocks, savings bonds and the like, and its nonliquid assets, such as real estate, the loan value of life insurance, business holdings and farms, all of which are listed at half their market value. From the total a general allowance of $4,000 for the family and an emergency allowance of $500 for each member are subtracted. Other allowances are made for widows, families with parents who have no provision for their own retirement and many other contingencies.

What is left is considered the family's net assets. Each parent is assigned two shares of this sum and each dependent is assigned one. The student's share is divided by four, to apportion it equally over the four years of college.

For example: The Smiths have two children, $5,000 in the bank, a $10,000 equity in their home and a $2,000 loan value on life insurance. To arrive at their assets for this purpose, the Scholarship Service adds the entire amount of the bank account ($5,000) to half the home equity ($5,000) and half the life insurance loan value ($1,000), for a total of $11,000. After subtracting the general allowance of $4,000 and four emergency allowances totaling $2,000, the net assets are $5,000. Dividing this into six shares, four for the parents and one for each child, reduces the student's share to $833. The Smiths would be expected to provide one-fourth of this ($208) from their assets for each of the four undergraduate years, in addition to payments from income. If the Smiths had rented an apartment and had $10,000 in savings instead of owning a house, the $10,000 savings plus the $1,000 constituting half the loan value of the life insurance would still add up to $11,000.

The student's assets are considered in C.S.S. computations. If he has less than $1,000 it is separated from his parents' assets; if he has more the excess is added to his parents' liquid assets. Families generally are not expected to increase their mortgages or borrow on life insurance to finance college, although data on these are included on the forms.

Colleges usually expect students to use all or most of their own savings for college, but not all in the first year. The savings usually are apportioned at a rate of one-fifth for each year in C.S.S. computations, to leave something at graduation or for use in graduate school.

Some typical cases

The following examples have been provided by the College Scholarship Service as typical of applications for aid and amounts allocated:

John and David apply for financial assistance at the same school, where the total cost is $2,500 a year per student. John comes from a family with a $4,000 annual income. He has three younger brothers and sisters. The family owns its $6,000 house and has no mortgage. Its assets total $600 in cash and there are debts of $200. Because the family assets are modest, John's parents will be expected to draw only on their income to help him. The amount usually expected from a four-child, $4,000-a-year family is $160 a year. John plans to save $300 from a summer job and he has $625 in savings. The college expects him to apply $125 a year toward college.

The contributions then add up this way:

$160 from family income
300 from summer earnings
125 from student savings
―――
$585

John thus needs an additional $1,915 in aid for the school year. After studying the financial statement, the college decides to offer him a $1,200 scholarship (his grades have been outstanding), a $300 term-time job and a $400 loan. He will make up the remaining $15.

David, the second student, has a father who earns $14,000 in his own business, which has a capital value of $51,000. The family has $15,500 in savings and securities. David's younger brother attends a special school costing $1,500 a year. His dependent grandmother lives with the family. The college estimates that David's father can afford to pay $3,100 a year for college—$1,700 from his income and $1,400 from his assets. Since this is more than the total cost of college for the year, David is not offered any financial aid *although he is an even better student than John.*

In another example, Paul has applied for admission to a college costing $2,000 a year. His parents work, earning a combined income of $9,000. There are two younger children, one of whom has received $600 in medical treatment. The family lives in an apartment and has $3,000 in the bank. Paul has saved $1,000 toward college and is planning to net $300 from a job during the summer before enrolling. Taking into account the fact that both parents work, the college expects the family to apply $600 a year from income to the college bill. Paul is expected to contribute his $300 summer earnings and $200 of his savings, for a total of $1,100 from him and his family.

The financial need is reckoned at $900, but the college financial aid officer allocates $700 in aid as follows:

$400 scholarship
150 loan
150 term-time job
———
$700

This means that Paul will have to find $200 elsewhere, either taking it from his savings, finding another job or asking his parents for more money. The family's assets, although too small to be included in the actual computations, were considered as a possible source for this additional financing.

Mary has applied to two colleges, one far enough from home so that she would have to live on campus, the other within commuting distance. There are two younger children in the family, which has a total income of $7,500 a year. They own their home, valued at $13,000, and have a $6,000 mortgage. The parents have saved $3,000 and Mary has $750 in her bank account. Under the need formula, the family is expected to contribute $670 from income and nothing from assets. Mary will provide $200 from a summer job and $150 from her savings during her freshman year. The total family share then will be $1,020 for the year.

It would cost $2,300 for a year at the school away from home. This college offered Mary:

> $400 scholarship
> 200 loan
> 200 term-time job
> _____
> $800

This meant she would still need $480 to finance the year.

If Mary goes to the college near home it will cost $1,850 a year. This school offered her:

> $500 scholarship
> 200 loan
> 150 term-time job
> _____
> $850

With the $1,020 she and her family can provide, this would cover her first year in college.

Which school will she choose? Probably the one nearest home and most easily financed.

In studying the examples just given, you will note that some colleges do not meet the total need because they do not have the funds available, while other can and do meet family deficits. Parents should understand, however, that when a college has estimated what it feels a family can afford, it usually is considered to be a *minimum* figure, not the most that can be forthcoming from home.

Family statistics

Perhaps it would be useful for you to study a completed Parents' Confidential Statement. The form on Pages 64-65, which contains fictitious information, is reproduced with permission from the *1962-64 Financial Aid Manual*, published in 1962 by the College Entrance Examination Board.

In submitting a completed form to a school, the College Scholarship Service makes no value judgments, as you can see. It simply passes on to the school a summary of the financial situation as stated by the family, along with an estimate of what the family can afford to spend to finance a child's education during the next academic year. It is then up to the director of financial aid at the college to interpret the data. Some schools apply the C.S.S. information to their own formulas for computing need; in some cases they simply add or subtract an arbitrary amount.

There is no evidence in the Scholarship Service's files that families have taken unfair advantage of the forms, but some people, of course, would misrepresent anything. Once in a while the C.S.S. or a college checks with a student's secondary school or with a credit agency, or occasionally a high school counselor will get in touch with the Service or a college when he hears that considerable help is going to a student in an obviously solvent family. Occasionally—very occasionally—a misrepresentation is uncovered. If aid has been awarded in such a case, the college concerned will take appropriate action that year—or the next. It is heartening to know that people have been found to be more frank with the C.S.S. than with the Collector of Internal Revenue!

The confidential form is revised periodically to keep up with economic changes. A computation committee of college financial officers meets annually to suggest changes for the next year. In 1964, for example, additional information about taxes was requested, while in the preceding year the special form completed by farm families was revised and expanded.

The C.S.S. is always aiming for greater standardization and less confusion, and for primary emphasis on the student and his needs. In the past, when scholarships were thought of mainly as prizes for academic excellence, school officials were not very thorough in considering pleas for aid and requests often were made informally and in person. Now, with more and more students who need aid, as well as a constant financial squeeze on the academic community, schools must be more careful in allocating their money. Some persons may object to the punch-card system, but it is the best that college administrators have been able to devise—and they are frank to say that they are still open to suggestions for improvement.

Aid for able Negroes

Another national organization meriting mention in this discussion is the National Scholarship Service and Fund for Negro Students, which in its first 15 years of operation helped nearly 9,500 Negroes gain admission to more than 350 interracial colleges and to receive more than $4.3 million in scholarships from the schools. An additional $450,000 in aid funds has been provided by the organization through gifts and grants to it.

Educators are increasingly aware of the fact that there is a large body of untapped talent among Negro young people, who are generally in greater need of financial aid than are white students. The National Scholarship Service and Fund guides the academically qualified Negro in his search for acceptance and financial aid at an interracial institution.

Applicants are required to take standard aptitude tests and fill out detailed forms. Every student rated as qualified then receives information about the interracial colleges to which he might be admitted and at which scholarship money is available. Data also are provided on other sources of aid outside the colleges.

The students apply directly to the schools for admission and financial assistance, but they are guided in their choices by the service. Upon acceptance by a school, a student informs the service and also lets it know how much aid has been offered. The service then may help the student get further aid if it is needed.

A generous allocation of scholarship aid to Negroes is described in the discussion of the National Merit Scholarship program in the next chapter, and another aid program to Negroes and whites on an equal basis is presented in Chapter 7.

A special kind of help

Of national scope also are at least three other major clearing houses that help guide students to colleges but offer neither financial aid nor assistance in winning admission. They were organized only recently, largely at the request of colleges and universities that saw many young people being exploited by commercial college placement organizations, some of which charge large fees and either give little service or direct students to nonaccredited schools. There also were instances in which the college placement concerns received kickbacks from academically substandard schools in payment for referring students.

The three nonprofit groups generally approved by accredited institutions of higher learning are the College Admissions Assistance Center of the New York City Council of Higher Educational Institutions, the College Admissions Center of the Association of College Admissions Counselors and the Catholic College Admissions and Information Center. These organizations exist to help bring students and colleges together—the right school for each student, and vice versa. Primarily they serve students who have been turned down by the schools of their choice and do not know what to do next.

300

PARENTS' CONFIDENTIAL STATEMENT	ACADEMIC YEAR 1963-1964	↓Do NOT write in this space↓
Return to **COLLEGE SCHOLARSHIP SERVICE**	**N⁰ 002501**	

Box 176, Princeton, New Jersey
or Box 27896, Los Angeles 27, California

	Last name	First name	Middle name	Date of birth			Sex	Marital status
1. Student applicant	Wendell,	James	Paul	Month 4	Day 17	Year 45	☒ M ☐ F	☒ Single ☐ Married

2. Student applicant's home address	Street 9236 North Elm	City Marshall,	Zone	State Ohio	Parents (check if living) ☒ Father ☐ Stepfather / ☒ Mother ☐ Stepmother	Are living parents ☐ Divorced ☐ Separated

FATHER OR MALE GUARDIAN / **MOTHER OR FEMALE GUARDIAN**

3. Name	The Rev. Arthur H. Wendell	Age 43	Mrs. Arthur H. Wendell	Age 43
4. Home address	9236 North Elm, Marshall, Ohio		Same	
5. Name and address of employer or firm	First Presbyterian Church			
6a. Nature of business	Church	Years with firm		Years with firm
6b. Position held	Minister	9		

7. Provision for retirement — Please check if you participate in: ☐ Social Security ☒ Another Plan ☐ Neither — Please check if you participate in: ☐ Social Security ☐ Another Plan ☒ Neither

8. Names of banks at which you have accounts: City Bank and Trust Company — Names of banks at which you have accounts: None

9. Please list here all children, student applicant first. Please give specific dollar amounts where requested.

Name	Age	Check if dependent for income tax purposes in 1963	Name of present school, college, or occupation (1963-63)	Year in School	Public School	Private School	College	a. Tuition plus fees 1962-63	b. Total amount of scholarship or gift aid, 1962-63	c. Difference (a less b)
Applicant James	17	☒	Marshall High School	12	x					
Other Children Katheryn	16	☒	Marshall High School	11	x					
Peter	12	☒	Grade School	7	x					
		☐								
		☐								
		☐								
		☐								

Total column "c"

10. Please list here other dependents receiving financial support from family. (Do not include those listed in 3 and 9 above.)

Name	Age	Relationship to student applicant	Check if living with family	Check if dependent for income tax purposes in 1963	Estimated amount of total annual support from family
None			☐	☐	$
			☐	☐	$

Total estimated amount of support from family $

11. Please give make and year of any family automobiles. 1955 Chevrolet — Present auto indebtedness. $ None — If one of these cars is owned or used primarily by the applicant, indicate which. ---

12. Please explain here any special family circumstances the college should know about: See Instructions for examples.

     In addition to my salary, the church provides me with a manse. I would place its value at about $100.00 per month.

13. List (in any order) colleges to which copies of this form are to be sent:

Enclose check or money order payable to College Scholarship Service: $3 for first college named and $2 for each additional college.

Do not write in boxes below

Muskingum College			1496
Westminster (Pa.)			2975

Amount enclosed $ 5.00

Middle name Paul   First name James   Last name Wendell   (Please print) Student applicant

PARENTS' ANNUAL INCOME AND EXPENSES

(14) Salaries and wages before taxes		Total 1961	Total 1962	Estimated 1963	For css use only
	Mother	$ ---	$ ---	$ ---	
	Father	7200	7200	7200	
(15) Other income	Mother				
16-Explat item	Father	1200	1200	1200	
16. Gross income (14 plus 15).		8400	8400	8400 css	
(17) Business expenses		550	765	765	
18. Net income before taxes (16 less 17)		7850 6650	7635 6635	7635 6635 css	8635
19. Federal income tax	1960 income tax	1961 income tax	1962 income tax	—If none, write "none."	
	$856.22	$702.52	$650 (est)		
Total Number Exemptions Claimed	5	5	5		

		Total 1961	Total 1962	Estimated 1963
(20) Annual home expenses		200	200	200
(21) Uninsured medical expenses (include cost of medical insurance)		358	840	800
(22) Other extraordinary expenses paid		---	---	----

PARENTS' ASSETS AND LIABILITIES

23. Life insurance Type: Life term and endowment	Annual premium	Face value	Amount of insurance loans outstanding	Present loan value less loans outstanding
	$ 376.01	$ 19,200	$ None	$ 3,000
24. Home (if owned)	Total amount of fire insurance	a. Present market value	b. Unpaid mortgage	Difference (a less b)
	$ Not owned			
(25) Other real estate	$ ---	$ ----	$ ---	$ ----
(26) Total capital value of business or farm			$ ---	
Dollar value of your share of business or farm			$ ---	
27. Bank accounts (personal saving and checking)			$ 1200	
(28) Other investments			$ ----	
29. Indebtedness (exclude mortgage, auto) insurance loans)				

Purpose of debt	Amount outstanding	To be paid in 1963
	$	$
Total	$ ----	$ ----

STUDENT'S OWN ASSETS

(30) Nature of assets	How obtained	Value
Savings account	work	$ 106.00
Total Student Assets		$ 106.00

RESOURCES FOR STUDENT DURING 1963-64

(31) Sources of financial support	If living at college	If commuting to college
a. From parents' income	$ 600	$
b. From parents' assets	100	
c. From student's own assets (30)	100	
d. From student's summer earnings, 1963	100	
(e) From other sources		
Total	$ 900	$

PARENTS' AUTHORIZATION
We have checked this form for omissions and errors. To the best of our knowledge, the information reported is complete and correct. We authorize its transmittal to the colleges named in Item 13 and its use by the College Scholarship Service as described in the *"Information"* and *"Instructions"* accompanying this form.

Signatures of both parents (or guardian)

Date

CC62 P650V   *Copyright 1962, College Entrance Examination Board.*

In the space below please explain all circled items.

Item (14) —Itemize source, explain any major differences ($500 or more) between years 1962 and 1963.

Items (15)(17)(20)(21)(22)(23) and (28)—Itemize and explain.

Item (26) Give total current assets, current liabilities, net fixed assets, and net profit. See Instructions.

Items (30)(31a)—Explain.

17. Business Expense
Contributions $400
Professional journals 30
Books 120
Dues to professional organizations 25
Professional entertainment 135
Supplies 55
$765

21. Orthodontist $390
Drugs and medicine 450
$840

20. This is expense which I must bear for utilities on my house, provided by the parish

7. I also participate in Presbyterian Church annuity plan.

Nº 002501

(DO NOT WRITE ON BACK OF STATEMENT)

REFERENCE FORM 1963-1964

(Please print) Student applicant	Last name	First name	Middle name
	Wendell	James	Paul
Student applicant's home address	Street	City	Zone State
	9236 North Elm, Marshall		Ohio

REC.

F.U.

RET.

Nº 002501

Note: In its confidential computations, the College Scholarship Service determined that the family could contribute $769 from income, $21 from the student's assets and $300 from the student's summer earnings, for a total of $1,090. This would mean that at a resident college costing $2,000 a year, he would need $910 in aid each year. At a commuter college costing $1,300, he would need $210. It is up to the college to decide how to allocate the aid funds.

Sometimes the students have been rejected because the schools demand a higher level of performance than they can maintain. Sometimes the students have applied too late. Quite a few of the rejected applicants have been Negroes or members of other minorities. With the help of the clearing houses about 80 per cent of those who have been turned down and who seek placement guidance have proved to have academic potential and have found schools.

For a nominal fee of $15 these nonprofit centers serve students by providing colleges with copies of high school transcripts, counselors' recommendations and completed application forms. The colleges and universities frequently send their representatives to the centers to review the credentials on file. The colleges also file their requirements with the centers.

The average student turned down by the college of his choice has received offers of acceptance from 29 different schools through the center maintained by the Association of College Admissions Counselors in Evanston, Illinois. One, a highly qualified boy, had failed to make an Ivy League school where standards were extraordinarily high. Through the guidance of this center he applied to an excellent school where he was accepted and where he did well. The center also was able to guide him to a job, which he needed.

A student who wants this kind of advice should consult his high school guidance counselor, a college admissions officer or one of these three centers rather than rushing out to the nearest college placement "service" listed in the telephone book. Unfortunately, most of the commercial organizations have names similar to those of the nonprofit groups.

For further information on clearing houses

Write to:

Catholic College Admissions and Information Center, Box 4582, Brookland Station, Washington, D.C.

College Admissions Center of the Association of College Admissions Counselors, 610 Church Street, Evanston, Illinois 60201.

College Scholarship Service, 475 Riverside Drive, New York, New York 10027.

Council of Higher Educational Institutions in New York City, 41 East 65th Street, New York, New York 10021.

National Scholarship Service and Fund for Negro Students, 6 East 82nd Street, New York, New York 10028.

6

A TALENT REGISTER

... the National Merit program

Shortly before the first day of spring each year, about 700,000 students pore over a three-hour battery of tests in some 17,000 high schools in every state and territory of the United States and in schools abroad enrolling Americans. A few months later, about 14,000 of them are invited to take still another test, and the following spring, 1,500 to 2,000 are notified that they have won college scholarships ranging in value from $100 to $1,500 for each of the next four years. Of the original 700,000 students, about 35,000 will win commendations, and the 14,000 who were tested a second time will receive special citations. The commendations and citations may help the recipients win scholarships elsewhere, but for most of the rest of the 700,000, chances for stipends are limited.

This is the way the National Merit Scholarship program works. The academic competition is stiff and the financial rewards go to only a small fraction of those who compete, but with an annual expenditure of about $4 million, it still is one of the largest independent scholarship programs in the history of education, and it is growing. On the surface National Merit's activities may not seem significant, because of the few scholarships it awards in relation to the total number of students who participate in its competition. If scholarships were the only reason for the program, it would not amount to much, but its importance is inestimable in spotlighting scholars in general, helping to single out able students and motivating young people to seek a college education or search for scholarships elsewhere. More than a third of the students tested in one year said they took the examination primarily to gain information about their own educational development, not in the expectation that they would win scholarships. The total result is important, therefore, far beyond the number of scholarships granted.

The General Motors Corporation's scholarship program is the only other giant in this field, with an annual budget of more than $5 million for 1,600 scholarships to students and gifts to colleges. No other programs come anywhere near those of the National Merit organization and General Motors. Most stipends, including those of G.M., are controlled by a few schools, which means that in the main scholarship students really do not have a free range of choice of where they will study. They go to the schools where the scholarships are, and the scholarships go where the smartest students are. While the National Merit program also benefits these same schools more than others, *it does give students a choice* of any accredited four-year school and also makes contributions of $100 a year to publicly supported schools and $250 to private schools for each Merit scholar (up to a maximum of 20) enrolled, in addition to the grants provided for the students themselves.

Who benefits?

There is one major difference between this program and most other scholarship plans. It is concerned with the matter of need. Merit scholars are chosen, regardless of their financial status, on the basis of their ratings in examinations and reports by the officials of their schools. *Every* winner gets a stipend, whether he needs it or not, but *the amount* of the grant is determined by need. Therefore, the student who is in no need of funds to get through college receives an honorarium of $100 or $250 a year for four years. The neediest winners may receive up to $1,500 a year, and sometimes more. The average has been running at just under $800 a year. In this way, the most brilliant and well-rounded student is given recognition even though he can afford college. He and his family are able to say that he has won a scholarship; the fact that it is only $100 a year is not important.

This program, like almost all the other major efforts to help students finance college, is a recent one. It was established in 1955 with a $20 million grant from the Ford Foundation and $500,000 from the Carnegie Corporation of New York to seek out intellectually able students. The Ford grant provided $1 million a year in scholarship funds for 10 annual selections of scholars, $2 million for administrative costs and $8 million in matching funds to encourage other sponsors. The Carnegie grant helped meet administrative expenses for the first five years of the program. In 1962 the Ford Foundation extended its original commitment to provide $14.5 million to support and expand the basic program through 1970 at least, with some of the funds earmarked for experimental programs.

Meanwhile, a number of businesses, unions and industries, and even colleges themselves, have become participants in the Merit program through scholarships with requirements they may stipulate. From the inception of the Merit awards through the 1963–64 program, sponsors paid or committed a total of nearly $16 million for approximately 4,000 four-year stipends. In the 1963–64 program alone, 951 sponsored scholarships were in effect; over a four-year period, their cost was approximately $3.7 million.

The grants provided with the Ford nestegg are known as *National* Merit Scholarships. Those from other sources are given the names of the donors, such as the *Sears* Foundation Merit Scholarships, the *Occidental College* Merit Scholarships and the *AFL-CIO* Merit

Scholarships. The Army and Air Force provide Merit awards for a limited number of children of active-duty personnel from the profits of post exchanges, theaters and the like. For individuals and organizations wishing to give small amounts, there is a President's Fund, which in a recent year attracted $42,000. A newer program is the college sponsorship of Merit stipends. Several schools are offering Merit awards through the national organization by drawing on their own scholarship funds. The colleges' development departments are finding this a good fund-raising tool; they establish a Merit award and then ask a donor to finance it, thus adding to their total pool of money for stipends.

Another recent program provides special awards to students who are not usually considered for such aid: those whose records indicate exceptional creative promise, those who can enter college without completing high school and those with academic ability who have shown exceptional determination to overcome severe financial handicaps and other disadvantages. In the first three years of this program, more than 300 students received special scholarships. Among them were a Maryland boy now enrolled in Harvard who got only average grades in high school but demonstrated artistic skills, a California girl outstanding in writing and history but poor in mathematics, a Massachusetts boy brilliant enough to be accepted by the Massachusetts Institute of Technology without taking the senior year of high school, and a severely deprived daughter of migrant workers who studied despite the fact that her parents forbade her to read books.

The last-mentioned student did not do particularly well in the Merit tests, but her difficulty was recognized by her teachers, who recommended her for one of the new scholarships. She did not even have the $1 fee to cover the costs of administering the tests, grading them, reporting the scores and selecting the winners. Small as the fee is, if a student cannot afford to pay it he is allowed to take the test for nothing.

Still another major opportunity for youngsters out of the mainstream of scholarship activity has been provided by the Ford Foundation through the National Merit organization. The Foundation launched a five-year, $7 million scholarship program in 1964 for outstanding Negro students. Unlike the standard Merit awards, there are no qualifying scholastic examinations for Negro applicants, though finalists take a special test to determine their strength of purpose and drive to succeed. The first of these National Achievement Scholarships, ranging from $1,000 to $6,000 for four years, were awarded in the fall of 1964 to 200 Negroes who were nominated by officials of their high schools on the basis of their past performance and their motivation. A total of 1,000 Negroes, at a rate of 200 a year, will benefit from this program during the five years. In the past, Negroes have won Merit grants under the general national competition, but only 13 of the 1,650 awards in 1964 went to members of their race.

The search lasts a year

The ninth annual Merit program began with the administration of the National Merit Scholarship Qualifying Test in March, 1964. To be eligible for scholarship consideration one had to be a United States citizen or in the process of becoming one and to be planning to study for a degree at an accredited college or university in the United States. The Merit test must be taken in the calendar year preceding completion of high school and entrance to college. That meant that a student planning to enter college in the fall of 1965 would have taken the qualifying test in the spring of 1964. It also meant that the student would have to complete high school and enter college in the same calendar year. Thus students pursuing the standard four-year high school course are expected to take this test in the second semester of their junior year or the first semester of their senior year.

Students enrolled in an accelerated high school program may take the test in the spring of their sophomore year provided that they plan to enter college the following year. A few students matriculate without actually receiving high school diplomas. They, too, may take the first test in their sophomore year in high school.

However it may be, in the September after the qualifying tests are taken some 14,000 top-scoring students are named semifinalists. Every state is represented in this group, with no more than 1 per cent of the high school seniors in any one state becoming semifinalists. The names of the 14,000 are published in a book distributed to colleges and universities and scholarship agencies. The names, addresses and scores of the 14,000 are also sent to the colleges of their first and second choice, on the chance that scholarships might be available to them there.

A month later, another group, usually around 35,000 students, receives Letters of Commendation. They have done well in the qualifying test but are no longer in the Merit scholarship competition. The Letter of Commendation makes a student eligible for some of the National Merit services, such as the sending of his name, address and score to the first two colleges on his list.

Only semifinalists are eligible for final consideration for Merit scholarships. To become a finalist a student is required to take the College Entrance Examination Board's Scholastic Aptitude Test, be endorsed by his school, have his school send his record to the National Merit Corporation, submit a biographical form and provide confidential family financial information. At least 97 per cent of the semifinalists make the final list each year, with every finalist receiving a Certificate of Merit.

About a year after the first qualifying tests are given, the Merit scholars are announced, often in appropriate ceremonies in the high schools. The stipends awarded the top winners who can prove financial need represent the difference between the money they can obtain elsewhere and the amount they need to go to college—up to a maximum that almost invariably is set at $1,500 a year, although some sponsored awards may be larger. The size of the scholarship may be adjusted if the winner's financial situation changes or costs fluctuate significantly during the four years he is in college.

Merit scholars are not allowed to accept other major stipends unless financial need is considerably larger than the maximum grant. Smaller outside grants of a maximum of $500 over four years as a single prize or $125 a year for four years are allowed, but all such gifts must be reported to the Merit Corporation.

How need is determined

The National Merit computation of need is based on the tuition and fees charged by the school, the cost of room and board, a flat $450 for books, clothing, laundry and incidentals, and five cents a mile for transportation between home and college for two round trips a year. These figures are totaled and set against the family's financial situation, which is based on net taxable income, the number of dependents, student earnings, and family assets and indebtedness.

So that you will know exactly what questions are asked, and to enable you to see for yourself how this system compares with that of the College Scholarship Service, discussed in the preceding chapter, the form on Page 75 is provided through the courtesy of the National Merit Scholarship Corporation, which filled out the fictitious but representative data and made the computations. You will note that the National Merit organization is a little more liberal in its analysis, allowing a working mother to deduct a fair portion of her income as a business expense that is not counted toward the family contribution for college and giving a family a larger "thrift" or "general" allowance from assets. The two systems are not so far apart, however, that they could not be merged into one need analysis formula that would enable families to file one detailed form where two now are required.

B

33-1234	SCOTT	JAMES	HENRY
NMSC Identification No.	Last name of student applicant	First name	Middle name

Sex	Marital status	Date of birth	Student lives with	☒ Father	☒ Mother
☒ M	☒ Single	Month Day Year		☐ Stepfather	☐ Stepmother
☐ F	☐ Married	12 12 46	Parents are: divorced, separated, deceased (father - mother)		

	Street	City	State
Student's home address	666 Valley Road	Kensington	New York

	Name	Age	Address (if same as student, write "same")
Father or Guardian	Harold T. Scott	46	same

Name and address of employer or firm	Fix-It City 31 Main St., Kensington	Years with firm 13
Nature of business	Radio-TV Repair	Position now held Repairman-Manager

	Name	Age	Address (if same as student, write "same")
Mother	Ethel L. Scott	42	same

Name and address of employer or firm	Kensington School Board	Years with firm ½
Nature of business	Teaching	Position now held Teacher

COMPLETE THIS SECTION IF STIPEND GREATER THAN THE MINIMUM IS NEEDED

(1) Dependents (in addition to parents named above) for Federal income tax purposes in 1964

	Name	Relationship to student applicant	Age	Check if living with family	Name of present school, college or occupation (1963-64)	Grade level
Applicant	James H.	same	17	☒	K'sington HS	12
	Marcia M.	sister	19	☐	Barnard	14
	Harold T., Jr.	brother	14	☒	Park JHS	9
				☐		
				☐		

If you contribute to the support of other relatives, please check here and explain on back.   3   ☒

A	For NMSC use only	I	For NMSC use only	C	For NMSC use only
	16600		11150		(SE + I + A)
B-F _____		IT 1490	3500		300
E 12500		WM 1050	7650		870
MSS _____		Med ____			80
Ret _____		Exp ____			1250
		Debt ____			
	12500	Col 760			
	2) 4100	Dep 200			
Sh: 7	2050		7650		

The chart explained

... the key to the boxes labeled A, I and C in lower left-hand corner:

A = Assets

B–F: business or farm
E: emergency allowance
MSS: mother sole support

Ret: retirement
Sh: shares

FINANCIAL INFORMATION FORM
Return to

1964-65
ACADEMIC YEAR

NATIONAL MERIT SCHOLARSHIP CORPORATION
1580 SHERMAN AVENUE
EVANSTON, ILLINOIS

PARENTS' ANNUAL INCOME AND DEDUCTIBLE EXPENSES

			Actual 1963	Estimated 1964	For NMSC use only
(2) Salaries and wages before taxes	Father		6850	6950	
	Mother		3000	4200	
(3) Other income	Father				
	Mother				
4. Gross income (2 plus 3)			9850	11150	
(5) Business expenses (deductible)					
6. Net income before taxes (4 less 5)			9850	11150	

FEDERAL INCOME TAX INFORMATION

	on 1961 income	on 1962 income	on 1963 income (est)
7. Federal income tax withheld and paid	975	980	1000
8. Number exemptions	1961 5	1962 5	1963 5

PARENTS' ASSETS AND LIABILITIES

	Unpaid mortgage	Equity	
9. Home (if owned)	3000	11000	
(10) Other real estate..................			
(11) Dollar value of your share of business or farm........			
12. Bank accounts (personal savings and checking)........		3000	
13. Other investments		2600	
14. TOTAL ASSETS (sum of items 9-13).................		16600	
15. Automobile indebtedness; give year and make..........		200	'59 Chev
(16) Other indebtedness			
17. TOTAL indebtedness (15 plus 16)			
18. NET ASSETS (14 less 17)		16400	

STUDENT'S OWN ASSETS

(19) Nature of assets	How obtained	Value
Bank Savings	Yard Work	200

PROVISION FOR RETIREMENT (Please check)

☒ Social Security ☐ Other plan ☐ Neither

PARENTS' CERTIFICATION

We have checked this form for omissions and errors. To the best of our knowledge, the information reported is complete and correct. We agree to inform NMSC of major changes in our financial status if the student applicant is awarded a Merit Scholarship.

Signatures of
both parents
(or guardian)   *Harold ... L. Scott*
                Ethel L. Scott

Date   12/20/63

S27-15M-63

I = Income

IT: income tax
WM: working mother
Med: medical
Exp: unusual expenses

Debt
Col: college for another child or children
Dep: dependents other than children

C = Contribution

SE: summer earnings
I: income

A: assets

This side of form to be used only where explanations are called for (see instructions)

(1) DEPENDENTS: If children other than the applicant will be in college in 1964-65, give name of institution, amount of family support, amount of scholarship aid if any.

Marcia - Barnard - $815 State Scholarship

(T = $1575) — $815 = $760

If you contribute to the support of relatives not listed in (1), give name, relationship, and dollar amount of support.

Thomas and Millie Luther
Maternal Grandparents
$200/year

(2) (3) INCOME: Include here any necessary explanation of salaries or other income.

(5) BUSINESS EXPENSES (allowable as income tax deduction)

(10) OTHER REAL ESTATE

(11) OWN BUSINESS OR FARM

(16) INDEBTEDNESS (excluding mortgage or automobile)

Purpose of debt

Amount outstanding ....

To be repaid in 1964............................

MEDICAL EXPENSES IN EXCESS OF $400 AND NOT COVERED BY INSURANCE (itemize)

          1963   1964 (est.)

Explain here any special family circumstances not shown elsewhere on form.

Analyzing the chart

In general, the National Merit need analysis procedures are based on those developed by the College Scholarship Service (see Chapter 5). A student's *need* is determined by subtracting the amount of money a family can be expected to contribute toward college costs from the student's total college costs. The family contribution consists of monies from three sources: income, assets and student's summer earnings.

Here is how the financial situation of the fictitious Scott family is broken down:

Contribution from income. In the Scotts' case, the expected contribution from income is based on their estimated income for 1964: $11,150. First, however, in order to determine what portion of this sum is available for college expenses, certain allowances for unusual family expenses must be made.

The first allowance, "IT," is the amount of income tax the family can be expected to pay, assuming it claims the standard deductions. The typical tax paid by a three-child family with an annual income of $11,150 is $1,490.

The second allowance, "WM," is that for a working mother. The Merit organization recognizes that part of an employed mother's salary must go toward expenses incurred solely as a result of her working. Twenty-five per cent, or a maximum of $1,500, of her salary therefore is subtracted from the family's net income. In the Scotts' case, the allowance is $1,050.

There are other allowances. Because the Scotts also contribute $760 a year toward college tuition for Marcia, James's older sister, and $200 a year toward the support of grandparents, as itemized on the back of the form, these amounts also are subtracted from the net income and are entered on the lines marked "Col" and "Dep." Allowances are always made for the cost of college tuition for other children in a family, minus scholarship help and up to a maximum of $1,600, and for the support of grandparents or other relatives up to a maximum of $600. The medical expense and debt lines have been left blank on the Scotts' form because they do not anticipate any unusual or major outlays for these items.

All the allowances listed are totaled, giving a figure of $3,500. This is then subtracted from the Scotts' net income of $11,150. The remaining $7,650 is the significant figure used to determine the expected minimum family contribution from income.

The tables developed by the College Scholarship Service listing expected contribution from income (see Page 55) show that a three-child family with a net income of $7,650, after allowances, should be able to contribute $870 a year from income toward college expenses.

Contribution from assets. The Scotts indicated that their total assets were $16,600. This figure included an $11,000 equity in their home, a $3,000 bank account and $2,600 in other investments. An automobile indebtedness of $200 has been subtracted from total assets. The result is $16,400 in net assets. In addition, since student assets are normally considered a part of family assets, James's $200 has been added to the $16,400; thus $16,600 is the amount used in computing the family contribution from assets. Again, however, certain allowances are made before determining the actual contribution expected from assets.

To avoid penalizing those families that, through great thrift or sacrifice, have accumulated assets, each family is automatically given a $10,000 "thrift allowance." This means that only net assets in excess of $10,000 are considered significant in determining the expected contribution from assets. In addition, an emergency allowance of $500 for each family member is subtracted. Therefore, the total emergency and thrift allowance, both listed in the space marked E, is $12,500 for the Scott family. This amount is subtracted from net assets, and the remaining $4,300 is divided by two for computational purposes. Each child in a family is entitled to one share of assets and each parent receives two shares. The tables provided by the College

Scholarship Service (Page 55) then show that James's share of his family's assets is $80 for 1964–65.

(If James's father owned his own business or farm or were retired, or if his mother were the sole means of support for the family, certain other allowances would be subtracted from assets.)

Summer earnings. In addition to the help provided from family income and assets, the student himself is expected to contribute a certain amount of money toward college expenses. While most students earn the required amount during the summer, the money may be acquired through campus jobs during the school year or from loans or other sources. Freshman girls are expected to contribute $200, while boys are asked to provide $300.

Total family contribution. James's expected $300 in self-help funds and his family's contribution of $870 from income and $80 from assets are totaled to obtain the family contribution, which comes to $1,250. To determine James's financial need for a year at college, the family contribution now is subtracted from the total cost of attending the school of his choice.

Total college costs and student need. The cost of a year at college includes tuition, fees, room and board (all reported by the college), miscellaneous expenses ($450 for all students) and travel (equal to five cents a mile for two round trips a year between home and college, for a maximum of $400).

It is apparent that James's actual need will depend on the cost of the college he attends. For instance, if he wishes to attend a state university costing $1,600, his need will be $350—the difference between his family's contribution of $1,250 and the cost of the college. If he wishes to attend a more expensive private college costing $2,700, his need would be $1,450. The stipend accompanying a Merit Scholarship may vary from a minimum of $100 to a maximum, in most cases, of $1,500 a year.

In general, as has been pointed out, the National Merit procedures for analysis of need are based on those developed by the College Scholarship Service and the C.S.S. expectancy tables are used. As is

true of most colleges, the National Merit organization adheres to
the principle that students and their families must share the responsibility for paying for higher education commensurate to their ability
to do so.

The results are widespread

Although Merit scholars are few, compared with the total number
of college students and even with the total number of recipients of
stipends of all kinds, the qualifying steps undoubtedly start many
toward college who might not otherwise think of seeking a higher
education. The program also encourages some to seek scholarships
who otherwise would not do so, and it helps the schools find the
most promising students. Further, by insisting on recognition of
students from every state in both public and private schools, the
program is a truly national one, developing talents in some areas of
the country that might be ignored. John M. Stalnaker, president of
the National Merit Scholarship Corporation, says that the program
actually generates more scholarship aid for deserving students than
the sum of its own scholarships. It provides what he calls "a national
register of talent."

About 40 per cent of the youngsters who participate in the
National Merit talent search receive offers of aid from other sources,
many of them unsolicited. The United States Military Academy at
West Point uses the results in confirming the academic ability of
candidates for its four-year training program, and the Woodrow
Wilson National Fellowship Foundation writes every finalist and
commended student a letter urging him to go into teaching and
offering information on opportunities for graduate fellowships.
Several state universities offer stipends to Merit finalists. An organization of journalism educators has been sending lists of semifinalists
and commended students interested in journalism to journalism
schools, which then send data on aid opportunities. In addition,
information about high-performing students is made available to

a number of large national, state, regional and local scholarship-granting groups and to foundations and businesses engaged in fostering higher education.

Also to be considered, of course, is the fact that not everyone who takes a National Merit Qualifying Test is aiming for a scholarship. Many students simply want to find out how well they are doing. In some schools the test is given to every student, while in others only promising pupils are tested.

To preclude the possibility that any student will do well in a test as a result of having seen the questions asked in previous years, new examinations are developed each year. All of them explore knowledge and understanding of English usage, vocabulary, reading in social studies and natural science, and mathematics. The examinations are designed to rate the ability of a student to use the information he has absorbed, to think critically and to apply factual information to problems. They are considered to be examinations of readiness for college and are designed primarily to single out bright youngsters who are using their talents.

When the time for selection comes, the individual sponsors, whether industries, unions or colleges, may choose their own scholars from the list of finalists or turn the job over to the National Merit judges. A sponsor may establish his own criteria, as, for example, ACF Industries, which awards stipends only to children of its employees. Ten scholarships are given annually to Arkansas students, and a major beer company gives first preference to chemistry majors and second to the children of its employees, wholesalers and distributors.

What the judges look for

The National Merit selection committee, made up of high school guidance experts and college admissions officers, has reported to the national organization that it looks for "that something extra" in a student—"a plus value." Often the recommendation of the school is the determining factor. In other words, if a recommendation is well thought out and clearly and enthusiastically written, it can have a decisive influence on the selection committee.

In the final judging, the goal is to find the ablest and most productive students. Extracurricular activities, in and out of school, are considered, as are the student's evaluation of himself and the recommendations of his school's staff. Although recognition of intellectual excellence is of prime importance, the committee also asks such questions as: "Do activities reveal creativity, special talents, dedication and effort to be of service?" One member of the Merit selection committee has said that "activities as they reflect depth or breadth of interest are of considerable importance. I find myself unimpressed by the *number* of activities certain candidates list, and deeply impressed when occasionally there is evidence that a candidate has found great meaning in, or contributed greatly to, a single activity."

Misunderstandings arise periodically about the method of selecting semifinalists or recipients of the National Merit and sponsored awards. Also often misunderstood is the stipend itself. Some persons are not aware that the Merit Scholars are chosen first and the stipend then computed on the basis of individual need. It is important to bear in mind that, *comparatively* large as it is, the Merit program *directly* benefits no more than 2 per cent of the nation's high school graduates, and that most stipends still are awarded by colleges.

Simplified procedures provided

A major achievement of the Merit program has been to eliminate many multiple competitions and sets of rules for allocating scholarships that used to exist when the present sponsors acted independently. Still more needs to be done in this direction, by National Merit and other groups. It would help considerably, for example, if all the local PTA's nationalized their little scholarship programs into one large one. The same can be said for the Kiwanis, Boy and Girl Scouts, the YMCA, YWCA and YMHA, and other organizations. Each could be more effective if it acted nationally, perhaps even by joining the National Merit movement and sponsoring scholarships bearing its name. In this way each group could still retain a measure of control over its awards and could continue to be identified with them while at the same time almost assuredly putting its funds to more efficient and beneficial use.

However, it was not the intention of the organizers of the Merit program to bring all independent scholarships under its aegis, nor to give the impression that they regarded theirs as the only way to conduct a scholarship program. They were hopeful that the Merit system would help to inspire others to leadership and attract new scholarship sponsors, as well as to provide a national program that would call attention to intellectually able young persons and encourage favorable public opinion toward intellectual achievement. It is felt also that the program makes life somewhat easier for both the high schools and the colleges by providing an orderly system of giving examinations and identifying able students.

Stalnaker summarizes the philosophy of the Merit program this way:

"As pressures grow for college admission and for scholarship help, selection will become more important and can become a tyrannical, pernicious device. If it favors the compulsive conformer whose only interest is top grades, it can discourage the independent and creative types. By demanding well-roundedness, it can encourage the able to dissipate their energies in a frenetic round of extracurricular activities just for the sake of the record.

"But selection can also be beneficial in its influences. It can encourage a recognition of the breadth and diversity of talent. It can encourage a variety of types of talented persons to strive for excellence, each in his own way."

For further information on Merit scholarships

Write to:

National Merit Scholarship Corporation, 990 Grove Street, Evanston, Illinois 60201.
Or consult your high school counselor or principal.

7

DOLLARS FOR SCHOLARS

... a grass-roots plan

It was a crisp autumn day in Fall River, Massachusetts, but Irving Fradkin's spirit did not match the weather. He was a discouraged and disappointed man.

Then he met a boy. That chance encounter not only changed Fradkin's life but brought something new to the lives of hundreds of thousands of young people from Fall River to San Diego.

At the time, Fradkin had just suffered a defeat. A long-nourished dream had been shattered—he thought. An optometrist in the town of Fall River, he had a successful practice and a happy family, but he couldn't forget how hard he had been required to work for his own education. He wanted to help others obtain their schooling in easier ways. That was why Irving Fradkin had run for the School Board of Fall River. His campaign had been waged on the promise of trying to establish some kind of scholarship program that would benefit every high school graduate in the city who wanted to have further education.

Fradkin was defeated. It was only his first participation in politics, but he still was discouraged—until he bumped into the son of his receptionist.

"Dr. Fradkin!" the boy called.

Fradkin stopped.

"I just wanted to tell you how sorry I am you lost the election," the boy said. "I had been counting on you to help me get through college."

They talked briefly, then Fradkin slowly walked on, thinking. "What if every person in town gave $1 a year to send that boy and others like him to college?" he asked himself. "It would be a very small contribution for each one to make, but it would be enough to help quite a few young people get started."

Fradkin thought quite a bit about it. He talked it over with his wife, Charlotte. Then he began discussing it with friends and leaders of the community. Although they were unenthusiastic at first, the men Fradkin appealed to decided to give him a chance. There were plenty of parents worrying about college costs who supported him, and a local organization resulted. It was called "Dollars for Scholars" at first and later the Citizens' Scholarship Foundation. Now it is known across the nation as the Fall River Plan, with Fradkin as president.

How it got started

The first chapter of the foundation elected the School Superintendent as chairman of the board and named an awards committee made up of a banker, lawyer, realtor, doctor, high school guidance counselor and Fradkin. That was in 1957. Now all they needed was the scholarship money!

A scholarship week was proclaimed by the Mayor. Youngsters were recruited to go through town wearing caps and gowns to sell $1 memberships in the Dollars for Scholars movement. Housewives rang doorbells. Contributions soon started coming in from religious groups and all sorts of business organizations, including an all-night diner and a Chinese restaurant. A truck driver stopped Fradkin on the street one day and handed him a greasy, crumpled bill; he was one of many donors who not only had never gone to college but who had dropped out of high school.

This effort in 1957 reaped $4,500 for scholarships—a modest beginning for what soon became a national movement. Three years later, when Dollars for Scholars had been incorporated as the Citizens' Scholarship Foundation, $56,500—enough for grants to 225 youngsters—was raised in Fall River alone. News of Fradkin's work reached every corner of New England, and soon he was receiving appeals from other communities to help them organize Dollars for Scholars programs. The Citizens' Scholarship Foundation movement spread across the country. Six years later, when there were 115 chapters in areas with a total population of more than 3,500,000 and they awarded $500,000 to 1,500 young people in one year, the movement still was growing rapidly. By mid-1964 more than 4,500 students had received nearly $1.6 million; 2,000 of them received $800,000 in that year alone.

Drives were conducted in communities throughout the nation. The city fathers of a small Arizona community auctioned themselves to perform manual labor for their "owners" at $1 an hour, and the elected officials of a Pennsylvania town shined shoes for $1 a pair. High school seniors in North Reading, Massachusetts, earned $200 by distributing local telephone books. Residents of nearby Mansfield held a hootenanny to raise funds. Cookie sales, car washes, raffles and all sorts of money-raising events were staged in other cities in behalf of this genuine grass-roots movement, in which each contributor is asked for only $1 a year (if he wishes to give more it is welcome). Organizations participating are expected to contribute a minimum of $100 annually.

What it does

This would be enough to make the program unique, but there are other unusual features in the Fall River Plan:

1. It reaches young people who otherwise might not consider themselves of college caliber. Many would not even graduate from

high school. A check for $100 or $150, labeled a scholarship, tells such a person that he is college material. It gives him academic status and motivates him to want to go to college, and if he *wants* to go, he can usually find ways to get the rest of the necessary capital.

2. It gives scholarship opportunities not only to superior scholars but also to the *average* students who have shown qualities of leadership, who have ambition and a sense of purpose, who have won respect in the community, and who can prove need. Although they may be B or C students, they can be superior young citizens.

3. It favors members of low-income groups rather than middle-income families, who today receive most scholarship aid.

4. It provides funds for several kinds of training beyond high school, not just for courses in colleges and universities. Some dollar-scholars are enrolled in junior colleges or trade schools. Funds have been made available to girls going to secretarial or nursing schools or to boys who wish to become auto mechanics or welders. Art students are also considered for these stipends.

Fradkin puts the philosophy of the Fall River Plan this way:

"Citizens' Scholarship Foundation of America is more than just another local scholarship plan. We are seeking to meet some of the deficiencies of existing scholarship programs. Present programs administered at the local level do not have rational systems of selection; Citizens' Scholarship Foundation of America has developed a point system to determine relative merit and a financial form to determine the need. Aid granted by colleges tends to go to the secondary school students in the very top of their classes; our grants reach deeper to help the qualified but less-than-brilliant high school graduate.

"In the past, most scholarship programs have favored students pursuing academic training; our chapters allocate a portion of all money raised to students desiring to pursue technical and vocational training, and these students compete against each other and not against students applying for college aid."

The philosophy of the Foundation is, then, to motivate young people to get ahead and to help equip them for service to community and country. In the view of the people who head the movement, the secretary and the telephone installer are as needed and worthy as the chemist or the law student.

The program is designed to:

Encourage local citizen interest in educating local youth;

Increase aid to students by broadening the base of contributions to include everyone, not just prosperous individuals and companies;

Emphasize student responsibility to the community and vice versa;

Help average as well as superior students;

Assist students in getting vocational and technical training as well as college degrees;

Cooperate with programs of other groups and help coordinate all local scholarship efforts to achieve the most effective use of all the funds contributed.

The last objective has resulted in producing some order in several confused local situations. In one community of 8,000 population, for example, there were 17 local scholarships worth a total of $1,900, financed and administered by eight different groups. When the Citizens' Scholarship Foundation came in, it persuaded the other groups to coordinate their efforts with those of the Foundation and in that way eliminate duplications. In its first year, the Foundation raised more than $6,000 and provided 16 scholarships for the community as well as a carefully planned system for allocating all the grants given locally.

Fifty annual scholarships valued at a total of $5,700 had been awarded by 40 groups in another community. Each grant involved a separate application and two letters of recommendation from the applicant's school. This meant hours of letter writing and application filing. With the arrival of the Scholarship Foundation, all the applications were coordinated so that every student submitted one form and the schools' paper work was reduced to two letters per applicant instead of a possible 80. All the groups cooperated in allocating the stipends so that no winner got more than one.

The local element

Because it is a genuine grass-roots program, Dollars for Scholars specifies that all money raised in a community must remain there for distribution by a local committee. Each chapter pays annual dues of $50 a year to the parent body in Fall River to help underwrite headquarters expenses and promotional literature, forms and other materials. Operating funds also have been provided to the national office by the Ford Fund for the Advancement of Education, the Alfred P. Sloan Foundation, *Time* Magazine and the General Electric Company, among others. The United States Junior Chamber of Commerce has adopted the program as a national project.

Sam Levenson, former high school teacher turned professional humorist, has lent the organization his name as honorary president. The national board is made up of prominent educators, including officials of the University of Notre Dame and Dartmouth College. Fradkin, as executive head, keeps the organization moving and growing, but all local groups determine their own ground rules for collecting money and making awards.

"We are an idealistic and altruistic organization dedicated to assisting any community in the United States in establishing chapters so they may help their own deserving students in college," Fradkin says. "We have eliminated any potential profit to the mother organization by having complete autonomy invested in each chapter.

"If we want to retain the reputation of an 'educated community,' we must all realize that the financing of the higher education of our youth is no longer a personal matter but has become a community responsibility. This is a brotherhood-in-action movement. It is a way of saying 'thank you' to America for the privilege and honor of being born and brought up in this great land of ours."

Lest anyone misunderstand, the Fall River Plan is not a massive give-away program. Every dollar granted to a scholar is regarded by the organization as a loan—interest free. There is no *legal* obligation to repay, but there is a *moral* obligation, and each recipient is expected to repay when he is able. In just the short time the plan has been in operation, Fradkin reports, there has been a high rate of return, with a few dollars added in voluntary interest in some cases. Several of the beneficiaries are giving time to help the Foundation obtain new sources of funds.

While informally regarded as loans, the grants are called incentive scholarships. Most are of modest size, although some have been as large as $1,000 a year; as the program grows, more generous allocations will be made. Regardless of the amount, all are based on financial need determined at first through a system recently developed by Dartmouth College and the University of New Hampshire and in the final stages by local committees using their own methods. The Dartmouth-New Hampshire system judges students on the basis of scholastic standing, scores on college board examinations and leadership, employment and other "intangibles"; the last three can weigh heavily in the final choice. Those with the highest scores are listed by the awards committee, with the scholarships finally going to members of this group on the basis of need as analyzed by members of each community. As for a set formula for discovering need, Fradkin says, "there just isn't one." All applicants for aid are required to fill out detailed financial forms, but the final determination of need is left to the local committees. "In a community, people have a way of finding out things," Fradkin explains. "Two people with the same income can have unequal needs. A family in one locality can have different requirements from a family with the same income in another. The local people can determine need locally and in their own way."

The incentive factor

Regardless of how recipients are chosen and the amount of the awards, the grants have proved to be incentives for individuals, families and even communities. They give students the little push they need to get started. Recognition bolsters their courage to borrow and their incentive to find part-time jobs. No one organization or means of support can solve the college cost problem, and many deserving young people must be turned down because there simply is not enough money to go around. But there is evidence in Fall River and elsewhere that the Citizens' Scholarship Foundation (and, undoubtedly, other plans) has inspired youngsters to go to college and also has cut into the high-school dropout rate by giving hope for help to underprivileged youngsters who might otherwise give up.

Before Fradkin introduced his plan, only 35 to 40 per cent of the students in the Hillsboro-Deering High School in New Hampshire went on to further education. The 1963 figure was 75 per cent. The B.M.C. Durfee High School in Fall River has graduated 50 per cent more students since the program started and the number going on to college has doubled. Fall River authorities say the scholarship program has been a key factor in this. Fradkin likes to tell about a girl who would have left high school if her hopes had not been raised by Dollars for Scholars. She was a recipient of Aid to Dependent Children and, although not a particularly good student, felt that college would change her life. When the Fall River Plan was introduced, she applied for money to commute to college. She worked for all the additional money she needed, first as a hostess in a restaurant after school and in the summer, then also as a tutor. Now she is teaching school, has paid back the money provided by the Foundation and is one of Fradkin's fund-raisers. Moreover, she is helping her younger brother through college.

The program not only has motivated young people to go to college but has encouraged parents to plan ahead. In Fall River, interest in college resulting from door-to-door solicitations of dollars has brought the sales of more insurance policies and a greater rate of savings.

There have been other so-called "fringe" benefits. Citizens who have found they could cooperate in Foundation work also have discovered that they could serve together in behalf of other worthwhile projects. When the Monroe County, Ohio, Jaycees wanted to build a swimming pool, they could not raise the money in the community. But in conducting a successful Dollars for Scholars program, they found their fund-raising machinery working so smoothly that they went on and got money for the pool, too.

"This type of program brings out the best type of persons to serve," Fradkin observes. "The people who join in the movement become a source of motivation for the kids. We are building a community spirit by bringing together people of all faiths and races, and representing labor and management. It is giving all of us a greater understanding and love for our fellow man."

Some chapters have extended their programs to include a "big brother" relationship in which each member "adopts" a scholarship student whom he advises and sometimes helps to find summer or weekend work. There have been cases in which big brothers have been able to arrange additional financial aid for particularly needy students.

This sort of system is easier to establish in smaller communities, which is one of the secrets of the success of the Citizens' Scholarship Foundation program. Even when they exist in larger areas, the individual chapters are kept small. Fradkin believes that wherever possible a chapter should limit its activities to the community surrounding a single high school to keep its program on a personal basis. Grand Rapids, Michigan, with 350,000 residents, is one of the largest communities in which the plan operates, but even there the individual chapters cover only small sections of the city. The average population of a Dollars for Scholars community is under 50,000.

With the rapid growth of the movement, Fradkin found that he could not begin to serve as personal adviser to a number of small groups scattered across the country so he began setting up state organizations to operate as clearing houses and supervise new chapters. Fradkin also has encouraged service clubs to institute Citizens' Scholarship Foundation programs on district or state levels. He concluded that he could best serve the largest number of people by conducting workshops on fund raising and scholarship allocation for groups of communities at once. The goal is one stipend for every 1,000 people in the United States—a total of 180,000 scholarships. The quota has been reached in New Hampshire, Rhode Island and Massachusetts, which, together with the rest of New England, have served as a pilot area.

Also on Fradkin's blueprint is an eventual fund to be administered by the national office and distributed to local Dollars for Scholars groups to support programs other than those that are locally financed. In the meantime, of course, some of the money allocated locally is coming back in the form of repayments by recipients, so that eventually there may be a sizable revolving scholarship program throughout the nation. As it stands, the Citizens' Scholarship Foundation is a beacon showing many communities the way to more help for more young people at a minimum cost and with a low operational budget.

Getting a chapter started

How does one go about organizing a Foundation chapter? It usually starts with one person who sees the program's merits, talks with others about it and then forms an organization or finds one that is interested in sponsorship. Once a decision is made to start a scholarship program, publicity is the next important ingredient—that and hard work on the part of the committee selected to recruit the actual fund-raisers. Going out and getting the money to give the students seems to be the easiest part of the task.

The statewide organization in New Hampshire, with 13 chapters representing 20 per cent of the state's population, took in a total of nearly $58,000 for 178 scholarships in 1963. The program in the New Hampshire community of Hillsboro was almost an overnight success. It began one spring with a Citizens' Scholarship Week. The first contribution was $100 from the high school student council. Other money flowed in—$175 from a benefit fashion show; $165 from a student carnival; $560 from 430 persons in a house-to-house membership canvass. By May more than $2,000 had been raised, and the following month 10 graduating seniors shared $2,450 in scholarship money.

The Allegan, Michigan, Business and Professional Women's Club voted in March, 1962, to organize a chapter. Members weeded out entrants with an essay contest to select finalists for scholarships. Within two months they had raised $3,000 for their fund and had awarded $2,600 to eight students. One of the early winners, a girl who made the honor roll in her sophomore year at Michigan State University, wrote Mrs. Francis Clair, president of the Allegan chapter, thanking the group for her scholarship. "I have a friend who is going to college without any financial assistance by working one term and going to college the next and by working part time while at college," the girl wrote. "This is proof that a college education is possible for every person without financial aid, but, thanks to the Scholarship Foundation, I can attend college without financial worries."

Mansfield, Massachusetts, with a population of 8,000, raised $10,000 in a scholarship week that began with a "kick-in" day rather than a "kick-off." Students in Claremont, New Hampshire, conducted a tag-day solicitation of shoppers and a house-to-house campaign in which they raised $5,000 one year and $10,000 the next. No one in that community with a definite financial need has been turned down in an appeal for a scholarship. Harry A. Rosenberg, chairman of the Claremont group, tells this story of one winner:

"A senior who ranked in the lowest quartile of his class had a flair for bookkeeping. To all concerned it seemed that he was not college material; however, the registrar of a large, standardized commercial college interviewed the lad and decided that there was a place in the business world for a boy like him.

"John was accepted. Now, where would he find the funds necessary? He had some savings. His mother is a widow. Despite his low grades in some subjects, the screening committee agreed with the registrar and granted him a $200 scholarship, enough to help finance his first year. He is in school now, doing a creditable piece of work. This would have been impossible without the C.S.F. donation."

The first town west of the Mississippi to become interested in the Citizens' Scholarship program was International Falls, Minnesota. Elvin Foss, a high school counselor, read about Fradkin and his program and wrote for information. Foss then went to the principal of the high school, who frankly doubted that his fellow citizens would support an egghead program in preference to sports, though he wished Foss luck anyway. Foss then took his idea to a city councilman who also was a Rotarian. The man liked the program so well that he presented it at a Rotary meeting. The response was instantaneous; the club voted $500 to launch the program.

After that the movement mushroomed, with other service clubs, religious groups and individuals joining in. Telephone operators and linemen volunteered their help, too. The chapter was incorporated and a drive was held in which residents of the town contributed more money per capita than had any other chapter of the Citizens' Scholarship Foundation. A total of $7,500 was given in this town of a mere 1,600 people.

The awards committee, fearful of being accused of playing favorites in such a small community, gave each of the 42 scholarship applicants a number. The names were known only to Foss until the decisions had been made. The committee awarded 24 scholarships, including one to an 18-year-old secretarial student who was one of five children of a totally disabled war veteran, and another to a service station attendant orphaned as an infant.

Members of the International Falls chapter recognize that the amounts they have awarded do not go far toward paying college bills, but they regard each grant as an incentive investment in young people who know that the whole town is behind them. "International Falls in the past has had a dubious reputation as a wide-open border town, a rough place," a town leader said. "Now we're living a new image of a town where brotherhood and democracy are being practiced without preaching."

Making the awards

The distribution of funds is not always as easy as collecting them. This process begins with the filing of an application by a student on three forms—a blue one, part of which he fills out and the rest of which is completed by officials of his school; a pink confidential financial statement, filled out by the student's parent or guardian; and a white form, filled out by a teacher. All three go to the local chapter for evaluation.

Now the scholarship committee meets to go over the forms and decide who deserves and needs help, and how much. A typical procedure is that of the chapter in Urbandale, Iowa, with a population of about 6,000. Its seven-member committee considers applications from seniors in four high schools who are planning to go to college or technical school. The committee studies all the data and then grants scholarships of at least $150 each until its funds are exhausted. Awards are made for one year only, which means that recipients must apply annually. Some foundation chapters make four-year awards that are subject to review each summer.

When a stipend is granted by a chapter, a check is made out jointly to the student and the school. Some rural chapters allocate as much as 50 or 60 per cent of their funds for nonacademic training, but in urban areas only 5 to 10 per cent goes for this purpose. The national organization recommends that no less than 10 per cent and no more than 40 per cent be used for helping to finance study in trade schools and other nonacademic institutions; the average runs about 20 to 25 per cent.

It is the general practice to process applications for grants to four-year colleges, junior colleges and technical schools separately to avoid competition between the three groups. Fradkin regards this as important, for one of the aims of his organization is to try to convince the public that "there is no shame in developing skills or gifts." Every community must believe in skilled manpower, he says, for every community needs it. The entire task of awarding financial aid is made difficult, in Fradkin's view, by the fact that "reasonable men differ on the factors that should be considered and the weight to be given various factors. Every individual has his special personality, talents and worth. In truth, there is no satisfactory way to measure such qualities."

He goes on to say that "poor academic performance does not necessarily foretell failure. Winston Churchill had trouble getting through the English school system. Some individuals are late in developing their particular genius. Albert Einstein spent his early career as a civil service clerk. No foolproof system has been developed to predict who will succeed and who will fail. In fact, most of us would find it difficult to give clear and full definitions of the words 'success' and 'failure.' "

Grants for Negroes in the South

One notable achievement of the Fall River Plan has been the awarding of scholarships to Negroes in some Southern programs. Five Negroes were among the first 26 winners in Charlotte Hall, Maryland, while in El Dorado, Arkansas, the only two Negroes to apply were awarded stipends. The board of directors of the chapter there voted unanimously to help students of all races and never has turned down *any* person who has applied. Four Negroes were among the first year's recipients of grants in the Jacksonville, Florida, program, in which $39,000 was raised for 65 scholarships. Only 10 Negroes applied. The Smithfield, North Carolina, chapter has an interracial membership. Of 16 scholarships awarded in its first year, several went to Negroes in what was believed to have been the first integrated public meeting of any size in the town's history. Murray

Bonder, then president of the chapter, wrote Fradkin at the time: "We are quite proud of the money raised and the scholarships given. But we are really proud of the fact that they were truly awarded on a completely unbiased basis. This in a little Southern town is something."

To Fradkin, a letter such as this is the finest reward for his work. He gives time and money of his own to the movement, which at the outset he never dreamed would spread beyond Fall River, now officially called the "scholarship city." Although he must keep up his practice of optometry, he often cuts his work week short to make himself available to the scholarship program. He has a small office staff, including an executive director, who shares the major work burden. Why is he doing it? "There's got to be a reason," he replied. "It's a crusade to perpetuate our form of government and to stimulate and motivate and inspire the use of our God-given gifts for mankind. It is a dream. We need proper leadership. I hope I can inspire and motivate some of the future leaders of the country."

For further information on "Dollars for Scholars"

Write to:

The Citizens' Scholarship Foundation of America, Inc., 100 Purchase Street, Fall River, Massachusetts.

8

LONG-RANGE PLANNING

... savings, investments, insurance

Financing an education looms so large in the lives of so many Americans that an increasing number of parents who talk about wanting their children to go to college are trying to do something about it in advance. The planners are in a minority, sad to say, but their ranks are growing, and the fact that some have managed to carry out long-range plans to help pay for college indicates that still more parents could do the same thing if they were to chart a course and adhere to it.

Saving, investment and insurance are the chief means of financial preparation. Both saving and investment have an advantage over insurance in that they are hedges against inflation; the money they earn tends to reflect the way the economy is going. In the case of savings accounts, interest rates fluctuate; with investments, there is the changeable dividend rate and the rise and fall in the value of the securities themselves. Insurance, on the other hand, has some advantages neither of the other two offer in that it provides a guaranteed income and assures college financing if the family wage-earner dies.

Saving for education

Obviously, you can set up any savings program you wish, whether it be $5 a week or $50, for as many years as you are able to put money aside. Ideally, a college savings plan would begin in infancy and continue through the December of the senior year in college, with the age for college entrance figured at 18. Let's see how this would work.

Suppose the goal is to have $10,000 available for financing college. The following chart presents several plans for saving this amount, based on 4 per cent interest compounded and credited quarterly. It allows for withdrawals of $1,250 on September 1 and January 1 of each of the four college years.

SAVING $10,000 FOR COLLEGE

If Your Child's Age Is Now	Period of Savings Accumulation	Monthly Deposit Required to Meet Goal	Cumulative Total of Deposits	Accumulated Interest (at 4%)
1	20 yrs. 4 mos.	$28.42	$6,934.48	$3,065.52
2	19 yrs. 4 mos.	30.57	7,092.24	2,907.76
3	18 yrs. 4 mos.	32.97	7,253.40	2,746.60
4	17 yrs. 4 mos.	35.66	7,417.28	2,582.72
5	16 yrs. 4 mos.	38.68	7,581.28	2,418.72
6	15 yrs. 4 mos.	42.12	7,750.08	2,249.92
7	14 yrs. 4 mos.	46.06	7,922.32	2,077.68
8	13 yrs. 4 mos.	50.60	8,096.00	1,904.00
9	12 yrs. 4 mos.	55.89	8,271.72	1,728.28
10	11 yrs. 4 mos.	62.14	8,451.04	1,548.96
11	10 yrs. 4 mos.	69.63	8,634.12	1,365.88
12	9 yrs. 4 mos.	78.74	8,818.88	1,181.12
13	8 yrs. 4 mos.	90.06	9,006.00	994.00
14	7 yrs. 4 mos.	104.51	9,196.88	803.12
15	6 yrs. 4 mos.	123.55	9,389.80	610.20
16	5 yrs. 4 mos.	149.78	9,585.92	414.08
17	4 yrs. 4 mos.	188.17	9,784.84	215.16

As the chart shows, if a parent begins depositing $28.42 a month when his child is a year old and continues this program for 20 years and four months, he will have saved a total of $6,934.48 and received accumulated interest of $3,065.52, for a total of $10,000. Should the plan begin when a child is six years old, it would continue for 15 years and four months at a monthly savings rate of $42.12. This would result in deposits totaling $7,750.08 and interest of $2,249.92, again for a total of $10,000.

You can also stockpile $10,000 in 20 years through a *graduated* savings program that may more accurately reflect the growing income of a young family. For example, if you save at a rate of $10 a month for the first five years, $20 a month the second five, $45 a month for the third five and $60 a month for the final five, you will reach your goal. The total deposited in this case would be higher, of course, since the bulk of the deposits would have earned interest for a shorter time.

Savings accounts really operate in an elementary way. The hard part is getting one started and then sticking to it by putting a set amount away for college each week or month. Banks assist such programs with systems under which funds are transferred automatically each month from checking accounts to savings accounts, but the budget must still be managed so that the money can be spared. Quite a few people have set out to save for only one or two years of college, with the idea of borrowing the rest. Certainly *any* savings program is better than none. Not only will the pressure be lightened at college time, but the interest *earned* now may help to compensate for the much higher interest *paid* on loans later. You will see in the next two chapters, which deal with loans, just how much money advance financial planning for college can save.

Government bonds as investments

Although the United States Treasury Department encourages the purchases of government bonds as investments for college, they cannot be recommended here. True, they are a "safe" way to save, but they offer the lowest yield in the current market. A government savings bond matures in 10 years and pays 3.75 per cent interest.

When held beyond the maturity date, the bonds continue to accumulate interest at the same rate. There was a time when the interest paid for this investment compared favorably with that of savings banks, but this no longer is the case.

Periodically, suggestions are made for the enactment of legislation to establish a special bond for educational purposes, one that would yield more than the 3.75 per cent now returned to investors and one that could be bought through a payroll savings plan. Congress has defeated one proposal for such a bond, but the idea has been revived by the Treasury in its search for ways to strengthen the savings bond program.

A major barrier in the way of a bond for education has been the lack of a foolproof way to insure its use for college. Suggestions have been made that the proceeds from the sale of an education bond be sent directly to a school, or that the total value of bonds a person might hold be limited, but the problem has not been satisfactorily solved.

Mutual funds for flexibility

A relatively new form of accumulating capital has become popular in the last decade or so among persons with moderate incomes. It is the mutual fund. The first such fund was established in 1924; in 1963 the National Association of Investment Companies estimated that there were about six million individual mutual fund accounts, with three million people involved. Of this figure, 250,000 persons were known to be accumulating money for college and more were believed to be so engaged.

Also known as an open-end investment company, a mutual fund organization is set up to enable individuals of moderate means to use their small investment capital to get benefits they would not otherwise readily enjoy, such as diversification of holdings and professional management.

The mutual fund company gets its capital by selling stock to individuals. It then invests this capital, most of it in the stocks and bonds of established corporations, and pays dividends on the basis of its average income from these holdings. Individuals may invest in mutual funds by outright purchase of shares without any formal plan when they have the cash available, by outright purchase of shares with a plan for reinvesting all dividends in more shares, or by an accumulation plan of systematic monthly or quarterly purchases.

There are several kinds of funds. A common stock fund invests almost all of its capital in common stocks, while a balanced fund puts a considerable part of its assets in "senior securities," which are bonds or preferred stocks. Because of the wide differences in the investment portfolios of various funds, there is one to suit almost every pocketbook or investing temperament. The balanced fund is for the more cautious investor and the common stock fund is for the person more willing to speculate. For the truly conservative investor there are funds made up of holdings in blue-chip companies with steady incomes, and for the adventurous there are funds made up largely of "growth" stocks, which pay modest dividends now but may provide much higher profits in the future.

A built-in advantage of mutual investments is the professional management provided. The mutual fund also offers a convenient way to invest with continuity of purpose. Some funds have as many as a hundred securities in their portfolios, whereas the individual investor, working on his own, might buy only a few.

A disadvantage, of course, is that the income from the investment and its value are not certain. The market could drop at the very moment money is needed for college. However, by their nature mutual funds have an averaging effect, avoiding the extremes of performance of individual stocks.

The Investment Company Institute has compiled a table for the potential college planner showing how mutual funds can be beneficial over the long range. The table gives the *averages* of 10 common stock funds and 10 balanced funds. The common stock funds selected had a broad investment policy, giving consideration to income as well as to growth and safety. They did not include the so-called "growth stock funds," which would have shown larger increases in value, reflecting a larger risk. Only past performance can be given in discussing securities, of course, but a study of the figures below may give you an idea of the potentialities of mutual funds as a means of planning ahead for college.

AVERAGE WORTH OF MUTUAL FUND INVESTMENTS

Amounts Invested	10 Years 1953–63	15 Years 1948–63
10 COMMON STOCK FUNDS		
$500 initial investment $100 a month thereafter	$19,300	$46,400
$250 initial investment $50 a month thereafter	$ 9,600	$23,200
$125 initial investment $25 a month thereafter	$ 4,800	$11,600
10 BALANCED FUNDS		
$500 initial investment $100 a month thereafter	$18,200	$37,700
$250 initial investment $50 a month thereafter	$ 9,100	$18,900
$125 initial investment $25 a month thereafter	$ 4,600	$ 9,400

In the common stock funds, based on past performance, an investment of $500 in 1953, with $100 added each month for 10 years, would thus have built a total investment of $12,500 into $19,300. Had this program been started in 1948, by 1963 there would have been mutual fund securities worth a total of $46,400 for an investment of $18,500. Again it must be emphasized that these figures represent *averages* of the yields of 10 common stock funds.

Using the same 10 funds, consider what would have happened to an investment of $125 to start and $25 a month thereafter for 10 years, beginning in 1953. This would have built $1,925 into a $4,800 holding. On a 15-year basis, an investment of $4,625 would have grown to $11,600.

Now look at what happened to the average of 10 balanced funds during the same periods. A $500 initial investment followed by $100 a month in purchases of these securities from 1953 to 1963 would have provided a total investment worth $18,200 at a cost of $12,500. In 15 years, purchases totaling $18,500 would have been worth $37,700. With $125 to start and $25 a month, the $1,925 would have grown to $4,600 in 10 years and the $4,625 to $9,400 in 15.

An independent mutual fund organization, Distributors Group, Inc., which is an investment advisory firm that sponsors Group Securities, Inc., and its three funds, has a program to encourage periodic investments. It has drawn up a table showing what happened to investments of $100 a month in its Common Stock Fund starting on January 1, 1943, and continuing for 10, 15 and 20 years thereafter. This was a period of generally rising stock prices and reflected the progress of the blue-chip securities held by this fund.

Keep in mind that if you were to put $100 monthly in a savings account paying 4 per cent interest, compounded quarterly with deposits on the first of each month, you would accumulate $36,744.80 in 20 years. That would be less than half the total from the mutual fund investment as tabulated here.

SUMMARIES FOR THE 20-YEAR, 15-YEAR AND 10-YEAR PERIODS
ENDED DEC. 31, 1962

	Total Monthly Investments	Total Dividends Reinvested	Total Cost Including Reinvested Dividends	Total Value End of Period
20 Years 1943–62	$24,000	$25,220	$49,220	$78,742
15 Years 1948–62	18,000	11,910	29,910	43,340
10 Years 1953–62	12,000	3,675	15,675	18,658

Mutual funds offer a potentially larger average earning on money invested than do savings accounts, but the element of risk is greater and the time required to realize an attractive profit may be longer.

Other investment plans

Mutual funds are not the only lane on Wall Street leading to college financing. In recent years small investors have been courted through the Monthly Investment Plan, which enables them to put as little as $40 every three months or 44 cents a day in the stocks of individual companies.

Suppose you have $75 a month to invest in stock. You begin by finding a common stock that you like, trying to make your selection on the basis of long-term growth. The stock you want costs $30 a share. You fill out an M.I.P. Purchase Order and mail it to your broker with a check for $75. A total of 2.3583 shares of the $30 stock are bought for you, with $4.24 subtracted from your $75 for the brokerage fee. You continue to make these monthly investments in the same stock. If you wish to diversify, you sign up for other plans covering other issues, with all dividends being reinvested for you. There is no binding contractual arrangement—it is entirely up to you. If you stop making payments, you simply do not acquire more shares of stock.

Over a period of 17 years, almost any blue-chip stock is expected by investment counselors to double in value. High-quality growth stocks increase their earnings by 5 to 10 per cent a year. The monthly stock-purchase plan should be maintained for at least 10 years in order to assure the best possible price when the stock is sold.

Insurance for college

Various forms of insurance have helped an inestimable number of parents solve the college cost problem, and insurance companies are constantly experimenting with basic policies aimed directly at this problem. A brief look at the types of insurance available will at least furnish a rough map to guide you in future exploration.

An endowment policy is primarily a savings program. If a man aged 35 with a 3-year-old son decides to accumulate $8,000 for college by the time his boy is 18, he would pay $530 a year for a 15-year endowment. In 15 years the policy would mature to provide the desired sum. If the father died during the 15 years, the money would be available when the son was ready for college.

If this same father bought an $8,000 straight-life policy, it would cost $185 a year. In 15 years it would have a cash value of $2,000. The father could stop payments and take the $2,000 or continue payments and borrow up to $2,000 on the policy.

The Travelers Insurance Company has developed a special educational endowment known as the Guaranteed College Fund, which offers a means of financing college whether the father lives, is disabled or dies. The fund provides an endowment on the life of the child, to mature when he is 18, and includes insurance on the father's life. Beginning when the child is 18, the company makes payments for each college semester. At this time, the father stops making premium payments to the company, diverting these funds into direct payments to the college. In other words, the father's obligation continues, but he sends the money to the school and the insurance company's payments are minus the amount of the father's installments.

The plan also provides that if the father dies or is disabled at any time before the child is graduated, the premium payments are stopped and the balance of the installments is paid by the company. In other words, the full amount of the plan's benefits is paid during the four college years regardless of whether the father is available to pay his share.

At least two other major insurance companies have announced elaborate plans for college insurance policies with great fanfare in recent years. Both were failures from the outset. Parents simply were not interested in them, largely because the programs did not take inflation into account. Other plans have been introduced, however, and almost every company writes policies tailored to cover college costs.

One of the men who sets up such plans is Murray Frankel, an agent for the Prudential Insurance Company, who described several insurance programs for this discussion of college financing. Frankel began by pointing out that a plan providing money for education through the use of insurance has built-in guarantees through a binding contract. The policy is automatically completed if the parent dies and usually continues without interruption in cases of the wage earner's temporary or permanent disability. Psychologically, an insurance plan is good because it is "semicompulsory"; that is, systematic and encouraging continuance through reminders in the form of premium notices. Of great importance also is the fact that it does *not* make the money available for any other purpose.

Here are the situations Frankel described:

1. A 24-year-old man went to Frankel asking for a program to plan for college for his newborn son. He wanted a minimum of $12,000 available in 18 years. Frankel drew up a plan calling for an annual premium of $538.80. This provided $10,000 insurance on the life of the child. For an additional $26.94 a year, the life of the father was insured, too, and a disability clause was added for him.

Eighteen years after the payment of the first premium this father will have a total of $12,562.70 available (based on the 1963 scale), in return for premiums amounting to $9,689.40. His net gain will be $2,873.30. Should the father die before his son reaches college age, all further premiums will be waived and the money will be available for the boy's education.

2. An alternative was offered the young father in the form of a plan placing the protection on his life. Some men prefer to take out a life policy and then put its cash value to use either through a loan or outright surrender of the policy for cash.

Here is how such a plan works: The 24-year-old father of a new-born son takes out a 20-pay life policy for $18,000 on his own life, at an annual premium of $555.48. In 18 years, $11,844 in cash is available in return for premiums totaling $9,998.64, for a net gain of $1,845.36.

All premiums would be waived if the father became disabled before the age of 60. His death would mean immediate payment of $18,000 in cash to his family. If the father lived and funds for college became available elsewhere, the insurance could be continued for life, with premiums ceasing after 20 years. The increase in cash value of the policy through the years could be earmarked for retirement.

3. A 30-year-old father wanted a program to finance college for a daughter just entering grade school, so that $12,000 would be available when she turned 18.

Two possible courses were suggested to him. One called for an annual premium of $845.80, insuring his daughter's life for $10,000, with an added $42.29 insuring him against death or disability before she turned 18. In 12 years he would have $11,799.10 in cash at his disposal after payment of $10,149.60 in premiums, for a net gain of $1,649.50. The other plan included a slightly higher premium that provided the same endowment policy written on the life of the father and offering similar cash results. The basic difference rested in the provision that if the father should die prematurely, the money would be available immediately for family needs or could be left to gather interest until the daughter was ready for college.

4. Still another plan involved a 30-year-old father with a boy of six. He wanted a 20-year endowment with $20,000 insurance on his own life. The annual premium was set at $987.20. By the time the boy is 18, there will be $12,542.20 available in cash. The premiums will have totaled $11,846.40 by then, for a net gain of $695.80.

Comparison of these various programs is difficult to make on a straight dollars-and-cents basis. However, it is possible to rate them according to the return and value to the investor. Here is the general picture:

An insurance program has the lowest rate of growth on a dollar basis but is the least risky and has the invaluable feature of some form of insurance protection. It also has the built-in element of providing a psychologically compulsory savings program.

Savings accounts also are virtually without risk (assuming that an individual account does not exceed the limitations set on federal deposit insurance) and at the same time they tend to have a higher yield than insurance. On the other hand, except for the gradual increase that has taken place in interest rates in periods of inflation, savings do not reflect the decline in purchasing power that has been characteristic of modern times. Insurance, of course, generally reflects the change in the purchasing power of the dollar the least.

Investments in securities offer the area of greatest risk—and of the largest potential return. Within this classification, there are opportunities to choose between the more conservative mutual funds, blue chip securities and more speculative issues.

Ideally, one should try to have a diversified investment program providing for insurance, savings and securities, but this is difficult for most persons to manage. Securities dealers have a general policy of discouraging would-be investors from putting money into stocks until they have made provisions for insurance and savings.

For the individual who can afford only one program for college planning, the savings account earmarked for that purpose would seem to be the most sensible.

Only a few possible ways to plan ahead—well ahead—for college have been included here, but they may help clarify your thinking about financing an education on the installment plan—in advance. For those who can manage it, planning ahead has advantages that no one need point out. But for those who either cannot plan ahead or have not done so, there are avenues of help, too.

For further information on savings, investments and insurance

Write to:

Savings
Savings and Loan Foundation, Inc., 1111 E Street, N.W., Washington, D.C. 20004.
U.S. Savings and Loan League, 221 North LaSalle Street, Chicago, Illinois 60601.
Or consult your local savings bank for advice on a savings program.

Mutual funds
Distributors Group, Inc., 80 Pine Street, New York, New York 10005.
Investment Company Institute, 61 Broadway, New York, New York 10006.

Monthly Investment Plan and other securities purchases
Eastman Dillon, Union Securities & Co., 1 Chase Manhattan Plaza, New York, New York 10005.
Merrill Lynch, Pierce, Fenner & Smith, 70 Pine Street, New York, New York 10005.
Or consult a broker.

Insurance
Equitable Life Assurance Society of the United States, 1285 Avenue of the Americas, New York, New York 10019.
Institute of Life Insurance, 488 Madison Avenue, New York, New York 10022.
New York Life Insurance Company, 51 Madison Avenue, New York, New York 10010.
Prudential Insurance Company of America, Prudential Plaza, Newark, New Jersey 07101.
The Travelers Insurance Companies, Hartford, Connecticut.

9

HELP FOR THOSE WHO DIDN'T PLAN AHEAD

... federal, state and college loans

"Learn now and pay later" has become an accepted practice among college students. Until only a few years ago youngsters and their families balked at the idea of borrowing for college. They regarded it as an unjustified mortgaging of the future. The same people were willing to buy homes, cars, refrigerators and clothing on the installment plan or to borrow for them, but when it came to college they could not accept the idea of going into debt.

With the passage in 1958 of the National Defense Education Act, which created an extensive program of low-interest, long-term loans to students, the national attitude changed almost overnight. Between 1955 and 1960 the amount of money lent students for education by all financing sources increased 600 per cent, largely under the impetus of the federal legislation. Accompanying this program are at least 20 state plans and more than 125 commercial loan arrangements. In the 1957-58 school year (just before the passage of the federal law), $115 million was lent for college. The figure in 1962-63 was about $600 million, according to the best available estimates. At this rate, it may not be many years before $1 billion a year is borrowed to finance college!

One of the more interesting—and distressing—figures to emerge from studies and surveys of loans for college is the average income of the father who finds borrowing his only recourse—$16,000 a year. As indicated in the first chapter, the high-income family may be less prepared for college than those not so well fixed.

A point that cannot be overemphasized is that borrowing should not be regarded as inevitable or intrinsically desirable. Savings and otherwise planning ahead are the best ways to finance college, for when you borrow you are putting a higher price tag on your education. However, many students who would not otherwise have been able to attend college have had the doors opened to them through loan programs.

Loans are available not only to parents but in some cases to the students themselves. They are becoming part of the college "package" of scholarships, loans and jobs, which will be discussed in detail in Chapter 12. Also, some state-sponsored commercial loans are available to students rather than their parents.

One argument favoring loans is that they free the student from day-to-day financial worry and the need for working long hours while in school, and that they therefore enable him to get more out of his education. It is also pointed out that a student is borrowing on his future income, which will be considerably more than his present earning capacity. Another argument is that, assuming the continuance of inflation, the money he borrows will be repaid in dollars that are less costly in relation to his total lifetime income than they were when he floated his loan.

Some new ideas

Seymour E. Harris, professor of political economy at Harvard, has estimated that a loan of $1,000 a year for the three years that the average student stays in college could be financed with a payment of 1 per cent of the lifetime income of the average college-educated person. He suggests that it might be best to arrange repayment on the basis of income rather than the amount of money borrowed. He also favors extension of the college loan repayment period to 20 to 40 years, like that of some home mortgages.

Another economist, Edward Shapiro of the University of Detroit, has proposed a federal program for educational loan repayments geared to income. A former student would not be required to pay back a cent until his taxable income was more than $4,000 a year. Repayment would then begin at a rate of 2.25 per cent of taxable income, rising to 19.4 per cent at $10,000. Shapiro estimates that the average student loan would be paid back in 10 years at this rate. How he would plan to "police" this program to assure repayment at the proper time was not disclosed.

In California, John L. E. Collier, a state assemblyman, called for an arrangement under which students would borrow money from the state to finance college and then repay it with earnings resulting from having a higher education. Upon issuing a loan, the state would estimate how much it would have to spend to educate a student in one of its tax-supported institutions. The student then would sign notes promising to repay the state (i.e., the taxpayers), beginning a year after graduation and at 1 per cent interest, with payments extended over 20 years.

The federal loan program

The National Defense Student Loan Program, the largest of all the plans for financing college on credit, is responsible for having made borrowing for education not only acceptable but popular. It has gone a long way toward democratizing student aid and spreading the money among more schools and more states. The National Defense Education Act (N.D.E.A.) is regarded widely as the most important advance in federal aid to higher education since the Morrill Act of 1862 established land-grant colleges in every state. The last direct loan effort of any size prior to 1958 was provided during the Great Depression of the 1930's, when the National Youth Administration allocated funds to colleges on a quota basis to support work programs. More than 600,000 students were aided during the 10-year life of that program, which was terminated when the Student War Loans program began in 1943. This enabled upperclassmen in professional training or science and health programs to borrow for their education if they agreed to work in the war effort upon graduation. During the two years this plan operated a mere 11,000 students took advantage of it.

The student aid program without parallel was, of course, the Servicemen's Readjustment Act, better known as the G.I. Bill of Rights, which was an outright government scholarship program to finance the education of men and women who served in World War II. The academic world may never see such a program again, for a total of 7,800,000 veterans were aided by it, 2,200,000 of them at colleges and universities. During the 1947–48 school year, when the program hit its peak, more than half the students in college were studying under the G.I. Bill.

Neither this nor the later G.I. Bill for Korean War veterans nor the Junior G.I. Bill for children of servicemen who lost their lives have involved loans. Under the current program, low-interest, long-term loans are provided to full-time students or entering freshmen. There is a scholarship aspect in a clause providing for forgiveness of up to 50 per cent of the money lent to students who go into teaching or certain technical fields. A full-time elementary or secondary teacher, for example, may have his loan forgiven at a rate of 10 per cent a year for five years—a total reduction of 50 per cent of his debt—provided, of course, that he remains in teaching during this time.

The loans are not administered by the government; individual schools have the job of allocating the funds and *collecting* them when the time comes. Loan funds are distributed among the participating institutions, which now include most colleges and universities. For every $9 the government provides, a school must contribute $1. New funds have been appropriated each year and allotted in proportion to the full-time college enrollment in each state. To obtain loan funds, a school applies to the United States Commissioner of Education, with a maximum of $800,000 going to any school in any year. If a school does not have the required 10 per cent to contribute from its own funds, it may borrow from the government.

To qualify for a loan one must maintain a good academic standing and show a *need* for the money. A student may borrow up to $1,000 in any academic year and a total of $5,000 during the period of his higher education. The average loan has worked out at slightly less than $500 a year.

Repayment begins one year after leaving school, with 10 years to pay. No interest accrues until the payments start, when it is set at 3 per cent a year on the unpaid balance. All obligations are canceled on death or in cases of permanent and total disability.

In line with the special forgiveness features for those going into teaching and technical fields, the program requires that participating schools give special consideration to loan applicants who are superior students and who want to teach or go into science, mathematics, engineering or modern language study. Financial aid officers of the colleges are advised to single out all academically qualified applicants and then select loan recipients from this list on the basis of need. About two-thirds of the loans have been made to the more favored students.

Some 1,500 of the nation's institutions of higher learning, enrolling 90 per cent of the students, are administering nearly $100 million in N.D.E.A. loans, with requests running well over that amount.

A survey of borrowers indicated that 90 per cent depended on loans to enter or continue college, 81 per cent had saved $250 or less, nearly a third had to finance their educations without help from their families and 80 per cent were paying at least half of their expenses themselves. The amount repaid by June 30, 1962, was more than twice the amount actually due, indicating both the desire and the ability of graduates to get out of debt. It also was reported that there had been an astonishingly small number of defaults.

One major result of the N.D.E.A. program has been to put colleges and universities into the business of lending money. Financial aid offices have had to expand their staffs greatly. It has become necessary to keep careful track of the whereabouts of debtor alumni. Some aid officers frankly fear that, as the program continues and becomes larger, the collecting business will become more difficult and far more expensive. They feel that the program will not have undergone its full test until it has been in effect long enough for the original borrowers to have graduated and then repaid their loans over a 10-year period. That would mean it will be 1972 before the first freshman borrowers of 1958 will have paid their debts.

The states and moneylending

At least 35 states provide some kind of direct student support. All the programs have been set up since World War II, a third of them in the last decade. About 20 states offer a form of "service loan" to encourage more persons to enter the teaching profession. These programs provide loans to needy students, who repay them by teaching in the public schools after graduation.

Most of the state aid funds available are provided by New York, California, Illinois, New Jersey, Virginia, Rhode Island and Massachusetts. The last-named state pioneered in lending money to students through HELP, officially listed as the Higher Educational Loan Plan, established by the Massachusetts Higher Educational Assistance Corporation in 1956—two years before the federal program began. At least 10 other states have adopted variations of this plan, which is operated by a nonprofit organization without drawing on public funds. The activities in Maine and New Hampshire and the United Student Aid Funds, which helps students in states without formal plans, are patterned after the Massachusetts program. Rhode Island, New York, New Jersey, Virginia, Ohio and Michigan have official bodies maintained through appropriations. Connecticut also has a liberal loan program.

The one feature nearly all have in common is that, although the lending is done by banks, the state organizations guarantee partial or total repayment in case of default. In Massachusetts, up to 80 per cent of the unpaid principal will be repaid. The HELP corporation also is committed to maintain a reserve fund of 5 per cent of the total of loans outstanding; this fund was built with tax-exempt contributions from corporations, charitable trusts, labor unions and individuals. The return on the reserve fund provides income, and the participating banks pay a fee of one-tenth of 1 per cent on each loan.

Most of the commercial banks and more than 20 mutual savings banks and credit unions in Massachusetts participate in the program, under which nearly $6 million in loans was outstanding in 1963. During the first eight years approximately 20,000 students borrowed nearly $9.5 million, of which more than $3.2 million had been repaid.

Freshman students are not eligible for these loans because of the high rate of first-year dropouts. However, anyone else living in Massachusetts who is attending college is qualified to apply to the bank of his choice. The student acts for himself, although his parents must approve if he is a minor. Loans usually are limited to $500 in any academic year, with an over-all maximum of $1,500, but the total can be more under special circumstances.

The student borrower signs a note promising to start payment six months after graduation. He is given three years to pay and an extension if necessary. The interest ranges from 3.5 to 5.5 per cent for the entire term of the note, depending on what the bank charges. (For a comparison of this pioneering program and the lending arrangements of other governmental bodies as well as banks and finance companies, see the chart in Chapter 10, Pages 134–137.)

The Massachusetts plan has been discussed here in considerable detail because it has set the pattern for other states. There are certain variations, however. While Maine and Virginia charge rates similar to those in Massachusetts, New Jersey's is a little lower—

5 per cent simple interest before and after graduation (see Chapter 10 for an explanation of "simple interest").

No state offers the lending bargain that is available in New York, but it should be added hastily that, though New York's program is a bargain to the students and a boon to the banks, it is quite costly to the taxpayers. Much of California's well-rated and relatively low-cost (to the student) higher education is financed by direct state aid to the schools. New York channels most of its aid money either directly to students or to lending institutions through outright incentive grants and low-interest loans for all persons accepted for college who want them. Together with scholarships, which are unusually generous, the total bill for state aid to education in New York in 1964–65 reached more than $58.5 million. A relatively small portion of this money went directly to the schools, but many of the schools managed to share in the bonanza by increasing their tuition or, as in the case of the many-branched state university, charging tuition for the first time.

Here we are interested mainly in the loan program, which is administered by the New York Higher Education Assistance Corporation, created in 1958 as an independent, nonprofit organization to certify and guarantee student loans made by banks in the state. During the first five years of the program, more than $63 million was lent to 57,000 students. The average loan was about $730 at first, but it rose to about $900. During the first five years more than $5.4 million was repaid, with defaults running at only one-half of 1 per cent; but here, as in the case of the federal program, it is too soon to make a definitive judgment of the credit responsibility—or risk—of college students. There is no doubt of the popularity of the program, however, for in 1964 the number of applications for loans reached 600 to 800 a day—50 per cent more than in the previous year.

A student borrower in New York may attend any institution of higher learning in the country that has been recognized and approved by the State Board of Regents. Included are colleges, business schools, nursing schools and technical institutes. There are no restrictions on study except that the student should be working toward a diploma or degree.

Parents do not become involved in this program. A qualified student deals with the lending institution, signing a promissory note for each school year in which he borrows. He pays no interest while in school. The state pays the total interest for him, which in New York is 6 per cent. Within 60 days after graduation or leaving school, the student begins repaying the loan at 3 per cent simple interest, with the taxpayers putting up the other 3 per cent. Payments may be spread over six years. This results in a gift of considerable size to the students, for in 1963–64 alone the taxpayers paid between $4 million and $5 million in interest.

A maximum of $750 may be borrowed in the first year, $1,000 in the second, $1,250 in the third, $1,500 in the fourth and $1,500 in each year of graduate school. Part-time students are restricted to smaller sums. Nursing students may obtain up to $500 in any year, with a maximum of $1,500. The same limit is set for other schools offering education beyond high school.

Although a student's transaction is conducted entirely with a lending institution, his application and his need for funds must be certified by the school he is entering or attending and approved by the state authority.

Perhaps a discussion of one more state body will provide a further understanding of college financing. This is the program of Michigan's Higher Education Assistance Authority, which is not quite so generous with its guaranteed loans. Student residents of Michigan may borrow from a bank to attend any accredited college, but a maximum of 6 per cent simple interest is chargeable on unpaid balances from the start of the loan until payment is completed. Monthly repayments of principal and interest do not begin until six months after a student leaves school, and he has up to five years in which to settle the debt.

The Legislature established this program in 1960 after a survey had shown that as many as 64 per cent of the state's high school graduates were not going to college, many of them for lack of money. The procedure for obtaining a Michigan loan is similar to that in New York, but the permissible amounts are $500 the first year, $650 the second, $800 the third and $950 the fourth, with $1,100 for one year of graduate school. The maximum one may borrow is $4,000, which if obtained during five years of study would be repaid at a rate of $91.06 a month for five years after completion of the graduate year. This would bring the total cost of a student's loan to $1,463.60, repaid in full about 10½ years after he enrolled as a freshman.

A program for others

Although a number of states have programs similar to those in New York, Michigan and Massachusetts, there still are many without sound, relatively low-cost sources for borrowing money. It was to meet the needs of students where there were no such programs that a group of educators, businessmen and bankers established United Student Aid Funds (U.S.A. Funds) in 1962. The supply of loan money had not been keeping pace with the demand for it created by the N.D.E.A. program, so U.S.A. Funds was developed as a national, nonprofit, tax-exempt corporation to endorse bank loans. Originally launched on a trial basis, the program is now a permanent one, with executive offices in New York and an endorsement center in Indianapolis.

The goal of U.S.A. Funds is to enable any needy student to borrow from his neighborhood bank without a tax subsidy or collateral. Funds to underwrite the loans have been raised by the corporation, which also serves other agencies interested in endorsing loans to students and provides free consultation services to banks, colleges and foundations.

U.S.A. Funds enters a student's life after he has been certified for admission. Now he must find the money to pay for his education.

He goes to a local bank to apply for a U.S.A. Fund loan. When the standard U.S.A. Funds forms are completed, the bank sends them to the U.S.A. Funds endorsement center. Upon being endorsed, they are returned to the bank, which then issues the loan.

Up to $1,000 a year, or a maximum of $4,000 for four years, may be borrowed, with repayment scheduled monthly beginning the first day of the fifth month after graduation. The usual payment period is 36 months if each installment is less than $100 or 54 months for larger loans. If a student leaves school before graduation, he must begin repayments in 30 days.

A limit of 6 per cent simple interest is set on unpaid balances. Loans may range from $1,000 borrowed by a student in his senior year and repaid at a rate of $32.09 a month for 36 months (total cost, $155.24) to $4,000 borrowed by a student in each of four years and repaid at a rate of $98.18 for 54 months, for a total cost of $1,301.72.

If a student dies, U.S.A. Funds repays the outstanding loan in full. Parents have no obligation at any time; they need only acknowledge that they know about the transaction. The participating colleges are involved, however, since each contributes to the U.S.A. Funds reserve. The amount the college deposits multiplied by 12.5 is the total that can be lent to students of that school; in other words, for every $1,000 deposited by a school, U.S.A. Funds endorses $12,500 in loans. Reserve funds come also from foundations, corporations, volunteer committees and individuals. Every participating college must be approved by U.S.A. Funds and the school in turn must certify the applicant's character, financial need and ability to do academic work.

One advantage of this program is that it helps the student with the greatest need, who often has the hardest time borrowing money through other channels, and it spares him from having to become involved in a high-interest commercial loan (see Chapter 10). In 1964 U.S.A. Funds reported that a total of more than 47,000 loans valued at nearly $25.6 million had been endorsed since the program's inception. Its services were available in all but a handful of states, and more than 630 colleges and 4,800 banks were participating.

While regular bank loans often carry high interest, U.S.A. Funds boasts that it can secure loans repayable at as little as 5 or 6 per cent simple interest a year. Its philosophy is one of combining philanthropy with self-reliance and of proving to the financial community that ambition and ability are good collateral. Perhaps the thinking behind such a noncommercial activity is best summarized by Allen D. Marshall, a former executive of General Electric and General Dynamics and president of U.S.A. Funds, who says: "Banks are willing to lend money to a student on the diminishing value of his second-hand car. They should be more willing to lend it on the increasing value of his education."

The schools concur

When it comes to installment financing of college, the schools themselves have been unequaled in their demonstration of confidence in students. Nearly 75 per cent of the nation's colleges and universities are involved in long-term loan programs, with nearly all providing the lowest possible interest rates and the least painful repayment schedules.

The Massachusetts Institute of Technology was a pioneer in extending credit to students. Its loan fund, established in 1931, is now the largest of its kind in the country. An undergraduate may borrow a total of $5,000 and repay it at a rate of $150 every six months after leaving school. Interest of 1 per cent a year accumulates during the time a student is in school, and 2 per cent a year on the unpaid balance is charged after he leaves.

"Our 30 years of experience have shown that students borrowing from the Technology Loan Fund have incurred no millstone of debt," an M.I.T. official says. "These students, rather, have merely transferred payments for their education from a time when their earning capacity was low to a time when it was much higher."

Other plans are available at M.I.T. One enables a student to pay all tuition and dormitory charges in monthly installments without interest or carrying charges. In a recent year 3,000 students availed themselves of this opportunity. Another is the M.I.T. Installment Credit Plan, providing that any costs in excess of $1,000 can be met through credit of as much as $700 for any academic year, with a maximum four-year credit of $2,800. No collateral is needed and initial payments begin six months after the first credit is received. Payments continue at six-month intervals for six years after graduation at a rate of 6 per cent simple interest on the unpaid balance.

Harvard offers a plan under which a student or his family can obtain up to $600 a year in credit on term bills, with payment deferred until after graduation. Interest of 6 per cent a year on the unpaid balance is charged, with repayment at a rate of $50 a month starting immediately after graduation or withdrawal from college. This plan was created especially for families in the middle and upper income brackets that have no pressing financial need and seek no other aid.

Also available at Harvard is a loan of up to $750 a year, with a maximum of $3,000 in four years. No interest is charged until repayment starts after graduation, at which time the rate is 3 per cent simple interest, with installments as low as $10 a month.

Thus, you see, there *are* bargains in money for needy and worthy students. These are the funds that students should seek first when they find they need help to finance college. Much of the loan money provided directly by the schools goes, of course, to recipients of package aid in the form of jobs and scholarships as well as loans. Nonetheless, the student who does not qualify for a scholarship but needs money should apply to his school first. If he lives in one of the states with liberal loan programs, this should be his next recourse, followed by an application for a federal loan and, finally, by a request for U.S.A. Funds financing.

As is the case with other college financing programs, whether through savings, jobs or scholarships, it is wise to apply as early as possible for the most advantageous loans. A large number of young people are helped by these programs every year, but there is not enough low-interest money available for all who want or need it. Inevitably, thousands of students and their families have to borrow money at commercial rates. Some of the programs and pitfalls in this area will be described in the next chapter.

For further information on federal, state and college loans

Refer to:

Student Borrowers, Their Needs and Resources, by Robert C. Hall and Stanton Craigie, Department of Health, Education and Welfare, Washington, D.C. 20002.

The National Defense Student Loan Program; Basic Facts, Department of Health, Education and Welfare.

Write to:

New York Higher Education Assistance Corporation, Albany, New York 12224.

New York State Department of Education, State Education Building, Albany, New York 12231.

Massachusetts Higher Education Assistance Corporation, 604 Statler Building, Boston, Massachusetts 02116.

Michigan Higher Education Assistance Authority, State Capitol, Lansing, Michigan 48902. —

United Student Aid Funds, 1 Rockefeller Plaza, New York, New York 10020, or College Square, Indianapolis, Indiana 46205.

Or any state department of education.

10

BANKING ON BRAINS

... commercial loans for college

When you buy an automobile, a suit of clothes or a bottle of milk, you know how much it costs, but when you buy money on the commercial market, you can be plunged into an almost impenetrable mystery. Students and their families, like other consumers thrust into the wonderland of commercial credit, often have no idea exactly how much they are paying for the use of money or even what they are paying for.

Perhaps if Alice's outrageous Red Queen could come from her Wonderland to this one and put her mad genius to work at the console of Univac, she might break the code used by finance companies in pricing loans for college. But there are those who fear that even public exposure or crusades by congressmen and the President's Consumer Advisory Committee will not force moneylenders to shed light on what they persistently refuse to disclose—how much they *really* charge for the use of their money.

The cost of attending college today is high, and it is the highest of all for the students and families that, for a variety of reasons, find they are unable to present themselves to financial aid officers as cases of genuine need, or are unable to obtain low-cost government or school loans. These families have as their last resort the commercial loan market, where interest rates are very high—often higher than the borrower is led to think because of hidden charges, piecemeal provision of funds, payments in advance and various other "gimmicks."

Obtaining lucid, straightforward explanations of the figures is just about impossible. Asking that interest rates be explained often evokes silence, double-talk or the mumbles from loan company officials. Some of the college financing operations are subsidiaries of commercial lending companies, but nowhere does their literature indicate the fact. Some work through colleges, making arrangements for the loans to be approved or issued by the schools, thus obtaining a kind of academic seal of approval. And one major consumer credit company insists that it provides a *service*, not loans, and that the service is to the schools, not students or their families, even though it is papa who pays for the use of the money.

Most commercial financing plans for education are relatively new. Only since 1956 have loan programs been adopted or expanded significantly by banks and the terms made reasonable enough for student borrowers. No one can say exactly how much is borrowed for college from all sources, because much of it undoubtedly is in the form of personal loans to parents. It may also be in the form of mortgages, although the United States Savings and Loan League said it had detected no indication of a trend toward paying for college through home financing or refinancing.

Straight commercial loans for college are generally available only to adult sponsors—parents or guardians. Some banks require that a student's family prove need in order to borrow for college, but they then extend the payment period to six or even eight years. There are instances in which the borrower never sees the money; the lending institution sends it directly to the school twice a year. Insurance on the borrower's life is included in most college loans; this is called a "peace of mind" clause.

How costly can borrowing be?

Interest charges on commercial loans run in the main from 5 per cent up—mostly *up*, reaching as high as 60 per cent (see the table on Pages 134–137) although lenders deny this. Not only should the borrower read the small print carefully to see what he is committing himself to—whether he is being charged simple or compound interest and whether the loan is discounted at the outset—he also should ask questions. What is the difference between the total he borrows and the total he repays? What are the discounts, the service charges, the insurance charges and other fees? It is the rare commercial brochure that quotes rates in such a way as to answer these questions, and it is difficult to get realistic figures in talking to lending agents. When taking out loans, borrowers should demand to know the *true* interest rate. If the lender hedges, perhaps they had better take their business elsewhere.

What is simple interest?

Before we plunge deeper into the jungle of loans for college, it would be well to come to an understanding of terms. Various interest rates are quoted for loans from all sources, whether it be 1 per cent simple interest charged by a college, 3 per cent simple interest charged for a government loan or 6 per cent interest (the "simple" is missing) from a bank. Several of the lending organizations sponsored by finance companies talk only in terms of dollars, and then somewhat vaguely.

The best place to begin trying to understand lending is to study an explanation of the term "simple interest." This is the actual cost of using someone else's money. When the cost of a typical loan is expressed in simple interest instead of some vaguer formula, it usually turns out to be about twice the rate quoted. Therefore, if a banker tells you that your college loan will cost 6 per cent interest a year, ask him what the simple interest rate will be. Almost invariably he will come up with a figure closer to 12 per cent than 6. A loan quoted at the outset in simple interest, as is the case with the money provided by the federal and state governments and colleges, usually is the most desirable.

Because of failures to disclose simple interest rates or efforts to hide them, many people think that installment credit is cheaper than it is. Say you borrow $1,000 for a year, payable in 12 monthly installments of $88.33 a month, totaling $1,060. This is not the simple 6 per cent interest it seems to be. The $60 "add-on" is 6 per cent of the *original* amount of the loan, to be sure, but the *actual* amount available decreases each month as you repay. As a result, one-twelfth of the $60 charge is 6 per cent during the first month only. Then the rate increases as the balance drops, making the average closer to 12 per cent, which would approximate the true (or simple) interest rate.

At the request of the President's Committee on Consumer Interest, the United States Department of Agriculture has issued a *Consumer's Quick Credit Guide*, which lists "typical" credit charges as follows:

If charges are based on the *original amount owed* and are included in 12 equal monthly installments:

Charge	Simple annual rate
$ 4 per $100 or 4% a year	7.4%
$ 6 per $100 or 6% a year	11.1%
$ 8 per $100 or 8% a year	14.8%
$10 per $100 or 10% a year	18.5%
A straight 1% a month	22.2%

If charges are based only on the *unpaid balance owed*:

Charge per month on unpaid balance	Simple annual rate
¾ of 1%	9%
⅝ of 1%	10%
1%	12%
1¼%	15%
1½%	18%
2½%	30%

A major problem is encountered in figuring true annual interest when contracts run for either more or less than a year. Even statistical experts cannot agree on a formula that will really enlighten the borrowing public.

The government also gave this formula for computing the dollar cost of credit:

Multiply the amount of each monthly payment by the number of monthly payments to be made.

Subtract from that total the amount financed—cash price minus down payment.

The *difference* will be the dollar cost of credit.

For example, a refrigerator costs $300 and can be paid for by making a $12 down payment and 12 monthly payments of $25.92 each.

Now, multiply the payments by months to pay

($25.92 × 12)	= $311.04
Subtract the amount financed (cash price minus down payment)	− 288.00
Dollar cost of credit	$ 23.04

The total cost equals $8 per $100 a year on the unpaid balance of $288. This is equivalent to a simple annual interest rate of 14.8 per cent, as the above chart of credit charges shows.

This information has been presented as the government computed it, but the formula could be applied to a college financing arrangement.

Other factors further complicate computing interest on loans for college. You may borrow a total of $4,000—$1,000 for each year. The money is provided by the lending institution at the rate of $500 each semester. Not only do you repay monthly, but your payments may extend over a period of perhaps six to eight years. The payments may even have started the summer before you got the use of any part of your loan. Thus you pay interest on money when you do not have the use of it and far beyond the time you do use it, and this makes calculating the true interest rate a job that would have challenged Albert Einstein.

While it is essential to know the actual cost of educational loans in terms of true interest rates, the situation is not quite the same as that of ordinary consumer credit, in which money is obtained for the purchase of a car, a refrigerator or a house. The consumer-borrower uses his purchase while he pays off his loan and after he has paid it off, while the college borrower is often paying for money he has not yet used or is no longer using. Strict comparisons of interest rates on consumer loans and college loans could therefore be misleading. Also, the difference in the net cost of a college loan should be weighed against such other factors as the duration of the repayment program, which may be more important to the parent than the lowest possible interest rate.

Be assured that no attempt is being made here to tell people they should not under any circumstance obtain commercial loans for college. It is evident that a large number of families have no choice. It also is possible that many persons who could qualify for cheaper loans are acting without investigating other avenues thoroughly enough. It must be noted, moreover, that the typical consumer loan has some form of collateral—an appliance, a house, a bank account—behind it, but the typical loan for schooling has none unless it is guaranteed by an outside agency, such as the United Student Aid Funds or state bodies described in earlier chapters.

What *is* being urged here is that you demand to know all the facts, no matter what kind of loan you seek.

In the realm of commercial lending, there is a variety of sources of money—credit unions, banks, savings and loan associations and, finally, the finance companies. We will also consider other plans that stress the inclusion of life and disability insurance. Before reading about these plans and while considering them, you may wish to study the chart on Page 134, reproduced with the permission of *The Credit Union Magazine*, published by the Credit Union Association, which engaged a professor to compute interest rates on

TYPICAL EDUCATION LOAN PLANS AVAILABLE TO PARENTS, GUARDIANS OR SPONSORS OF STUDENTS

	Amounts Which Can Be Borrowed	Length of Repayment Period	Amount Borrowed	Examples of the Plans Offered					Comparable Interest Rate*	Eligible Borrowers
				Monthly Payment	Total Interest Charges	Total Insurance Charges	Other Charges	Total Cost		
First National Bank of Allentown, Pa.	Up to $10,000 for 4 years of study	Up to six years	$500 a semester repaid in six years	$ 63.60	$320.00	$259.20 (90c per month per $1,000)	$15 initial investigation fee**	$ 594.20	11.36%	Parents under 60 years of age who live in the Lehigh Valley area, or who have children attending school in the area.
			$1,250 a semester repaid in six years	$159.00	$800.00	$648.00 (90c per month per $1,000)	$15 initial investigation fee**	$1,463.00	11.12%	
Wachovia Bank & Trust Co., Winston-Salem, N.C.	Up to $10,000 for 4 years of study	Up to six years	$500 a semester repaid in six years	$ 64.32	$307.04	$216.00 (75c per month per $1,000)	$15 initial investigation fee** plus 50c monthly service fee ($36) and 25c per $1,000 monthly administration fee ($72)	$ 646.04	12.36%	Any responsible adult with typical credit qualifications and who is acceptable to the insurance company.
			$1,250 a semester repaid in six years	$160.05	$767.60	$540.00 (75c per month per $1,000)	$15 initial investigation fee** plus 50c monthly service fee ($36) and 25c per $1,000 monthly administration fee ($180)	$1,538.60	11.70%	
Wheeling Dollar Savings & Trust Co., Wheeling, W. Va.	No maximum	Up to six years	$500 a semester repaid in six years	$ 63.30	$320.00	$201.60 (70c per $1,000 If age 45 or less)	$15 initial charge** plus 50c monthly service fee ($36)	$ 572.60	10.94%	Parents, under 60 years of age, anywhere in continental U.S., except those whose children have less than two years of college remaining.
				$ 64.50	$320.00	$288.00 ($1 per $1,000 If age 46-55)	$15 initial charge** plus 50c monthly service fee ($36)	$ 659.00	12.62%	
				$ 66.50	$320.00	$432.00 ($1.50 per $1,000 If age 56-60)	$15 initial charge** plus 50c monthly service fee ($36)	$ 803.00	15.45%	
Bank of America, California	Up to $10,000 for 4 years of study	Up to six years	$500 a semester repaid in 4 years: 5 years: 6 years:	$ 87.02 $ 72.78 $ 63.36	$176.96 $366.80 $561.92	Included at no extra cost	None None None	$ 176.96 $ 366.80 $ 561.92	13.17% 11.18% 10.62%	Residents of California who have children attending school anywhere in the U.S. Students are eligible if their income is sufficient.

Institution	Maximum term	Amount	Repayment					Total cost (incl. insurance)	%	Eligibility
Central National Bank of Cleveland, Ohio	Up to eight years	Up to $10,000 for 4 years of study	$750 a semester repaid in 8 years	$78.84	Unknown	Unknown (first year's premium based on amount borrowed plus length of time, is payable in advance)	Unknown	$1,636.56 (includes initial insurance premium of $67.92)	11.06%	Residents of Ohio under age 65 who have children attending school anywhere in world.

In the preceding plans, insurance on the borrower provides funds for completion of study by the student in case the borrower dies.

Institution	Maximum term	Amount	Repayment					Total cost	%	Eligibility
Lincoln Rochester Trust Co., Rochester, N.Y.	Up to six years	Up to $10,000 for 4 years of study	$1,250 a semester repaid in six years	$154.16	Unknown	$300.00 (50c per $100 per annum)	None	$1,099.52	8.29%	Parents living in the 7-county banking area, or have children attending school in the area.
Boatmen's National Bank of St. Louis, Mo.	Up to six years	Up to $10,000 for 4 years of study	$600 a semester repaid in 4 years:	$104.68	Unknown	Unknown	None	$224.64	13.92%	Parents living in the greater St. Louis area.
			5 years:	$86.75	Unknown	Unknown	None	$405.00	10.26%	
			6 years:	$74.88	Unknown	Unknown	None	$591.36	9.31%	
The Tuition Plan, Inc., New York, N.Y. (Subsidiary of C.I.T. Financial Corp.)	Up to five years	No maximum	$250 a semester repaid in 40 mos.:	$106.00	None	Included at no extra cost	$240 service charge (6% of cash price)	$240.00	60.02%	Parents under 60 years of age who have children attending schools participating in the Plan.
			60 mos.: (payments begin on June 1 preceding start of school year)	$73.30	None	Included at no extra cost	$398 service charge (9.95% of cash price)	$398.00	23.38%	
Funds for Education, Inc., Manchester, N.H.	Up to six years	Up to $10,000 for 4 years of study	$500 a semester repaid in 4 years:	$89.59	Unknown	Unknown	None	$300.32	22.24%	Families anywhere.
			5 years:	$75.59	Unknown	Unknown	None	$535.40	16.24%	
			6 years:	$66.96	Unknown	Unknown	None	$821.12	15.65%	
American Fletcher National Bank & Trust Co., Indianapolis, Ind.	Up to eight years	No maximum	$500 a semester repaid in 4 years:	$87.28	$189.44	Included at no extra cost	None	$189.44	14.09%	Parents under age 60 who reside in Indiana.
			5 years:	$72.88	$372.80		None	$372.80	11.36%	
			6 years:	$63.28	$556.16		None	$556.16	10.51%	

In the preceding plans, insurance on the borrower provides funds for completion of study by the student in case the borrower dies or becomes totally disabled.

Examples of the Plans Offered

	Amounts Which Can Be Borrowed	Length of Repayment Period	Amount Borrowed	Monthly Payment	Total Interest Charges	Total Insurance Charges	Other Charges	Total Cost	Comparable Interest Rate*	Eligible Borrowers
Education Funds, Inc., Providence, R.I. (Subsidiary of Household Finance Corp.)	Up to $14,000	Up to five years	$500 a semester repaid in 40 mos.**: 48 mos.**: 60 mos.**:	$105.06; $88.18 (begin Aug. 1); $73.98 (begin June 1)	$202.40; $232.64; $438.80	Included at no extra cost	None; None; None	$202.40; $232.64; $438.80	54.80%; 35.90%; 26.39%	Parents living anywhere in the United States.

In the preceding plan, insurance on the borrower provides funds for completion of study by the student in case the borrower dies or becomes totally disabled. Life insurance on the student pays off the loan balance outstanding in case the student dies.

	Amounts Which Can Be Borrowed	Length of Repayment Period	Amount Borrowed	Monthly Payment	Total Interest Charges	Total Insurance Charges	Other Charges	Total Cost	Comparable Interest Rate*	Eligible Borrowers
The Philadelphia National Bank, Philadelphia, Pa.	Up to $10,200 for 4 years of study	Up to five years	$525 a semester repaid in 5 years; $1,275 a semester repaid in 5 years	$70 plus 1% per month on balance outstanding; $170 plus 1% interest	$420.00; $1,050.00	Included at no extra cost; Included at no extra cost	None	$420.00; $1,050.00	12%; 12%	Any financially qualified adult.

In the preceding plan, insurance on the borrower pays off only the balance outstanding and does not provide funds for completion of study by the student in case the borrower dies.

	Amounts Which Can Be Borrowed	Length of Repayment Period	Amount Borrowed	Monthly Payment	Total Interest Charges	Total Insurance Charges	Other Charges	Total Cost	Comparable Interest Rate*	Eligible Borrowers
Canadian Imperial Bank of Commerce, Canada	Up to $8,000	Up to eight years	$500 a semester repaid in six years	From $57.46 to $65.45 (depending upon balance outstanding and interest due)	$370.00	No insurance provided	None	$370.00	6%	Parents with a regular income and good credit rating may borrow up to 80% of costs for tuition, books, room, board and travel.
Royal Bank of Canada	Up to $500 a year if student lives at home; otherwise $1,000 a year	No set schedule. Students usually repay out of summer earnings; parents can reduce loan on monthly repayment plan worked out at the bank or its branch offices.				No insurance provided	None	Depends upon repayment schedule	6%	Usually parents, but students are also eligible.

* Because the amounts borrowed and length of repayment periods vary in many of the plans, THE CREDIT UNION BRIDGE MAGAZINE engaged an authority to obtain a standard of comparison for all the plans. The standard decided upon was to consider all the costs (interest, insurance, extra fees and service charges) as interest and compute what would be comparable to a true annual interest rate. For ease of comparison, all plans except those noted were treated as if advances were made on Sept. 1 and February 1, with the monthly repayments beginning on Sept. 30. In reality they do vary to some degree, depending upon when the school year begins and other factors.

** This fee is paid only once and, although not a part of the monthly payments, is included in the total cost of the plan.

TYPICAL EDUCATION LOAN PLANS AVAILABLE TO STUDENTS

	Amounts Which Can Be Borrowed	Repayment Begins	Length of Repayment	Annual Interest Rate	Life Insurance	Other Charges	Who May Borrow	Additional Information
National Defense Student Loan Program	Up to $1,000 a year for 5 years	1 year after leaving school	Up to 10 years	3% once repayment begins; none until then	Included	None	Students attending U.S. schools participating in the program	Apply at college or university. Public school teachers receive a 10% reduction of the loan for each year they teach, up to a maximum of 50% of the total loan.
North Dakota State Department of Public Instruction	Up to $500 a year for 4 years	1 year after leaving school	1 year for each school year financed	3% from date of loan; payable annually	None	None	North Dakota residents attending school in the state and who have completed their first semester	Similar plans are available in other states. Check with the school or the State Department of Public Instruction.
Wisconsin State Loan Fund	Up to $750 a year	1 year after leaving school	1 year for each school year financed	1% while in school; then 5%	None	None	Wisconsin residents attending school in the state	
New York Higher Education Assistance Corp. (NYHEAC)	$500-$1,500 a year, depending on grade	Arrangements to be made 60 days after leaving school	Up to 6 years	None in school (paid by NYHEAC); then 3%	NYHEAC guarantees the loan	None	New York residents in need of financial assistance. May attend school out of state	NYHEAC established by New York State legislature. Similar plans are operating in Ill., N.J., R.I., Va., and Wyo. Corporation guarantees student's loan from financial institutions participating in the plan.
Massachusetts Higher Education Assistance Corp. (MHEAC)	$500 a year in final 3 years	6 months after leaving school	Up to 3 years	3½-5½% (depending on prime rate in Boston) while in school; then MHEAC sets rate	MHEAC guarantees 80% of loan	None	Massachusetts residents who have completed their freshman year and are in need of financial assistance	MHEAC financed by contributions from businesses, individuals and charitable foundations. Maine has a similar plan. Corporation guarantees student's loan from financial institutions participating in the plan.
United Student Aid Funds, Inc. (USAF)	Up to $1,000 a year in final 3 years	4 months after graduation	Up to 3 years	No more than 6% from date of loan	USAF guarantees loan	None	Students who have completed their freshman year, are in need of financial assistance, and are residents of state in which they apply	USAF guarantees loans made by banks in areas where plan has been endorsed by state bankers associations. Thirty states have already endorsed the plan, others are considering it.
Province of Ontario	Up to $500 a year for 4 years	1 year after leaving school		4% once repayment begins; none until then	None	None	Students in Ontario schools	Other provinces have similar plans.

college financing plans. The chart covers some of the cheapest of all loans—those provided by governmental sources—as well as loans arranged by the federal and state governments and the United Student Aid Funds and those of banks and finance companies. Senator Vance A. Hartke of Indiana used these figures in a criticism before Congress of the secrecy of finance companies, and officials of the United States Office of Education refer to them when asked if they have been able to fathom the mysterious depths of consumer credit.

Credit unions

Among the cheapest loans are those provided by credit unions. They also are the least accessible to the general public since one must belong to a credit union in order to borrow from it, and to belong one must work for an organization, company or labor union that has such a mutual savings and loan group. Credit unions are more numerous than many persons think, but they are not as large or as available as banks and other more expensive sources of borrowing. The sums they are able to lend individuals for college are not large either.

Borrowing from credit unions belongs in this discussion, however, for they are figuring increasingly in college financing and may someday become an important factor. A number of individual credit unions arrange for college loans, usually through one of two plans. One allows a member to borrow each college semester or quarter; the other allows him to borrow the entire amount needed for college and deposit funds not in use in an interest-bearing share account.

Under the first plan, a parent engages in a regular installment-loan transaction with the credit union to which he belongs, repaying at rates ranging up to 6 per cent simple interest. Under the second, a member borrows the entire amount needed for four years of college at once. For example, John Smith obtains an $8,000 loan from his credit union. He spends $1,600 for tuition the first year and puts the $6,400 balance into a regular credit union share account. His interest payments in the first year total $480, but he receives a $304 dividend (interest payment) on his shares. His cost in interest that year, therefore, is $176 for the $1,600 he actually used, and he has the assurance that the remaining $6,400 is available when he needs it.

It was through such an arrangement that a truck driver earning $103 a week put his son through Colgate University. A factory worker was able to finance training in a college and a theological seminary for her son. The Hereford, Texas, Federal Credit Union has made special-rate education loans for more than 20 years in a community of 8,500 people. The loans are limited to $300 a year at 3 per cent simple interest.

In addition to the low interest, an advantage of dealing with a credit union is that if you are able to repay your loan before it is due, you may do so without any penalties or further interest charges.

Bank loans may be your best bet

Of all strictly commercial lending operations, banks generally charge the lowest interest. Their rates may run from $2.25 per $100 on a note repayable monthly, for a true annual rate of about 4.5 per cent, to $6 per hundred, or a true 12 per cent. Very few charge the lower rate but quite a few limit their return to 6 per cent.

The American Bankers Association has described in detail the program of one unidentified bank, which combines saving and lending. The arrangements go into effect at the start of a student's freshman year in high school, with the maximum plan providing $15,000. A note is signed covering the amount agreed upon plus charges. The customer makes a monthly deposit in a special account on which the bank pays interest as the funds accumulate. When the student is ready for college, the interest payments stop and the bank starts making tuition payments semiannually to either the borrower or the school. When the savings have been spent, the bank uses its own funds to make the payments each semester, with interest charged only on bank funds actually in use. The depositor is now a borrower. He continues to make payments throughout the student's college career and for two years longer. This makes it possible to spread the cost of college over a period of 10 years—four years before, four years during and two after—with the borrower's life insured for the amount of the loan throughout the decade. It is a workable plan for the person with foresight enough to begin preparing four years before college. However, most bank loans for college are designed as last-minute measures.

Bankers are of the opinion that the risk in college loans is reduced sharply when the money is advanced in installments, with monthly repayments. That is why loans made to parents under bank plans almost always call for regular repayment to begin immediately. Loans made to students under various guarantee arrangements usually defer repayment until after graduation.

Increasingly banks are offering special college loan programs. One of the leaders has been the Chase Manhattan Bank in New York, which has its own plan in addition to its participation in New York State's system of guaranteed loans to students. Chase's program is strictly a transaction between the bank and the parent of the student, with the terms tailored to educational needs. One can negotiate a single loan for a college program covering four years, with a check mailed at the start of each semester. *Interest is collected only on the amount the parent receives*, but it is discounted, or charged, at the beginning of the transaction. That means that if you take out a loan of $960 for four years, payable in eight years, you will be advanced $101.60 each semester and the total discount will be $119.55. Therefore, you will have the actual use of $812.20—not the full amount of the loan.

Chase Manhattan, which advertises that "you have a friend" in its sanctuary, allows eight years for repayment of college loans. Most banks give six to eight years, which, though it costs the borrower more, permits smaller monthly payments.

Some bankers feel that parents should foot college bills—that they are more predictable credit risks and that a student should not be saddled with a mortgage on his future running to four or five figures at the time he is starting a job. There is also the problem of girls who borrow money for college and then take a debt instead of a dowry into marriage.

The chart below shows a typical repayment schedule for a four-year Chase Manhattan loan program providing eight years to repay. Note that insurance charges and discounts are stated. The discount is deducted in advance, meaning that if you borrow $9,600, you get $8,127.84, the difference being $1,195.68 in interest and the $276.48 insurance fee.

CHASE MANHATTAN FOUR-YEAR COLLEGE PLAN WITH EIGHT YEARS TO REPAY

Amount of Monthly Payment	Amount of Loan	Total Proceeds	Advance Each Semester*	Discount	Insurance Charge
$ 1	$ 96	$ 81.28	$ 10.16	$ 11.96	$ 2.76
2	192	162.56	20.32	23.91	5.53
3	288	243.84	30.48	35.87	8.29
4	384	325.12	40.64	47.82	11.06
5	480	406.40	50.80	59.78	13.82
6	576	487.68	60.96	71.73	16.59
7	672	568.96	71.12	83.69	19.35
8	768	650.24	81.28	95.64	22.12
9	864	731.52	91.44	107.60	24.88
10	960	812.80	101.60	119.55	27.65
20	1,920	1,625.60	203.20	239.10	55.30
30	2,880	2,438.40	304.80	358.66	82.94
40	3,840	3,251.12	406.39	478.29	110.59
50	4,800	4,063.92	507.99	597.84	138.24
60	5,760	4,876.72	609.59	717.39	165.89
70	6,720	5,689.52	711.19	836.94	193.54
80	7,680	6,502.32	812.79	956.50	221.18
90	8,640	7,315.12	914.39	1,076.05	248.83
100	9,600	8,127.84	1,015.98	1,195.68	276.48

* Paid twice a year.

Two programs are offered by the College Assured Plan (CAP) of the Wachovia Bank and Trust Company of Winston-Salem, North Carolina (see chart on Page 134). One involves loans, the other budgets. The first provides a personal signature loan for education, with monthly payments for up to six years. The other, the budget plan, is prepaid, with the parent making monthly payments in advance for expenses *before they occur*; the bank then makes lump tuition payments in September and January of each year. Both plans are covered by life and disability insurance and range from $500 to $2,500 a year, with the maximum for four years set at $10,000.

A parent may start depositing money in the budget educational fund in the spring preceding the fall semester to be covered. By fall he has saved enough for the first semester's payment. His fee to the bank is $1 a month per $1,000 deposited, plus an application charge of $15. Termination is arranged at any time for a $5 fee. Payments are made to either the parent or the college. No loan is involved and there is always money for college. But, like many Christmas savings programs, the money deposited earns no interest. Instead, the parent pays the bank, in return for which his plan is insured and there is a built-in motivation to make payments. This is designed for the person who finds saving difficult without the discipline of a "plan." The same result could be accomplished through an ordinary savings account, with interest.

The CAP loan program provides for a repayment period extending two years beyond the length of schooling. A parent makes monthly payments, which are credited to his individual account. When the time for school comes, the balance in the account is withdrawn, with a loan discounted in advance (a true 10 per cent interest) and computed on the amount outstanding each time a loan is made, not on the total amount of the contract. Charges include the $15 initial fee, a 50-cent-a-month service charge, interest on the loan and an additional monthly fee of one-tenth of 1 per cent of the total amount contracted. The fees on a four-year, $4,000 loan program would be $4.50 a month.

A four-year CAP loan of $1,000 a year would involve repayments of $64.32 a month for 72 months, for a total of $4,631.04, or the equivalent of 12.36 per cent true interest.

Advantages of the CAP plan are that no collateral is needed and that the school receiving the money need know nothing about the transaction. Many loan programs have a goldfish-bowl aspect, with parents being required to divulge their financial situations to college officials. For those who cherish their secrecy a plan costing a little more might be more than worth the difference.

Insurance and loans

A well-known loan plan that is usually listed in brochures advising students and their families about college financing is the Insured Tuition Payment Plan, which is operated by the Richard C. Knight Insurance Agency, Inc., in Boston. The program is carried out as a service under a trust with the State Street Bank and Trust Company of Boston. It provides low-cost life and disability insurance to the sponsor of a student along with tuition payments directly to the college at the start of each semester. If the parent dies the program continues without further cost to his family; if he is disabled he must continue his payments for six months, when, if he is still disabled, the insurance company reimburses him for the payments made for the six months and continues paying for the schooling.

An individual plan is based on the amount of school expenses, with installment payments running for four, six or eight years and tuition payments beginning on the date the program begins. Each monthly payment includes $6.40 for insurance and a 50-cent banking fee (rates are somewhat lower for young parents and higher for older ones). A plan providing $2,000 a year for four years financed by a parent between 40 and 60 would cost $173.57 for each of the 48 months, or a total of $8,331.36.

Parents able to plan ahead can start paying into the fund and drawing interest when their children are in high school or even younger and continue receiving interest until the date of the first withdrawal for tuition. The longer deposits are made into the account, the smaller the monthly payments are when a youngster starts college and the longer the term of insurance protection is.

The insurance feature is emphasized in the case of one family that was able to plan only five months ahead. A father enrolled in

May to pay $1,500 a year for four years—a total of $6,000. He made five payments through September 1. Two weeks later the bank paid the college $750 to cover the first semester. A few days later the father died. The payments were canceled and the rest of the $6,000 was supplied by the insurance company in $750 installments every semester at no cost to the student's family.

Another plan not affiliated with any small loan or finance company but emphasizing its association with the Washington National Insurance Company of Evanston, Illinois, is Funds for Education, Inc., which does not disclose its interest figures or even its insurance fees but which, you will note in the chart on Page 135, charges high rates. In its promotional literature, this organization, with headquarters in Manchester, New Hampshire, describes its origin as follows: "Funds for Education was established in March, 1960, by trustees of nationally known educational institutions. Students from all 50 states are now using its facilities at more than 800 schools, colleges and universities."

One interesting aspect of this program is that a *minimum* as well as a maximum loan is set. The minimum is $700 for one year and the maximum is $10,000 for four years, with repayment schedules in equal monthly installments ranging from 11 months to more than eight years, depending on which of several plans is selected. Advance payments are made at the start of each term to either the parent or the school, with insurance covering the life and health of the sponsor provided under the terms of a group policy.

In comparison with other plans, and using the information that was available, the chart on Page 135 lists the interest rates charged by Funds for Education at from 15.65 to 22.24 per cent. This seems high for an organization disclaiming finance company ties, although a form letter signed by Paul V. Carrier, President, says Funds for Education aims "to finance education expenses in much the same way that the costs of a home, a car and other major family needs are met." In any case, the charges are such that a nice profit must be made from them.

When there is no place else to go

The last resort in seeking funds for college is the finance company. When there is no place else to look and it is a question of whether you can complete your schooling, then go to a finance company for help, but go with full awareness that it will cost a lot of money before you are through.

Major finance company plans are Education Funds, Inc. (E.F.I.), of Providence, Rhode Island, a subsidiary of the Household Finance Corporation, and Tuition Plan, Inc., and Tuition Plan of New Hampshire, Inc., which are subsidiaries of the C.I.T. Financial Corporation. All three seem to have the blessings of many college financial aid officers, who distribute their literature and often appear to present their high-cost programs as having at least quasi-official status on the campus. Education Funds issues a handsome brochure bearing a picture of a bust of Socrates with a book propped against it and the label, "the modern dimension in education financing." It also "personalizes" brochures for individual colleges, with monthly payment rates tailored to their costs, their names on the cover and the return address of Education Funds on the back.

Both Tuition Plans also work through schools with an air of exclusivity. Robert K. Keir, president, explained the program this way:

"Available to parents only through associated schools, the Tuition Plan ... was founded in 1938 as a financial service for private schools, colleges and universities. The company was acquired in 1955 by C.I.T. Financial Corporation, which continued its policies and expanded its facilities on a national basis.

"Through this service the college offers any parent the free choice of paying tuition in monthly installments instead of in lump sums. The college enters into a contract with the parent which provides for the cash price of up to four years of tuition and fees to be spread over as much as 72 monthly payments. Parent life insurance is automatically included on all contracts covering two, three or four years of tuition and fees."

Nowhere in the literature disseminated by either of the Tuition Plans or Education Funds is their association with large loan companies indicated. This writer learned of the E.F.I. link to Household Finance only when a query addressed to the Providence headquarters pleading for interest rates elicited a response from an official of the parent corporation in Chicago. The lending organizations do not try to hide the fact that they sponsor the school loan groups, mind you, but neither do they state these affiliations in the literature soliciting student business through the good offices of college aid advisers.

These plans have come under heavy fire in Congress and from the Credit Union Association, presidential advisers and various organizations because of their high and *hidden* charges. Senator Hartke's charge that Tuition Plan interest rates ran as high as 60 per cent brought general denials but no clarifying information. However, his allegation that E.F.I. charged from 26.39 to 54.80 per cent on some loans finally elicited a declaration from the lending company that its true interest on some loans was 14.4 per cent after the heretofore hidden insurance fees and service charges were subtracted from the payments. Hartke's original figures had been compiled, on the basis of available information, by the professor hired by the Credit Union Association.

A subsequent exchange of correspondence with H. W. Van Baalen, vice president of Household Finance, inspired an explanation of E.F.I.'s credit charges on loans issued at the start of each semester and repaid in monthly installments. He said they were broken down into three categories:

1. Insurance charges computed on the basis of $1 per month per $1,000 of insurance risk.

2. Interest charges on the actual unpaid principal balance at the rate of 14.4 per cent per year (1.2 per cent per month), computed at the time disbursements are made. During these periods, when a credit balance develops, the customer *earns* interest on the balance at the same rate.

3. Service charges of $1 per month.

Van Baalen said insurance charges are computed on the actual balance owed plus the total funds arranged for but not yet disbursed. The entire loan commitment is covered by the insurance. He gave the following examples of how the charges break down:

Total Advances	No. of Monthly Payments	Amount of Payment	Total Payments	Total Charges Insurance	All Others
$ 2,500	12	217.34	2,608.08	13.73	94.34
5,000	24	218.67	5,248.08	57.64	190.44
10,000	48	218.96	10,510.08	236.33	273.75

"Because of the unique nature of this type financing—with disbursements made at frequent intervals and payments being made on a regular monthly basis—you can appreciate that the balances, both credit and debit, change quite rapidly," Van Baalen said. "As a result, the quotation of a percentage, as related to an average amount outstanding, can be quite misleading. In reality, the total cost to the parent is modest and, in fact, in most cases the insurance protection furnished would, if purchased independently by the parent, cost more than the total charges for both the loan and the insurance.

"We believe a more realistic way of quoting the charges is a percentage of the total amounts disbursed." Van Baalen supplied the following table of percentages:

FINANCING PLAN				TOTAL CHARGES (Including Insurance)	
Disbursements		Payments		Multiply Total Disbursements by this %	Service Charge at $1 Per Month
No. of Years	Dates of Disbursements	No. of Months	Starting Date		
1	9/15 & 2/1	12	9/1	3.8420	$12
2	9/15 & 2/1	24	9/1	4.4804	24
3	9/15 & 2/1	36	9/1	5.1488	36
4	9/1 & 1/1	40	10/1	4.0550	40
4	9/15 & 2/1	48	8/1	4.6208	48
4	9/15 & 2/1	60	6/1	9.4685	60

He then cited this example: "An $8,000 program, calling for disbursements to the college of $1,000 each on September 15 and February 1, for four successive years, repaid in 48 monthly payments:

"8,000 × 4.6208 = $369.66, plus $48 service charge or a total repayment of $8,417.66, which divided by 48 produces a monthly payment of $175.37."

When pressed for an explanation of the percentages used in the multiplication table and the above example, Van Baalen responded:

"We are sorry we did not better identify the percentages used in our multiplication table at the end of our letter. These are 'add-on' percentages which point out the total cost (exclusive of the $1 per month service charge) of all charges—including insurance. These percentages are arrived at by subtracting the $1 per month service charge from the total scheduled repayment in excess of the principal amount of the 'loan' and dividing this amount by the principal advanced."

This procedure is illustrated further in the chart of "monthly payment program examples" (Page 136) prepared by E.F.I. for students of Duquesne University, in Pittsburgh.

The "pay as you learn" loan concept

Tuition Plan, Inc., operates in a different manner, but its program still involves loans. When officials of Tuition Plan and the parent C.I.T. organization branded Hartke's figures as incorrect and declined to provide any substitutes, they said they did not have "the slightest idea" what their interest charges were. Keir insisted that no interest could possibly be involved for the reason that, in the view of the C.I.T. organization, Tuition Plan did not provide loans at all, only a *service!* And that service was not provided to the parents but to participating schools. The parents just paid for it. Keir said the amount the parent paid could not be computed on the basis of interest or percentages. Here is his explanation of the program:

EDUCATION FINANCE, INC., PAYMENT SCALE

1 SCHOOL YEAR		2 SCHOOL YEARS	
Total Advances	12 Payments Start 9/1	Total Advances	24 Payments Start 9/1
$ 700	$ 61.57	$ 1,400	$ 61.95
1,000	87.54	2,000	88.07
1,500	130.80	3,000	131.60
2,000	174.07	4,000	175.13
2,500	217.34	5,000	218.67
3,000	260.61	6,000	262.20
3,500	303.87	7,000	305.73

3 SCHOOL YEARS		4 SCHOOL YEARS		
Total Advances	36 Payments Start 9/1	Total Advances	40 Payments Start 10/1	48 Payments Start 8/1
$ 2,100	$ 62.34	$ 2,800	$ 73.84	$ 62.03
3,000	88.62	4,000	105.06	88.18
4,500	132.44	6,000	157.08	131.78
6,000	176.25	8,000	209.11	175.37
7,500	220.06	10,000	261.14	218.96
9,000	263.87	12,000	313.17	262.55
10,500	307.68	14,000	365.20	306.14

The above monthly payments cover the entire cost of the program. There are no additional charges. A contract can be written for any amount from $700 to $3,500 per year.

"In addition to the cash price of tuition, the parent pays a service charge in his contract based upon the total amount of tuition and fees covered and upon the repayment schedule selected. Under its arrangement, the college then assigns the contract to the Tuition Plan. The Tuition Plan undertakes to pay tuition fees as due to the college, to guarantee the parent's credit to the college and to bill, collect and credit to the parent's account the series of monthly payments as they are made, thus relieving the college of the overhead expense burden that otherwise would be entailed in providing parents with monthly payments.

"Because the program operates through the college, all fees financed are exact and contracts may be increased or decreased to reflect changes in tuition, room and board, receipt of scholarships, etc.

"For performing the above services on a more economical basis, for both parent and institution, than the college could do itself and for meeting the cost of the insurance protection provided, use of the Tuition Plan involves, as examples of two plans, total service charges of $50 per $1,000 of contracted expenses for two years of college expenses, or $60 per $1,000 for four years of educational expense.

"The nominal dollar cost is charged directly to the parent by the college as an explicitly stated addition to the regular schedule of fees. In turn, this extra payment is then assigned to the Tuition Plan to compensate the latter for relieving the college of any credit responsibility and the billing-crediting-collecting procedures, as well as for providing insurance that will protect the parent's plans for the education of his child. No physical examination is required in qualifying for this insurance coverage.

"Under this program, no loan of money is made directly to the parent and the school-parent contract is not interest-bearing. No interest is charged to the parent for the advance of funds to the college and it is impossible to express in terms of interest-bearing figures any such charge. What is charged for and paid, as explained above, is the dollar-cost of a program, voluntarily elected by the parent, involving the administration of credit, collection and accounting procedures and the provision of life insurance on the parent's behalf."

Keir made available the following examples of the various contract terms offered by Tuition Plan and the dollar cost to the parent, based on $1,000 of tuition a year. Again he said it was impossible to compute percentages.

Keir was willing to state that Tuition Plan, Inc., had "served" schools through 250,000 families who had signed contracts and paid money to Tuition Plan since 1938, and that the finance company had contractual arrangements to provide money to students through 700 colleges, at an annual profit to the C.I.T. Corporation of an average

Fees For	Total Fees	Number of Payments	Amount of Monthly Payment	Dollar Cost to Parent (add-on)
1 year	$1,000	8 monthly	$130.00	$40
1 year	1,000	10 monthly	104.50	45
2 years	2,000	20 monthly	105.00	100
3 years	3,000	30 monthly	106.00	180
4 years	4,000	40 monthly	106.00	240
4 years	4,000	60 monthly	73.30	398
4 years	4,000	72 monthly	64.97	678

of $500 per school—a total of $350,000. But he would not say how many individual "service" contracts were covered by this figure, explaining that there was no way to make such a computation, just as there was no way for this large enterprise to compute its percentage of return on its business.

While Tuition Plan, Inc., operates through schools, the newer Tuition Plan of New Hampshire deals directly with borrowers, and, even in C.I.T. terminology, may be referred to as a loan operation. The New Hampshire organization is for parents of students going to schools that have not signed agreements with the C.I.T. subsidiary. It will make payments to the parent or the school; it is up to the parent to decide. Because it deals with the borrower, the New Hampshire company makes a credit investigation and operates in a more traditional manner than does Tuition Plan, Inc. All applicants are asked to seek a Tuition Plan "service" contract through a school first; if that fails, they may be able to obtain funds from Tuition Plan of New Hampshire, which charges slightly higher rates than Tuition Plan, Inc.

What should a borrower do?

Should you consider taking out a finance company loan now that you know it is the most expensive way to borrow and that it often contains hidden charges? The answer depends on your financial situation. A bursar of a large university that guides hundreds of its students to Tuition Plan, Inc., every year says that although it is more costly (and he always tells students so) than any other form of borrowing, the finance company loan can fill a real need. Many students want money in a hurry and can get it "right now" (or their parents can) through a finance company. The families of some students are such poor credit risks that they cannot bear investigation and therefore do not apply for bank loans at lower rates. Students who are below the scholastic rank required of most federal and state programs may not be able to qualify for any but finance company loans. These loans also have the advantage of being more elastic; you can borrow a set sum but increase or decrease the amount any time you wish.

Still, if you are combating the high cost of college—and the borrower certainly is as deeply involved in this battle as anyone—you should look into every other possible source of funds before signing a finance company agreement containing the most expensive terms. You may only *think* you are too poor a credit risk to seek cheaper ways of borrowing. In actuality, it may be possible for you and your family to obtain funds at lower interest from one of the many other sources.

Why not shop around?

The best approach to borrowing for college, obviously, is to seek the cheapest source of credit first. This is one order of preference you might consider:

1. A college or university's revolving loan fund calling for low interest on loans repayable after graduation.

2. A National Defense Student loan administered by a college.

3. A state-guaranteed or U.S.A. Fund loan.

4. A long-term, low-interest loan provided by a PTA or a service, civic or religious organization in your community. You can find out about these by getting in touch with officials of the groups.

5. A deferred-payment plan offered at nominal cost by many schools.

6. A credit union loan.

7. Bank or insurance company loans.

8. Loan organizations sponsored by finance corporations and similar credit agencies.

In borrowing from any one source, you cannot be reminded too loudly or too often to make sure of *what* you are paying for and *how much* you are paying for it. In other words, always find out the interest charge as well as the dollar cost. Try to get the rate expressed in simple annual interest. Investigate the possibilities thoroughly, and when you finally do sign yourself into debt, be sure in your own mind that you have obtained the best deal you can possibly get.

For further information on commercial loans

Write to:

American Bankers Association, Banking Education Committee, 12 East 36th Street, New York, New York 10016.

Chase Manhattan Bank, 1 Chase Manhattan Plaza, New York, New York 10005.

College Assured Plan, Trust Department, Wachovia Bank and Trust Company, Winston-Salem, North Carolina.

Credit Union National Association, Inc., P.O. Box 431, Madison, Wisconsin 53701.

Education Funds, Inc. (a subsidiary of the Household Finance Corporation), 10 Dorrance Street, Providence, Rhode Island 02903.

Girard Trust Corn Exchange Bank, Education Division, Second and Chestnut Streets, Philadelphia, Pennsylvania 19106.

Insured Tuition Payment Plan, Richard C. Knight Insurance Agency, Inc., 38 Newbury Street, Boston, Massachusetts 02116.

National Consumer Finance Association, 1000 16th Street, N.W., Washington, D.C. 20006.

Tuition Plan, Inc. (subsidiary of the C.I.T. Finance Corporation), 1 Park Avenue, New York, New York 10016.

Write also to individual colleges and universities and to the United States Commerce Department. If you are a veteran, seek loan advice from the Veterans Administration. Get as much information as you can from as many sources as you can find.

11

EARN WHILE YOU LEARN

...jobs for students

Working to earn money for college has become a way of life on the campus. Only a few students can boast that they are completely financing their higher education in jobs, but more than three-fourths of all undergraduates—90 per cent on some campuses—are earning at least part of their way, either in the job-scholarship-loan packages offered by their school or in term-time or vacation jobs that supplement other sources of income. Many young people try to find work whether they need it or not, to put their spare time to constructive use or to fulfill a desire for independence.

The idea of mixing work and study has become universally acceptable in the last few decades. Only really poor boys worked their way through college in the early years of the century. In the mid-19th Century an impoverished Denison University student, earning his keep as a janitor, was the first recorded person to work while attending school. A few years later, three Dickinson College students made their mark by supporting themselves, two of them by pressing suits in their room and one by operating a shoe-repair shop in his.

Today institutions of higher learning are paying at least $100 million a year to students in exchange for their services in term-time work, usually as part of the package plan offered the more promising students. The jobs may involve taking a count of the bacteria in the Vassar swimming pool or removing litter from the lawns at U.C.L.A. And they usually do not pay very well.

Summer jobs seldom are provided by the schools. Generally it is up to the students to find such employment; business, industry and government announce a limited number of summer openings for young people each year. Work off campus throughout the year is sometimes available, particularly in the direct-selling industry, which has some high-paying opportunities for industrious, highly motivated young people. A large number of students make their own opportunities to earn and there are many places to look for work.

Much of what has gone before in this book has been addressed to parents as well as students. This segment, although possibly of interest to parents, is directed mainly at young people who want to work while in college, or who have to. It may be helpful to describe some of the openings available to students—and some of the things young people have found for themselves—in the hope that they will give clues to how one can help defray the high cost of college.

Campus opportunities

Colleges and universities are constantly increasing their control of student finances through administration of the government's guaranteed loans, allocation of nearly all the major scholarships and assignment of campus jobs. In regulating where the money is coming from, and in what quantities, the schools also like to put a limit on the number of hours a student may work at a term-time job. Most college employment offices try to see to it that students work no more than 15 to 20 hours a week, and freshmen are often restricted to fewer than that. The average student is encouraged to limit himself to 15 hours. Campus jobs generally pay only moderately; $1.50 an hour is about the average, but it may go as low as 45 cents. A student working 15 hours a week at $1.50 an hour makes enough to pay for room or board, but 15 hours at 45 cents is scarcely worth the effort.

Let us look at some of the programs at individual colleges and universities so that you can reach your own conclusions.

At Harvard, Dustin M. Burke, director of the student employment office, reports that there are few students who have the time to spare to earn enough to pay all their expenses, but 40 per cent of the undergraduates fill term-time jobs paying an average of about $400 a year. About 75 per cent work every summer. Burke is convinced that any student who really wants a job during the academic year finds one at Harvard, but he acknowledges that summer placement presents a more difficult problem.

Harvard has two major employment programs. While they may not be unique, they certainly are unusual enough to serve as patterns for other schools to follow. One is the Harvard Student Agencies, Inc., which fosters earning while learning through free enterprise; the other is the Faculty Aide Program.

How to become a campus tycoon

The Harvard Student Agencies is a nonprofit corporation with a number of subsidiaries engaged in a variety of activities, including operating a refreshment business and stadium concessions. It has made money booking transportation on charter flights to Europe and publishing a best-selling European travel guide. The typing service always operates in the black. Several students set up a mutual fund sales agency that has harvested good dividends, and a prospering year-round catering agency provides service anywhere in the Boston area complete with bartenders, butlers, waiters and prepared hors d'oeuvres. Back Bay hostesses, needless to say, are delighted to have their guests served by Harvard men.

One of the corporation's most successful enterprises is the Student Linen Agency, which distributes blankets and linens to dormitory residents during the school year. Equally solvent is the Calendar Agency, which publishes and distributes a free weekly schedule of events and information that is financed entirely by advertising. A corporation subsidiary is in the business of renting refrigerators to students for use in their rooms. To keep the refrigerators stocked, another subsidiary employs students in distributing orange juice, milk, sandwiches and other foods. One door-to-door team solicits sales of Harvard class rings in the dormitories and another distributes newspapers and magazines. A year-round earning opportunity is afforded by the house-painting subsidiary, which hires students to paint both interiors and exteriors, hang paper and even do minor carpentry and masonry. Three hundred men earned $350 each during one summer of such work.

Jobs for eggheads

Under the Faculty Aide Program, which was originated in 1957, teachers select qualified undergraduates at Harvard and Radcliffe as paid assistants to help them with research and administrative work. This program enables students to participate in projects in their fields of study and, at the same time, gives professors expert and interested helpers. One aide was employed to study the backgrounds of Harvard professors, comparing their educational and social histories with those of the past. Another searched the Congressional Record for the use of certain rules in the passage of legislation. A third earned money by enlarging photographs for an archeologist.

The school pays the bill for such help, with the aides working 8 to 10 hours a week for a yearly minimum of $400—about $1.50 an hour. Some make more but none receive less. The hours are fitted into the student's schedule and it is the university's intent that such assignments be part of his educational program, not just a job.

Vassar girls work, too

At least 300 campus jobs are regularly assigned to students at Vassar. An additional 100 girls do baby-sitting for professors and other residents of Poughkeepsie, New York, at prices set by the student employment office—65 cents an hour if a child is asleep and 75 if awake. This covers a maximum of four children. There is an extra 10-cent hourly charge for each additional child.

On-campus jobs are varied, with the library providing the largest number of opportunities. There also are jobs operating business machines, washing the keys of the 52 pianos in the music department and keeping the water pans in the practice rooms filled when the heat is on so the pianos stay in tune. Bacteriology majors are employed to test the milk served at meals and the kitchen utensils as well as the swimming pool.

All campus jobs are posted in the spring and are awarded according to experience and seniority, with most girls being restricted to working 12 to 15 hours a week. Girls in their final year usually get the managerial posts, while the least demanding and desirable jobs go to freshmen.

Like Harvard, Vassar has student aides who help faculty members with research and other tasks. A few years ago the college had only 150 campus jobs, but with the development of package programs, the Board of Trustees appropriated a special fund to finance student assistance for the faculty.

Opportunities are varied

Most jobs filled by college students fall into the now traditional categories of waiting on table, clerking, typing, chauffeuring, performing custodial services, baby-sitting and the like. Once in a while an unusual opportunity comes along, as for example at the University of Southern California, where the employment office was able to place a student as a folk singer in a restaurant. Placement experts failed, however, in a search for a student who could saddle and ride horses and was willing to take two children riding every morning.

At U.S.C., as well as some other schools in big cities, job placement officers say it is easier for women students to find white-collar jobs than it is for men because of the demand for office help on and off the campus. While boys find higher paying seasonal employment as laborers and truck drivers, a girl who can type and knows shorthand can earn money throughout the year. Most of the requests from Los Angeles offices for student workers are for women.

Students generally try to find work that relates to the professions for which they are training, according to Mrs. Florence Watt, director of the U.S.C. placement bureau. "For instance," she says, "if we can place a premedical student as a hospital laboratory assistant, he will be delighted. A journalism student directed to a small job in an advertising or public relations firm will be ecstatic.

"Sometimes the jobs get too good and the students begin to work full time and quit school. This is unfortunate. I had a call from a young man whom I had sent to a little corner of a public relations firm. He wanted to tell me it was the best thing that had ever happened to him; his salary had been raised to $1,000 a month for full-time work, and he was dropping out of school. I told him I disagreed, that I felt I had done him a disservice. In four or five years he will find out what I meant."

A *scholarship program*

"Work scholarships" have been developed at some schools. This is just another label for the job compartment of the package plan. One of the better-established work scholarship arrangements is offered at Tufts University, which guarantees work for needy students. The recipient of such a "scholarship" is credited with $500 at the bursar's office at the opening of the school year. He then is required to earn $350 during the school year in campus jobs. The remaining $150 is a grant-in-aid. Since the average campus job at Tufts pays $1 an hour, the student must work 10 to 12 hours a week to earn his salary and grant. The school also has a partial work scholarship of $275, requiring $175 in campus earnings in five to seven hours of work a week and providing the rest in a grant. Job assignments for both full-time and part-time work scholarships include serving as dormitory receptionists, laboratory aides, film projectionists, statistical analysts and poll takers.

"Help wanted" signs are up elsewhere

Stanford University reports that 60 to 70 per cent of its students earn money for college whether they need to work or not. More than half the girls at Barnard College in New York work during the academic year and a larger proportion find employment in the summer. During one school year the jobs ranged from teacher of the flute to restaurant hat-check girl, with earnings averaging $200 a student. Term-time campus jobs are provided at Yale for all recipients of financial aid who want them.

Most universities in big cities have active employment offices that canvass business and industry; one of these is the University of California at Berkeley. Columbia University helps its students get well-paying part-time jobs by providing them with training in such skills as typing, proofreading and editing.

John M. Buckey, director of placement services at New York University, says that, generally speaking, any student with initiative and the need to earn money will get some kind of work. Getting a job in New York is relatively easy for an undergraduate, despite the fact that there are well over 200,000 college students in the city. Large and small businesses and government agencies ask for referrals. Insurance companies have been using a large number of students as temporary workers to help with the huge job of transferring all their data to punchcards for use in computers. The psychology laboratory at Yeshiva University sent out word to N.Y.U. and other schools that it needed students who walked or talked in their sleep to undergo observation for $10 a night. A N.Y.U. laboratory hires students to work as "sitters" for experimental animals. The government missile agency hired several young men to live in confinement in a capsule for two weeks. There have been openings also for students to fill

A.S.P.C.A. water troughs for police horses. One student was retained as houseboy for a famous actor.

Campus jobs at N.Y.U. include an attractive tuition remission feature. Students receive not only cash for working on the university staff but also refunds of up to half their tuition. A student working in Buckey's office can make up to $118 a week and also have half his tuition refunded. Stenographers make between $50 and $70 a week and a mail clerk can earn up to $75 a week by the time he is a senior. Thus, with both income and tuition remission, a student can make his own way at N.Y.U.

Buckey feels strongly that while jobs make college possible for many young people, one gets far more out of a higher education if he does not have to work. It is Buckey's opinion that in most cases the parents of working students could have done more to prepare financially for college. "No matter who you are, if you have to work after school, you need a lot of physical and mental stamina. And everyone still needs recreation, socializing and stimulating discussion with his professors and fellow students to get the most out of college."

Since the economic realities of life on the campus mean that some students must work, Buckey is there to help them as much as he can.

Summer opportunities

Traditionally there are a number of jobs for college students to fill in the summer. Young people are in demand to work in resorts as waiters, waitresses, dishwashers, busboys, secretaries, lifeguards and recreational directors. Some 20,000 college men and women earn from $300 to $2,500 between Memorial Day and Labor Day every year in the Catskill Mountains resort area, for example. One student headwaiter saved more than $2,000 in a summer and a young waiter put $1,000 in the bank. Those who worked as bellhops earned between $650 and $1,200, in addition to room and board.

The National Park Service has hundreds of jobs for young people during the peak tourist months and camps are staffed almost entirely by college students. There usually are openings for sales clerks, soda-fountain attendants, waitresses, cooks, nurses, service-station attendants and telephone operators, and miscellaneous jobs for others willing to do unskilled work.

Camps and resorts across the country list about 12,000 student openings with the University of Michigan employment office alone every year. The camps look for students with more than arts and crafts skills; they want young people who can teach dancing, swimming, tennis, drama, horseback riding, music, archery, boating, dueling and even how to operate a ham radio. The salary range is from $175 to $600 for a summer—plus room and board and sometimes transportation—with the median about $250 for six to eight weeks of work.

Year-round employers need vacation helpers, too

Companies regularly in business around the year have various openings for students in the summer. Offices hire boys and girls to replace regular employees on vacation, and seasonal outdoor farm and construction work is frequently open to men students, to mention a few.

About 75 per cent of the students at Knox College in Galesburg, Illinois, find summer work, with a few landing high-paying jobs. A draftsman, for example, earned $3,000 in one summer; an insurance salesman banked $2,700, and a cement mason received $2,000. This kind of job jackpot is unusual, however, as we have seen.

The summer experiences of Vassar girls are varied, too. During a recent vacation period, several worked in social agencies and as occupational therapists. An art major catalogued books in a private library and an anthropology student worked for the famous anthropologist Margaret Mead at the American Museum of Natural History. There were other interesting assignments, such as that of chaperone for a cross-country bus trip organized for foreign students by a travel agency. A sophomore picked blueberries on a commercial farm while several of her classmates worked in canneries. Another found employment in a toy factory, where it was her task to put a leg on an item labeled Big Bill the Pelican. Openings as junior bank tellers were snapped up by several girls, and two made money by operating a day nursery in a back yard. About 60 per cent of Vassar's student body works in the summer, with earnings averaging about $400.

All but a handful of Barnard girls held paying jobs during a recent summer, some of them rather unusual. A chemistry major did research in the structural analysis of the enzyme under a grant from the National Institutes of Health. A mathematics major was one of 90 students who served as junior technicians at the Brookhaven National Laboratory on Long Island at salaries of $350 to $475 for the summer, plus room, board and transportation.

Amherst reports that up to 80 per cent of its students find summer work, averaging $500 each in jobs ranging from manual labor to technical writing. The top wage of $2,400 was earned one summer in road construction. Almost inevitably the highest paying work for male college students is in manual labor; the future white-collar workers fare better while in college in blue-collar or no-collar jobs.

Travel for pay

Among the many vacation replacement positions in business and industry are those provided by Pan American World Airways, which carries its peak passenger loads in the months students are out of school. Pan Am hires and trains college men and women to serve as stewards and stewardesses on its global flights at standard pay. The girls then return to school to serve as campus representatives and encourage other girls to become interested in being full-time stewardesses after leaving school. Men are recruited from the Cornell School of Hotel Administration and the San Francisco City College for summer training and service as stewards.

Summers with a future

International Business Machines Corporation has what may not be a typical program of hiring college students during the summer in a variety of technical jobs. More than 500 students are employed each summer, with standard wages being paid on the basis of skill and rating. There always are far more applicants than there are jobs, so I.B.M. seldom hires the same students for more than one summer. It prefers to provide opportunities for new candidates each year, to have a chance to look over a wider range of potential employees. Apparently this policy has paid off, for between 40 and 50 per cent of the summer workers go to work for I.B.M. after graduation.

Similar summer internship programs have been adopted by other leading companies, among them General Motors, U.S. Steel, the First National City Bank of New York and the Harris Trust & Savings Bank of Chicago. Most companies with internship programs hire young men between their junior and senior years, in the hope that the promising ones will return for full-time jobs upon graduation. General Motors employs some summer student-workers in the lower classes but most are juniors or seniors. The pay ranges from $350 a month for freshmen to $515 for seniors and $565 for graduate students. First National City sends a handful of students abroad each summer to work in its overseas branches, and a larger number fill jobs in domestic offices. About half eventually go to work full time for the bank.

Co-ed "hello" girls

The New York Telephone Company—and other members of the Bell System—place college girls in temporary summer posts as operators, typists and clerks. Some are held over for part-time work during the school year. More than 100 men students, most of them in their junior year, are assigned to various departments in the New York company, where they have a chance to find out whether they would like to work for it, and it can take a good look at them, too.

Government jobs

Summer internships in the federal government and at the United Nations provide more experience than money, as a rule. A few of the 12,500 students in nonclerical federal positions do reasonably well financially, earning as much as $1,000 a month. Before anyone rushes to apply for a summer government job with the idea of getting rich, however, let me assure you that only one student made the highest salary one summer, while 119 made the lowest—$265 a month. The largest number received from $310 to $360 a month, out of which they had to provide their own living expenses.

On the state level, Connecticut's Department of Mental Health has a summer service corps program, patterned after the Peace Corps, that gives eight weeks' employment at $100 a month plus room, board and laundry to about 30 men and women students who work in wards in a state hospital for four weeks and then in a patients' summer camp for the other four.

Individual enterprise

There always are inventive students who make their own opportunities, in the summer or during the school year. At the University of California two men undergraduates sold lox and bagels to students on Sunday mornings; another pair distributed sandwiches to sororities and fraternities during lunch hours. A California girl worked her way through college as a labor-relations expert for a maritime union.

Knox College's students tend to use ingenuity and make money while home from school in the summer. One boy raised worms and sold them to fishermen. Another was a professional musician who sometimes did so well during the summer that he kept right on playing through the fall term to earn enough money to return for full-time study. Knox students have been known to run computers, read water meters, roof houses, work in iron mines and even pack pickles during summers. One made mousetraps. Quite a few work as golf caddies or farm hands. A Knox girl had the distinction of serving as a summer typist in the White House.

Here are some other money-making ideas that have paid off:

A Midwestern student earned her expenses making and selling novelty hats for as much as $17.

An Ohio boy banked more than $1,000 by selling reptiles to zoos, schools and private collectors.

A Maryland girl made extra money as a church organist.

Three Southern Methodist University students made a good living as a popular trio and even recorded several songs.

A Mississippi student defrayed most of his college costs as a photographer.

A puppeteer and ventriloquist did well entertaining at fraternity dances and off-campus gatherings in the Midwest.

An Eastern co-ed coated ivy leaves with copper for earrings and other jewelry.

Two girls in the Northwest painted designs to order on sweatshirts.

A student at Reed College, in Portland, Oregon, started a repair business for the increasing number of bicycles on campus.

Perhaps these will give others ideas how to develop their interests and skills profitably.

Campus representatives

In the days when cigarette companies aimed much of their advertising at young people, lucrative jobs were available across the country for personable undergraduates who served as campus representatives. They were paid by the companies for passing out free samples of cigarettes. This practice was abandoned with increasing evidence linking cigarettes and cancer, but other campus representative jobs are still available. Insurance companies recruit students to sell various kinds of policies, and in urban areas department stores retain girls to serve as campus representatives and work Saturdays and during vacations in their college shops.

Two success stories

On every campus there is also at least one of those rare students with awesome capacities for work and study. Blake R. Patterson, a recent engineering graduate from the University of Michigan, was one of these. He maintained a straight A average during most of his college career while playing the bassoon for pay. During his senior year he was first bassoonist with a symphony orchestra in Detroit on Monday nights, a Grosse Pointe orchestra on Wednesdays, the University Extension Orchestra on Fridays, the Michigan Youth Symphony on Saturdays and the Detroit Metropolitan Band on Sundays. Tuesdays and Thursdays were his nights to study.

Patterson trained himself to get by on fewer than eight hours of sleep and took a reading course that enabled him to cover up to 1,800 words a minute. When he had the time he took mile-long swims so he would get tired. On graduation he received a fellowship to study for a graduate degree in the communication sciences. How did he do it? "I try to work all the time, I guess," he explained. "The guys in the dorm waste a lot of time playing bridge and baseball. Instead of doing that, I work or practice."

If you are wondering whether such industry pays off in the long run, the story of Charles Harting Percy may push you in the direction of gainful employment. As one of the nation's leading young business executives, Percy has been serving as chairman of Bell & Howell, which manufactures photographic equipment. He began his career at the University of Chicago, where he operated a $150,000-a-year business engaged in selling furniture, linen, food and coal to fraternity houses. During summers he worked for Bell & Howell and so impressed its president that he was hired on graduation, going on to become a board member at 23 and president when he was only 29. Within a few years Percy gained national prominence, entering the race for the Illinois governorship in 1964. (He lost.) This, of course, is an unusual story, but it shows what can be accomplished.

Direct selling

There are, as you can see, some notable exceptions to the generally low pay provided college students in return for their services. Probably the most notable of all is direct selling, in which the worker sets his own goal and then makes as little or as much as he wishes. At least three major companies in the industry have college programs through which young men and women manage to make good money without infringing on their study time. Stanley Home Products, which sells household supplies at parties; Wear-Ever Aluminum, which deals in pots and pans from door to door; and the Vita Craft Corporation, which distributes cutlery, cooking utensils, tableware and china in sales made by appointment, not only recruit student salespeople but also give scholarships to those who do the best business and keep up their grade averages. Other companies also are involved in such programs, but on a smaller scale, and Tupperware Home Parties, makers of plastic containers, has a major program for putting the wives of college students to work.

Door-to-door to a diploma

College men have made as much as $10,000 a year in earnings and scholarships by selling pots and pans for Wear-Ever, which has a college program dating back to 1902. Until the early 1920's, in fact, the Wear-Ever force consisted mainly of college boys who sold during their summer vacations. Today Wear-Ever operates the year around and only a fraction of its dealers are students. Some collegians work part time during the school year and full time in the summer, not only paying their school expenses but buying cars, homes and furniture while in college and having money in the bank on graduation. More than 3,000 college men are recruited by Wear-Ever and its Cutco cutlery division every year in addition to the men carried over from year to year until they graduate. Some stay on with the company after they finish school.

"We feel the college program is more important than ever today," a company official explains, "because direct selling is the one way a young man can put himself through college and graduate entirely free of debt despite the high cost of an education."

Some prominent men have worked for Wear-Ever while in college, among them Dr. Norman Vincent Peale, one of the nation's most famous preachers and authors. Educators have followed the door-to-door route, too, including Dr. Robert Gordon Sproul, president emeritus of the University of California, and Dr. Buell Gallagher, another noted educator.

A student at Arkansas State College tells how he became involved in direct selling. His parents struggled to finance his first two years of college and then found out they could not help him further. Reluctantly, they told him he would have to make it on his own if he was going to make it at all. A fraternity brother invited the boy to a Wear-Ever recruiting class and that got him started. He did so well in the business that he financed his last two years in school, bought a new car every year and lived comfortably.

Pots and pans made it possible for a young man to attend classes full time at Burdett College and at the same time earn $100 a week in direct selling. A down payment on a $19,000 home and a new car were the major bonuses a liberal arts major was able to award himself while selling door to door and studying at the University of Missouri. A Delta State College man found he had a choice between a full football scholarship and selling for Wear-Ever. He chose pots and pans. Another student earned $3,000 during his junior year at Middle Tennessee State College and $5,000 during his senior year and then went to work full time selling Wear-Ever at an average income of $14,000 a year.

This is a big improvement over earning 45 cents an hour, or even $1.75 an hour, in a campus job. In addition to the financial possibilities, one advantage of direct selling is that it enables the student to work on his own time and at his own pace, devoting as much or as little effort to it as he wishes.

Getting paid for giving parties

Stanley Home Products usually has about 1,500 students selling its wares during the summers, with about 800 continuing through the winter. One of the youthful successes is an Emerson College student who began selling when he was only 12 and proceeded to make $2,000 a summer when he was in college. Anne Roberts, a student at Alma College in Michigan, made enough to support herself throughout the school year and received several Stanley scholarships. A Stanley dealer can make $10 to $12 for each sales party, at an expenditure of a total of three hours.

The Stanley College Division was organized in 1957 to help students and at the same time to find potential future executives. Foster Goodrich, president of the company, worked his way through Colgate University selling Stanley products, and others on the managerial level have done the same. If Stanley college dealers want to stay with the company after graduation, they go through an 18-month training period to qualify to head branch offices. Such opportunities are available equally to men and women.

One of Stanley's student dealers led all the company's 30,000 salespeople while going to college full time. He managed to make $5,000 in a single month during a company contest. Another boy, forced to go it alone, enrolled in the Rochester Institute of Technology, a work-study cooperative school (see Chapter 13), but found he could not make enough money during the work periods to support himself. He heard about Stanley and became so successful that he paid his way through college and bought a small apartment house as an investment in his senior year. This convinced him to make Stanley his lifetime career.

Other selling opportunities

Every college placement office in the country has received literature on the Wear-Ever and Stanley programs and others, too, including that of the Vita Craft organization, whose college program draws between 750 and 1,000 summer workers, only a few of whom remain in the winter. The average summer salesperson earns around $1,000, though a student at Western University made more than $3,000 during a canvass of a six-state territory. A Southern student earned enough in one summer to finance his education for a year and help his sister with hers as well. A dentist worked his way through eight years of college and dental school selling Vita Craft products and a Baptist minister made an average of $1,500 every summer he worked while in seminary.

While students, both male and female, are welcomed as Tupperware party plan sales people, the company, in a search for something "different" in the way of a college program, decided to stress the idea of working wives. This has proved to be a successful plan, for the wives of students on hundreds of campuses are earning an average of $50 to $75 a week selling plastic housewares at parties. Brochures on the plan, called "PHT," for "putting husbands through" college (Tupperware Home Parties' initials in reverse), have been sent to the financial aid directors of 1,000 colleges and universities so that they can inform married students of this opportunity.

A typical Tupperware PHT story is that of a student in a college in the Northwest who earned a few dollars a week in a part-time job in the library to eke out the money his parents and his wife's family were able to send them. When his father died, he faced the choice of quitting school or putting his wife to work. Since he was a premedical student with his heart set on being a doctor, his wife decided to leave school. She consulted the college job placement office, which told her about a number of opportunities, including Tupperware.

Within a short time, the young wife was earning $50 a week selling at parties, with enough time left not only to perform her household duties but to return to her studies part time.

Here it should be added that many mothers have helped finance college for their children by working in direct selling. Fathers have "moonlighted" in this business, too.

How does one find such opportunities as these? By consulting college placement directors and getting in touch with the direct selling companies. This is a field in which there never are enough salespeople.

Where to look for work

In trying to find work while in college, bear in mind that, as a rule, off-campus jobs pay better than those on campus. When you decide to look for part-time work, consult the local office of your state employment service, your state department of labor and the nearest office of the Federal Wage and Hour and Public Contracts Division. Get advice from your high school counselor, teacher or principal on where to look. Visit the nearest office of the Civil Service Commission. Check with the various branches of the armed forces on career possibilities (and see Chapter 16). Visit your chamber of commerce and get a list of companies that hire part-time workers. Talk with the local druggist, grocer, cleaner and hardware dealer. Try when you can to adapt your search to your own talents and interests.

Part of planning ahead for college should include preparing for a job if you have to be partly self-supporting. A student who knows typing or shorthand or can run a business machine has no trouble finding work. Those who have served in their high school or public libraries get the best campus library jobs. If you know how to play a musical instrument, you may do well financially in a collegiate band or combo. Don't turn your nose up at doing manual labor, which, as has been pointed out, often pays better than any other work available to students.

Learning good work habits in high school can stand one in as good stead as developing proper study methods. Also keep in mind that you are going to college to learn. The job that benefits a student most is one that allows time for study—night clerk in a hotel, chauffeur, baby-sitter or night watchman, for example.

To get a summer job one should start looking early—long before school is out. For weekend opportunities, check bus terminals, restaurants and hotels, which do their biggest business on Saturday and Sunday. Watch the want ads recruiting people for taking censuses or making tax-assessment surveys. Ask everyone you know or deal with in business if he knows of an opening. Then survey the businesses in your area. Get in touch with resorts, clubs, camps and parks and ask if they need lifeguards, locker room attendants, gardeners, etc. Go to seasonal employers such as operators of amusement park concessions or excursion boat lines. Write the National Park Service, resort hotels, the YWCA, the YMCA, the Boy Scouts and Girl Scouts, camping associations and agencies specializing in part-time and temporary work. Consult your minister and doctor.

Start by making a list of all the places to look for work and all the persons to consult. If your list is long enough and you search hard enough, a summer job is likely to be yours.

This chapter has dealt with some of the things a student can do to *help* pay for college by working, but in most instances without actually working his entire way through school. There are almost endless possibilities for the ambitious and tenacious young person. The few that were cited may help him to a realization of the variety of opportunities and the range of pay. It all adds up to the fact that a little ingenuity and a lot of ambition and diligence can help a student go a long, long way.

For further information on term-time and summer jobs

Refer to:

Job Guide for Young Workers, 1963–64 edition, United States Department of Labor, Washington, D.C. 20025.

Summer Employment in Federal Agencies, Civil Service Commission, Washington, D.C. 20025.

Use of Time During 1961 Summer by Students Registered During 1961 Fall Semester, University of Wisconsin.

Write to:

Civil Service Commission, Washington, D.C. 20025.

Department of Commerce, Washington, D.C.

International Business Machines Corporation, 590 Madison Avenue, New York, New York 10022.

National Industrial Conference Board, 845 Third Avenue, New York, New York 10022.

Stanley Home Products, Westfield, Massachusetts.

Tupperware Home Parties, Orlando, Florida.

Vita Craft Corporation, 632 West 39th Street, Kansas City, Missouri 64111.

Wear-Ever Aluminum, Inc., New Kensington, Pennsylvania.

Your local telephone company.

12

WRAPPING THE PACKAGE

... scholarship–job–loan combinations

The college aid package usually comes neatly bundled, but it also may have a number of strings attached.

One string may be a stipulation that a scholarship can be awarded only if the prospective recipient agrees to work in term-time and summer jobs and to borrow money. At some schools it is all or nothing; if the student turns down one part of the package, the school will not let him have any of it. Other institutions offer a choice, but almost invariably with the provision that a scholarship cannot be the only source of aid; a student may choose a job or a loan or both.

There are at least 10 different packages, including:

> scholarship and job
> scholarship and loan
> scholarship, job and loan
> job and loan
> job and option of a loan
> loan and option of a job
> scholarship and option of a job
> scholarship and option of a loan

scholarship and job with option of a loan
scholarship and loan with option of a job

Of the packages, scholarship and loan are the most frequent combination, with scholarship, job and loan ranking second and scholarship and job third.

Perhaps it would be helpful to single out a few colleges and universities and describe how they package their educational aid. The philosophies behind their approaches to needy students might be useful, too. But remember that these do not tell the whole story by any means; they merely tell some stories that are representative and others that may be unique. In any event, they should clarify the possibilities open to the student with scholarship potential and financial need and give him some idea of what to look for as well as what to expect.

Also keep in mind that scholarships and other financial aid in considerable sums are most important in the private institutions. Since tax-supported schools are not so expensive, the help they give in the form of scholarships is far smaller. Therefore, most of the information that follows concerns programs at the private, expensive, prestige school—the school that most often is at the top of a student's list.

The old school ties on the package

With these factors in mind, let us look more closely at the college aid package. A survey sponsored by the College Scholarship Service, the American Association of Junior Colleges, the American Council on Education and the United States Office of Education showed that 94 per cent of all American colleges and universities provided financial help to undergraduates. Two-thirds of these offered some kind of financial aid packages. Thus most institutions of higher learning with any kind of aid program attempt to offer funds in such a way as to help the greatest number of needy students in a manner least burdensome to them and their families and, at the same time, to enable the schools to admit the students they choose.

One of the most ambitious and successful programs is that of Stanford University, in northern California, which calls its program PACE, for "Plan of Action for a Challenging Era." Through PACE, every Stanford graduate and friend was asked to give financial support to a program providing some form of aid to about 40 per cent of all Stanford students. In a little more than 10 years the program grew from an annual total of less than $300,000 to nearly $5 million. PACE now has a $100 million fund to enable Stanford to carry on its tradition of trying to make college available to all who are qualified academically, regardless of financial status. Stanford was opened in 1891 as a free college, but 30 years later officials confronted with rising costs reluctantly set a $120-a-year tuition. The figure has been rising ever since, to more than 1,000 per cent of the original fee, with an accompanying aid program combining a "gift" in the form of a scholarship, fellowship or grant-in-aid; a loan, and a part-time job.

If Stanford authorities wished, they could fill every classroom with students who could afford to pay all costs, thus eliminating the need for financial aid. Of 6,100 applicants for the 1,270 available freshman places in 1961, for example, about 3,000 did not ask for aid, which meant that there were more than twice as many financially able candidates as were needed to fill the class. But admission of only those who could afford it would have violated the wish of the school's founder, Senator Leland Stanford, who had decreed that a Stanford education should be available to poor as well as rich. The result is that two-thirds of Stanford's students are earning at least part of their way and a large number of young people with no need are in a sense penalized because they must study elsewhere. These affluent casualties of the democratization of American education may, indeed, be attending the low-cost, tax-supported University of California in Berkeley, only a few miles away, while the poorer students are enjoying the fruits of the PACE program at high-priced, privately supported Stanford.

Some schools avoid the word "scholarship." One of them is Pomona College, also in California, which organizes aid packages for about a third of its 1,000-odd students. The combination consists of the now usual stipends, jobs and loans, with school officials making it clear that they feel that any student who qualifies to stay in Pomona after the freshman year is of scholarship caliber, intellectually speaking. Need is the only criterion after that.

Yale University's term for a grant is "financial aid," which goes to about 40 per cent of freshmen, who are offered gifts, loans and jobs and are free to accept all or decline either the loan or the job, but not both. A new scholarship policy was introduced in 1964, making each undergraduate eligible for annual scholarship renewals after the freshman year without regard to his grades. Kingman Brewster, then Yale's new president, reasoned that every man smart enough to be in "good standing" at Yale was of scholarship caliber, whether he received A's or C's; average at Yale is still excellent, in other words. This replaced a policy under which any student who ranked in the bottom 20 per cent of his class was ineligible for renewal of a stipend.

A few months earlier Yale liberalized its philosophy of financial aid by providing that undergraduate grants would be made without requiring proof of financial need. Any man on campus who asked for a stipend would receive one as long as the money was available. This step was taken on the assumption that no one would ask for aid if he did not need it and also with the full knowledge that eventually the school might run out of money to support such a policy. One reason for adopting the program was a growing awareness that rising costs and highly publicized tuition increases were frightening some promising candidates away from Yale. The school's leaders did not want to lose a single good prospect to inflation.

"The youngster whose father earns $5,000 a year is frankly terrified at the thought of entering an undertaking that will cost over $3,000 per year, however generous the scholarship award may be," said Arthur Howe Jr., dean of admissions and student appointments.

Harvard, too, is concerned lest its high costs divert good students to other schools, and repeatedly assures the public that anyone accepted can be sure of getting through four years of undergraduate work—as far as finances are concerned. Officials insist that no capable, vigorous student should hesitate to consider Harvard because of the cost. If Harvard really wants you, it will find a way for you to get a degree through a package of aid. Scholarships are regarded at Harvard as a form of motivation, encouraging the student to borrow and work to fill the remaining financial gap.

"Financial aid today is definitely more important than it was a generation ago," says Wallace McDonald, secretary of the Harvard committee on general scholarship. "However, the cost of education which the preceding generation faced was not nearly so extravagant as it is today. Most of our scholarship students find that they need to work term-time and during the summer, and the majority of them borrow to pay for their education."

A Harvard package for a year of study costing between $3,200 and $3,400 (depending on travel expenses) might work out this way: The average freshman grant would provide $1,250. Summer employment would be expected to bring $400 to $800, with students receiving aid *expected* to produce a total of $750 to $1,000 from work during school and in the summer. Loans could be substituted by students wishing to devote more time to study. No Harvard undergraduate is required to take a job or a loan as a condition of holding a scholarship, but if he needs more money he is responsible for finding alternate sources should the elements of the package not appeal to him. This is up to him and his family. Jobs are available to students who need them regardless of whether they hold scholarships, and a student may work part time whatever his level of academic standing. The school likes to limit working time to 10 or 15 hours a week.

Harvard invests about $3.2 million a year in scholarships, loans and jobs. About one-third of the students receive stipends from the school, while others have outside grants. Most of the men also get some help from home, but there still are an impressive number who are getting through college on their own; that is, with help from the college but not from their families.

There are other schools that consider all their students of scholarship caliber, not because they are "average" but because they all are rated as unusually bright. Among them is Reed College, in Oregon, which grants freshman scholarships to the best students but allocates funds after that to any student showing need and academic qualifications. Davidson College, in North Carolina, makes awards to every student who is accepted for admission who can prove need. To remain eligible a student need maintain the equivalent of only a C average. Davidson, one of the better small colleges, has a remarkably low dropout rate and about 70 per cent of its graduates go on to advanced training. Among the graduates of this residential college for men have been 14 Rhodes Scholars, seven of them since 1950.

Where the girls are

Wellesley College, one of the Eastern prestige colleges for women, established its package plan in 1961. It provides a combination of scholarships and interest-free loans of 10 to 20 per cent of the total need, with forgiveness of loans incurred by those who go into teaching. As of 1961, all entering freshmen who received aid were given a stipend and a loan in each of their four years and also were *expected* to make a contribution from their own earnings. Students are not offered campus jobs during their freshman year, during which their needs are met through gifts and loans. If a qualified freshman needs $1,000, she receives $900 in the form of a gift and a $100 loan. In subsequent years she may also work on campus, but no student is ever required to devote more than five hours a week to gainful employment.

Upon graduation a loan automatically converts to a gift for each woman who teaches, with the rate of forgiveness set at 25 per cent for each full year of teaching during the first four years after graduation, or 25 per cent for one satisfactorily completed year of graduate work and 50 per cent for two years, provided the study is followed by teaching within five years of graduation.

"In the years ahead most students will have to assume an increasing share of the cost of their education by taking loans and by working," says Wellesley's president, Margaret Clapp. "Moreover, willingness to take a loan and to work are significant measures of the importance to a young person of his or her education. If a combination of gift, loan and work becomes the typical pattern of financial aid in all institutions of higher learning, the problem of spreading available funds among the many qualified students who need and deserve help will be markedly easier for the nation."

In contrast to Wellesley's program, Vassar offers what appears to be a more flexible arrangement, which it calls GAP. The word GAP is used not because it is an acronym for a longer title but because the aid program is literally designed to fill financial gaps. Mrs. Elizabeth M. Drouilhet, dean of residence and chairman of Vassar's committee on student employment, explains it this way:

"The scholarship committee, in making financial awards, often finds it cannot give a girl the maximum possible scholarship. This leaves a *gap* between her financial need and the award allotted to her. We then list the opportunities open to the girl, explaining that every student should make some contribution to her education but at the same time giving her a chance to choose how she shall make it."

A scholarship recipient therefore may agree to take a part-time campus job, a summer job and a loan, or she may decide on only a loan, only a part-time job or only a summer job, or any combination, in addition to a stipend.

"We like our program," Mrs. Drouilhet says. "It gives a girl a choice. She may borrow now and work later, if she likes, or pay as she goes, through a campus job. The students like this plan, too."

Vassar has a generous scholarship endowment and its officials hope that no able student will have to give up college for financial reasons. Most of the girls on financial aid have been found to have parents who did not plan ahead as carefully as they might. Mrs. Drouilhet believes that GAP is fairer on that score than the former program of basing scholarships solely on need as computed more strictly under the College Scholarship Service formula (see Chapter 5). When that system was used at Vassar, those who did not plan ahead were often rewarded with aid while those who had prepared were penalized. Now, for example, if a girl has built a college fund through her own efforts, she can still receive a scholarship. On the other hand, the fact that she has worked and saved ahead makes it unnecessary for her even to consider taking a campus job if she does not want to. The GAP rules count her savings as earnings and not as part of her family's total resources.

Also, GAP allows a girl to go to summer school instead of working if she wishes, then to borrow what she needs to pay for the next year. If a girl has an opportunity to travel and work as an American Field Service Representative in Europe for a summer, in a job that barely covers her expenses, she is encouraged to take advantage of this opportunity and to borrow or work during the academic year.

Mrs. Drouilhet believes that this program gives the student the basic responsibility for planning to meet her needs while a down-the-line package arrangement may take the element of choice away.

"It is important," she says, "for a young person to feel she has some financial responsibility for her own education instead of having it handed to her on a platter."

These are but a few of the package programs; they are among the best-known pace-setting plans being offered. The ideal way for a prospective student to find out what is available, of course, is to write to the financial aid officers of the schools on his priority list. Students doing this should unfailingly ask whether scholarship aid received from sources not controlled by the school is subtracted from what the institution itself offers. Also ask whether your own savings, built through hard work, will help or hinder you in proving you need a scholarship.

But be ready for a package offer that will obligate you to a job or a loan or both, and consider yourself fortunate when the postman drops it into your mailbox.

For further information on aid packages

Write to the financial aid officers of the schools in which you are interested and ask them to send you details of the packages offered on their respective campuses.

Complete lists of colleges and universities with their addresses and admissions officers may be found in almost any public library and should be available in all high school guidance offices.

You may also obtain lists of schools and general summaries of the aid available from the United States government. The chief source of this information is *Financial Assistance for College Students: Undergraduate*, Department of Health, Education and Welfare, Washington, D.C. 20002 ($1.25), and may be obtained by writing to the Government Printing Office, Washington, D.C. 20402.

Also see the listings on Page 50 at the end of Chapter 4.

13

THE ACADEMIC APPRENTICE SYSTEM

... work-study programs

The ancient apprentice system has gone to college. On-the-job training programs under which young men acquired skills by virtually indenturing themselves to their masters as early as the golden days of Babylon, Egypt, Greece and Rome have undergone some refinements on the 20th Century American campus, however. In the earliest days, the apprentice, who almost certainly could not read or write, received room, board and clothing while learning a trade, but no money. Today's academic apprentice receives the going wage, in cash, for the work he performs in connection with his college course, which in most cases is highly technical.

Known popularly as "cooperative" education, the work-study concept calls for alternate periods of working at paying jobs and studying at college. Such a program usually involves five years of work and study toward a degree instead of the traditional four years of campus residence. It is labeled cooperative because it relies for its existence on the cooperation between schools and employers and because educators and employers alike regard each phase of a student's activity under such a program as being of equal value to his education.

It must be emphasized that although much-needed cash for college financing often *results* from the work phase of a cooperative educational experience, the *basic reason* for the existence of this system is the provision of a meaningful educational experience. Dr. Ralph W. Tyler, chairman of the Commission for Cooperative Education and director of the Center for Advanced Study in the Behavioral Sciences at Palo Alto, California, maintains that a "cooperative education gives a student an education qualitatively superior in some respects to a conventional college education. Cooperative students become more mature, and their records in graduate school and in employment show that cooperative education is first-rate education."

Money earned in this manner is regarded by educators as a by-product, although admittedly an often important one, as several student surveys have attested. A good many of the "co-op students" are convinced that if it were not for the money earned during their work periods, they would have been unable to afford college. The importance of such earnings toward financing an education varies from school to school. At Northeastern University, in Boston, one of the pioneering ventures of this kind of experience, the students' financial gains are acknowledged by school officials to be an important factor, although not the only one. On the other hand, the cooperative programs at Antioch and Bennington Colleges are regarded as more educational than financial in content, and in most cases do not contribute measurably toward paying college bills; about the most a student at one of these schools can hope for is enough cash to support himself during his work period, although there are some exceptions, of course.

History of the movement

What was regarded at the time as a revolutionary event in higher education occurred in 1906, when Herman Schneider, who later was to become its Dean of Engineering, started the first American work-study cooperative program at the University of Cincinnati, the nation's oldest municipal university. His idea, which has been emulated widely, was to provide a program under which work and study would be combined as part of higher education so that students could apply what they learned in school to actual work in their fields—and vice versa.

The program began with 27 engineering students; today more than 30,000 are involved in similar courses in more than 60 institutions. Most of them major in engineering, but increasing numbers are studying business administration, home economics, science, teaching and various liberal arts subjects. The National Commission for Cooperative Education, established in 1962, is campaigning for at least 75,000 cooperative students a year by 1972.

Schneider's first students alternated a week of work and a week of classes through the school year. Today's co-op students alternate quarters or semesters on a year-round basis. At most institutions using this kind of program, each class is divided in half, with one group working while the other studies, which makes it possible for the schools to put their faculties and facilities to maximum use. It also can make it possible for more students to be accommodated in one school than the traditional college program allows. Employers like the system because it is an ideal way for them to train expert personnel and also to try out potential employees without making any commitments. The students receiving practical training are likely to gain increased motivation as well as some financial aid.

But money is not the main object

Most officials of cooperative schools with whom I have communicated have tried to soft-pedal the financial aspect of the work-study program, although they acknowledge that it exists. Cooperative students earn a bigger proportion of their college expenses than do others, largely because they have regular employment periodically through the year and receive standard wages, not the nominal sums available for most part-time student work. The average annual earnings of the co-op student are about $500 more than those of his counterpart at a traditional school.

A survey of work-study financial programs showed that the average total earned by a student over the five years of his education was $5,600. The amounts ranged from $1,500 for students at a four-year liberal arts school that de-emphasized the earnings factor and had only one work term a year to $7,300 for a five-year engineering course with several work terms. The engineering students surveyed received an average of $7,000 over the five years, while business administration majors reported an average of $5,600 and liberal arts undergraduates $2,000.

To put the wage benefits another way, it has been estimated that it would require an endowment of $75 million to provide scholarship funds large enough to replace the annual earnings of cooperative students at the Georgia Institute of Technology, where 1,000 engineering undergraduates make about $3 million each year in their work programs. The 2,300 co-op students at the Drexel Institute of Technology, in Philadelphia, earn about $4 million a year, a sum that would require an endowment of $100 million to duplicate in income.

Regardless of the amount, the student in the program usually earns a much larger part of his college expenses than the regular student—and also has to rely less on his parents. On the other hand, it must be emphasized once again that cooperative education is not a program for providing part-time work or an institutionally sponsored method for working one's way through college.

Schools offering such programs include coeducational universities, men's and women's colleges, public municipal institutions in large cities with commuting student bodies and evening classes, and residential colleges in small towns. The work-study program lends itself particularly to helping to solve the chronic shortage of work for students in schools in small communities.

Technical school opportunities

Most schools using work-study programs have departments devoted to arranging jobs. The University of Cincinnati, for example, cooperates with 500 companies in 30 states; Drexel works with 600 in 16 states, and Northeastern has arrangements with 900 companies, most of them in New England. On the other side, General Motors employs 237 co-op students from 18 schools every year. Nearly 400 students from 22 colleges alternate classroom study and work at the Ford Motor Company. Wages are paid directly to the students by all employers.

At Cincinnati, students in the Colleges of Engineering, Commerce, Design, Architecture and Art have the option of work and study, with the year divided into quarters, or of taking a regular four-year course with vacations in the summer. Some 3,000 students of the school have chosen to join the program. As is the case with other institutions that have work-study programs, the freshman year at Cincinnati is devoted to study. A regular year consists of 21 weeks of classes, 26 weeks of work and five weeks of vacation. A student receives a "certificate of cooperative work experience" in addition to a degree on graduation.

Northeastern requires full-time study in the freshman year, after which jobs are assigned to all students, many of whom remain with the same employer throughout school and then go to work for him after graduation. As a student progresses, so do his job assignments and wages, which means his college financing becomes easier as he advances.

Founded in 1896 as the Evening Institute of the Boston YMCA, Northeastern became a cooperative institution in 1909 in response to a need for trained workers. It began with a four-year day program alternating six weeks in class and six weeks in jobs. This later was changed to 10-week periods, and a night school was added for persons with full-time day jobs. The first work-study class consisted of eight engineering students; now all the day students are involved.

The years of study at Northeastern are labeled freshman, sophomore, *middler*, junior and senior. An engineering student gets his first job as a tester of laboratory equipment in his sophomore year. The job is assigned to him; he does not have to go out and look for it. As a middler, he may serve as a liaison agent between departments of a manufacturing concern. Then he may move to quality control and finally he may actually design and build equipment. An education major begins as a recreation leader in an orphanage and proceeds to intern in an elementary school, first as observer of teaching methods and then as student teacher and substitute. The would-be journalist starts as a copy boy on a newspaper and then takes dictation, reports local high school events for the school page and finally covers a police beat before he graduates to full-time work in a city room. One Northeastern business management student was paid during one work period for organizing a chain store convention in Atlantic City. Another worked as a traveling public relations and sales representative for a tool company.

The cost of attending Northeastern, including tuition, fees, books, supplies and room and board, is around $1,800 a year, with tuition at $855. Thus the student who commutes to school can earn his own way entirely through the work-study program and perhaps even have something left over.

Students at Drexel average better than $1,800 a year per student in their jobs. S. B. Collins, director of the institute's department of industrial coordination, deplores the fact that this figure is often emphasized instead of the educational impact of the program. "I must admit," he says, "that the students' earnings are extremely helpful and, in many cases, have been primarily responsible in directing them to the doors of cooperative education. At that point, program philosophy must take over, and we continually point out to them the educational aspects rather than the financial aspects. We, along with the other cooperative colleges, are most interested in creating the educational image over the financial image of cooperative education."

On the other hand, research among Drexel students supports the idea that a large segment seek cooperative education for financial reasons. A survey of upperclassmen showed that a majority had earned at least 40 per cent of their expenses in their co-op jobs. It also showed that 24 per cent earned at least 40 per cent of their way in other work. A whopping 64 per cent doubted they would have been able to finance college without the co-op earning opportunities. In fact, 51 per cent held part-time jobs *in addition* to their co-op work; in other words, they were "moonlighting" work-study students. George H. Baughman Jr., program director at Drexel, says it is unfortunate that such a "financial by-product" of the program gets so much publicity. He says that "this sometimes is so much so that the top students financially able to go to any college deny themselves of a cooperative education because they mistakenly identify it with the necessity to earn money." Drexel's students generally agree that by the time they are ready to graduate they have gained a good deal more from the work experience than the income it has provided.

As with the case of Northeastern, the founding of the school preceded Drexel's move into the cooperative field. Drexel was established in 1891 by Anthony J. Drexel, financier and philanthropist, and joined the work-study movement at about the time World War I was drawing to a close. Its work periods are considered to be laboratory experiences and therefore require the participation of all engineering students. Undergraduates in the business administration, home economics and library science departments may choose whether they wish to take part in the program. The placement department tries to arrange for cooperative work assignments within commuting distance of home for all students, thus enabling them to use the major part of their earnings toward financing their study periods.

Many other schools have noteworthy cooperative programs, especially the Rochester Institute of Technology in western New York, where students earn up to 85 per cent of their total college costs in the years in which they work part of the time. A recent addition to the roster of work-study schools is Pratt Institute, in New York, which in the fall of 1964 began cooperative education for engineering and science students. School officials estimate that an undergraduate can earn $7,000 or more in five years—enough to cover tuition and fees.

Liberal arts cooperatives

Antioch College in Yellow Springs, Ohio, was the first liberal arts college to adopt the work-study plan, while Bennington College, a women's school in Bennington, Vermont, is one of the more recent institutions to introduce it. Both de-emphasize the earnings aspect of the program to such an extent that they may be understating it.

Coeducational Antioch, which was founded in 1852 and boasts of having had Horace Mann as its first president, converted to the work-study plan in 1921 as a means of enriching educational experience. Today its program is known throughout the world despite its relatively small size—the student body is limited to about 1,700, of which no more than half is on campus at any time. Each half alternates work and study throughout a full four-quarter calendar year, with some students spending a year on foreign work-study assignments. Although the regular curriculum calls for graduation in five years, the brightest students can win degrees in four if they want to.

Undergraduates at Antioch earn cooperative credits as well as grades toward degrees. They are rated for their work in offices, plants, laboratories, settlement houses, government agencies, newspaper offices, schools, hospitals, museums and department stores, where they receive regular wages. In addition, financial aid is provided in the form of scholarships and loans to students who cannot meet the $2,300-a-year cost of study at Antioch. Opportunities during work periods vary; while one student may be a clerk in a store, another may be assigned to serve as a gull bander for the Audubon Society. Other assignments have involved working as assistants to ophthalmology or mathematics professors or as psychiatric aides. Interestingly, the most engrossing jobs often are the lowest paying, but Antioch is more concerned with educational than monetary values. Because of this emphasis on learning over earning, about 25 per cent of the new students need stipends of $1,300 a year and more.

Bennington was established in 1932 as a new departure in higher education for women. Each student's program is planned just for her, so that no two need follow the same course through college. The academic year is divided into three terms: the fall term of class attendance from September until Christmas, a nonresident (work) term for nine weeks just after New Year's Day followed by a brief vacation, and a spring academic term running from mid-March to mid-June. Bennington girls earn about $150 working for the college in resident-term jobs on campus and up to $500 in part-time nonresident jobs during the school year and full-time summer work, which are part of the program. But the cost of education there comes high—nearly $3,500 a year—so financial aid of up to $2,400 a year is available to the neediest students in the form of loans and scholarships. Of the 350 students, 30 per cent receive some kind of aid.

Offbeat efforts

Two unusual work-study experiences are offered in the Southern mountains—one in Kentucky, the other in the Ozarks. Both are designed primarily to help youngsters from the impoverished hill counties in the Southern states. Berea College, in Kentucky, charges no tuition, but every able-bodied student is required to work to help meet expenses—his own and those of the school—during the academic year. The School of the Ozarks, at Point Lookout, Missouri, permits a student wishing to attend its college to work 540 hours during the summer preceding admittance to establish his right to a scholarship. Then during the school term, he works a minimum of 18 hours a week to pay for room and board. Each of Berea's 1,500 students is there with the aid of a scholarship or loan as well as a job to sustain him through his quest for a degree in agriculture, liberal arts, business administration, home economics, industrial arts or nursing.

Berea College was established in 1869 on a scenic 40-acre campus that now contains 100 buildings housing classrooms and living facilities and various industries that help support the school—a bakery, candy kitchen, ceramic factory, print shop, needlecraft work-room, bookcraft factory, woodcraft and fireside weaving shops, creamery and dairy farm. The students also run the Boone Tavern Hotel (no tipping allowed) on the campus, a popular stopping place for tourists.

Each student's room, board, health insurance and incidental fees come to the modest sum of about $530 a year. This rate is a result of the work program, which involves every student. The school guarantees that no one will have to drop out for lack of money and maintains a special work program providing at least 24 hours a week of gainful employment for the neediest. These students receive special grants-in-aid of $75 applied to each semester's bills. The balance due for board, room and fees is paid out of earnings from campus and summer employment. Loans can be obtained during the school year but must be repaid during the following summer.

This program is no experiment. Work opportunities have been provided for every student enrolled at Berea since 1906. In fact, every student is *required* to work at least 10 hours a week, unless excused for good reason, and about 200 participate in the special work program, which meets about two-thirds of their expenses, with the rest obtained by working in the summer. It requires five years to complete a four-year course in the special work program.

The regular work program of 10 hours a week keeps the cost of college for all the students at the lowest possible level. By performing the housekeeping and maintenance tasks made necessary by their presence instead of having nonstudent help, the youngsters hold down both the cost of operating the institution and their own expenses. The wares of the campus industries are sold through stores and a mail-order catalogue, bringing income that helps pay the student wages.

At the start of every semester each student applies to the labor superintendent for a job. Freshmen take what they can get, while other students work up to better positions as they advance. A student who refuses to work or quits without going through proper channels is subject to dismissal from school. How one does in a job may have an important bearing on his future, for records are kept for the reference of future employers.

The pay at Berea is low—15 to 18 cents an hour to start and increasing by 2 or 3 cents an hour each semester a student remains in the same department until a maximum of 34 cents an hour is reached. These rates are not as inequitable as they may seem for they are in line with the low living expenses and absence of tuition; the students actually work partly for "hidden wages" in these respects.

The School of the Ozarks was established in 1906 as an earn-as-you-learn high school, the same year that Berea began its work-study program. A few years later, the college was added for the benefit of graduates of the high school and of other schools as well. No one is turned away from the high school or the college because of a lack of money. Jobs are found on the campus for all students who need them and work hours are so carefully tabulated that when the required summer work toward tuition has been completed, a student may go home for a vacation before the school year opens.

Students completing two years of college may receive degrees as associates in arts or science. They may take preliminary courses in engineering, medicine, dentistry, agriculture, journalism, law, veterinary medicine, nursing and home economics. The college is accredited and has worked closely with the University of Missouri in establishing its curriculum.

As is the case with Berea, the School of the Ozarks has various industries. Midwestern supermarkets carry canned goods bearing the "S. of O." label, and hundreds of fruitcakes are baked and sold each Christmas. Nearly all the campus construction is done by college work crews. The weaving industry turns out products sold through the college gift shop.

The School of the Ozarks has never received state or federal funds, relying on voluntary help and on its own work force, which holds costs to a minimum.

Another program benefiting young people and communities in the Southern mountains is that of Alice Lloyd College in Pippa Passes, Kentucky. This two-year school in the heart of depressed Appalachia has a student body numbering about 250. Those who can afford it pay $20 a semester; deserving students who cannot pay even that much study free. All agree to serve their communities on graduation or on completion of further courses elsewhere. In 41 years the college has helped to train about 1,000 teachers who serve Appalachia. It also has sent a number of students on to become doctors, dentists, lawyers and nurses.

Although the opportunities offered by Berea, the School of the Ozarks and Alice Lloyd are almost entirely for residents of their areas —and the poorer ones, at that—these programs have been so successful that it is surprising that they have not been copied at least in part by colleges in other areas. The administration of one of the Ivy League colleges created a stir a few years ago when it announced that, as an economy measure designed to forestall a rise in the room rent, it was eliminating dormitory maid service and that residents would have to make their beds and keep their rooms tidy. The outraged cries of protest from young men who wore leather patches on their elbows for effect were enough to bewilder the industrious and sometimes involuntarily threadbare youngsters in the mountains of Missouri and Kentucky.

What the government does

Various government agencies have become involved in work-study programs. The United States Civil Service Commission provides opportunities for co-op students and non co-op students wishing summer training in specialties ranging from the study of the ocean floor to investigation of the weather. Students take Civil Service examinations for some posts. To be accepted for a federal cooperative program, one must be enrolled at a work-study school, while the trainees not in the co-op program are expected to have had at least one year of college and to remain in school during their on-the-job period.

Both the co-op and summer training programs give students a chance to earn as they learn and also to help them decide whether they want to make a career of working for the government. The agencies have an opportunity to appraise the young people for future opportunities, and with positive results, for a high percentage of trainees return after graduation, mainly in engineering, science and other technical fields.

Cooperative student programs in government were introduced in 1919, but have been most popular in recent years as the involvement in science and technology has grown. A young man at New Mexico State College, for example, served as a trainee at the White Sands Proving Ground during his undergraduate days and went on to become a government missile engineer. The Army hires technical students in pairs, with each member of a team working and studying in alternate periods. Engineers, scientists, mathematicians and accountants are being trained this way by the Army, and the Coast Guard has an engineering program. The Navy was able to use its cooperative program to solve a recent shortage of technical personnel by paying up to half the cost of college for a number of men in return for their pledges to work for the Navy as civilians for several years after graduation (see also Chapter 16). Every summer the United States Weather Bureau hires meteorological students for $62 a week to train in making weather maps, using radar to locate disturbances, reading instruments and doing other technical work.

As evidence of interest in the federal program, particularly in science and engineering, 45,000 students applied to take trainee examinations in 1963 and about 30,000 were tested. Nearly 16,000 were ruled eligible for jobs and 2,000 were placed in work-study positions leading to careers on graduation. The cooperative education program in the federal service works much as it does in industry; students alternate study periods and work periods in jobs in many parts of the country, mainly at installations of the Army, Navy and Air Force and the National Aeronautics and Space Administration. The Departments of Agriculture, Commerce and Interior and some independent agencies, including the Federal Aviation Agency and the Federal Communications Commission, also use the program.

Work-study participants are paid on the basis of their academic attainments; high school graduation alone brings a salary at the annual rate of $3,620. One year of college merits $3,880 and two and one-half years $4,215.

There are many opportunities. Those who wish to investigate them should get in touch with the Civil Service Commission or agencies having departments specializing in particular fields. College placement offices should have files of this information, too.

Study-work in business

There is another kind of work-study program that should really be called study-work, for it involves working full time for a business or industry and going to school part time, with remission of all or part of the tuition, depending on the policy of the company, for all satisfactorily completed courses. Hundreds of concerns do this, but only a few need be mentioned here by way of illustration.

The Chase Manhattan Bank in New York refunds as much as $200,000 a year to employees who have completed approved college courses related to banking. It also has established a special fund from which money is lent to worker-students who cannot afford to pay their tuition in advance. The loans are paid off through payroll deductions.

International Business Machines also matches tuition payments of employees who go to school part time, while the Combined Insurance Company of America has two programs designed to encourage its employees to go back to school. W. Clement Stone, president of the company, was himself a high school dropout who was able to complete college later on a part-time basis. He has instituted a program under which the amount of the refund to the student is based on the grade and standing he attains in a course. A grade of C or better brings a 50 per cent refund; B or better and in the top quarter of the class, 75 per cent, and A and first in class, 100 per cent. Some employees have completed more than two years of college while working full time. Another program of the company provides college-level language courses at the concern's Chicago headquarters, where employees can study Spanish, French or German after working hours. Grades are not given for these courses, but those who have completed them can take proficiency tests at some colleges and receive credit.

General Motors has industry's most intensive work-study plan at its G.M. Institute at Flint, Michigan. This is a five-year cooperative engineering school for outstanding high-school graduates wishing to become mechanical, industrial or electrical engineers. As is the case with other work-study programs, the students alternate periods of class with jobs at G.M. plants. They earn enough to pay almost entirely for their educations. During the fifth year each man works on a special project while employed full time by G.M. and receives a bachelor's degree on completing a comprehensive report. The Institute program is open to about 650 entering freshmen each year, with the total student body made up of about 2,500 potential General Motors engineers.

Work-study, whether through a cooperative plan or financed entirely by a college or an industry, can and does provide a partial solution to the college cost problem for many persons, even if that is not its *raison d'être*. For the student who is not of scholarship caliber it may be the only solution, short of going heavily into debt or seeking an educational opportunity that costs little or nothing. Most of the cooperative programs benefit engineering students and others planning to enter technical fields, while low-cost or no-cost college opportunities generally do not offer much to them.

It would seem that, despite the schools' reluctance to build up the earning aspect of the learning program, the work-study concept, if expanded, could help more students finance their educations and benefit from the experience gained in meaningful jobs.

For further information on work-study programs

Refer to:

Work-Study College Programs, by James W. Wilson and Edward H. Lyons, Harper & Row, New York, New York.

Write to:

Alice Lloyd College, Pippa Passes, Kentucky.
Antioch College, Yellow Springs, Ohio.
Bennington College, Bennington, Vermont.
Berea College, Berea, Kentucky.
Drexel Institute of Technology, Philadelphia, Pennsylvania 19104.
Educational Relations Section, General Motors Technical Center, Warren, Michigan.
Ford Motor Company, Detroit, Michigan.
Northeastern University, Boston, Massachusetts.

Rochester Institute of Technology, 65 Plymouth Avenue, South, Rochester, New York 14608.

The School of the Ozarks, Point Lookout, Missouri 65726.

University of Cincinnati, Cincinnati, Ohio 45221.

14

SHOPPING FOR EDUCATIONAL BARGAINS

... the junior college and other opportunities

When teachers and public school administrators joined early in 1964 in a proposal that two years of tuition-free formal education beyond high school be made available to every American who wanted it, regardless of brain power and ability, they stepped into a long-standing controversy over whether college should be financed almost entirely by the taxpayers or whether it should entail some direct payment by students. The basic idea presented by the National Education Association and the American Association of School Administrators was not new; 16 years before they went on record in the matter President Harry S. Truman's Commission on Higher Education had urged that two free years of college be made available to all who wanted them.

What seemed to many a revolutionary concept was in actuality largely an old one containing some new terms. The only apparently fresh idea of the teachers and administrators was not only that the 13th and 14th years of schooling should require no tuition but that "if there is to be equal educational opportunity for youth, the student who has no public college close by must be provided with transportation to and from the nearest one or with the means of living away from home." In other words, either transportation costs or room and board would be provided to needy students by the taxpayers in addition to the educational opportunity itself.

The proposal included an argument aimed at winning over the taxpayer. It pointed out that the more education a person has, the more money he is likely to earn, and the higher his income, the more taxes he will pay, thereby more than repaying his educational debt to society. "In other words," the statement said, "most persons whose incomes rise as a result of advanced education *do* pay the cost of that education in the form of higher taxes. The Veterans Administration has suggested that the G.I. Bills of Rights—the largest and most generous scholarship program ever undertaken by the national government—ended up costing the people nothing; the beneficiaries have paid back in increased taxes more than they received in benefits."

Soon after the educators had presented their platform to extend free education for all through the sophomore year in college, Secretary of Labor W. Willard Wirtz strongly supported their stand and added a plea for compulsory education for all to the age of 18, instead of 16. His reason for such a program was different from that of the educators, however. Wirtz felt that keeping young people in school longer would go a long way toward solving the unemployment problem.

The timing of the proposals was interesting, for they came at the height of a boom in the construction and expansion of two-year junior colleges (called community colleges in some areas) and of a bitter argument between educators in New York State over New York City's persistence in offering tuition-free four-year university courses despite the protests of the State Board of Regents, which found the city's policy in conflict with the state's $300-a-year tuition charge at two-year public colleges. State officials wanted the four-year Brooklyn, City, Hunter and Queens Colleges to start charging tuition so they would have funds for more rapid expansion. At the same time, the Regents asked for a relaxation of entrance requirements so more students could be accommodated.

Unlike many free, publicly financed colleges, the four-year institutions sponsored by the City of New York have rigid entrance requirements. They are not open to all high school graduates who apply, as is the case with the two-year community colleges and some large publicly supported universities in other parts of the country. In standing up to the Board of Regents, New York's Mayor, Robert F. Wagner, was adamant, declaring that tuition-free higher education was "the wave of the future."

"There is no more sense to an undergraduate tuition charge at a public college today than for a tuition charge at a public kindergarten," the Harvard-educated Mayor said. "It can no longer be considered a privilege to attend a public college. It is a right for all who qualify."

While the New York State legislature did not overrule the no-tuition policy at the city colleges, it did express its doubts about such a program by voting against *mandatory* free tuition in public universities. It also refused to restore the no-tuition policy that had been in effect at the State University until the fall of 1963. The new practice, as spelled out by the legislature, provided that no fees would be charged to students whose families had incomes of less than $7,500 a year. For those with incomes larger than that, the fee was set at $425 a year. Members of the legislature urged New York City to follow a similar pattern, but as of late 1964 the Mayor still refused.

In fact, he later responded by allocating the funds needed to put the city's five two-year community colleges on a free tuition basis, thus giving them the same status as the four senior colleges, at which free tuition had been a tradition for nearly 120 years. Prior to Wagner's action in 1964, the tuition at the community colleges had been $300 a year. Wagner's course was heartily endorsed by Dr. Jonas Salk, developer of the first antipolio vaccine, who said

that if it had not been for New York City's free tuition policy in its
senior colleges, he never would have gone beyond high school. To
this, Dr. Gustave G. Rosenberg, president of the city's Board of
Higher Education, responded, "When I think that, during the last
years, we haven't had one single case of polio [in the city], I say
what better indication could we have, what more could be said for
free tuition, than this."

The junior college boom

The wave of the future described by Mayor Wagner started roll-
ing across the country some years ago. By the time he spoke out,
there were, it was estimated, 400 accredited, public two-year community or junior colleges in 35 states, enrolling nearly one million
students or almost one-fourth of the nation's college population.
More than two million junior college students are expected by the
fall of 1975, with 25 to 30 new campuses being opened every year
until then. Several states foresee that by 1975 three-fourths of their
lower classmen will be attending tuition-free junior colleges, a goal
already being approached by California and Florida.

It is the aim of these two states, as well as of Texas, Maryland,
North Carolina, Mississippi and others, to establish networks of
junior colleges within the reach of every resident. This coincides
with the basic goal of the teachers and administrators.

California had 70 public junior colleges and several private ones in
1964, with more than 100,000 full-time students, and it plans to
spend $350 million on junior college installations in the five-year
period ending in 1967. By 1970 California education authorities
expect to see 800,000 students attending these schools.

In 1955 Florida had five publicly supported junior colleges with
7,200 students. By 1962 there were 29, with 38,000 students. The
speed with which a single junior college can grow was demonstrated
when a two-year institution opened in Dade County, Florida, in

1960. It was designed for 1,300 students but began with 3,000. Within three years it had 8,000 students, and it is expected to serve 28,000 by 1968.

With the development of its network of junior colleges, Florida also built a two-year senior institution, Florida Atlantic University, at Boca Raton, for students wishing to transfer from the junior colleges in order to earn baccalaureates. A second such institution was in the planning stage. The first buildings at Florida Atlantic were erected on a 1,200-acre campus at a cost of $5.3 million to serve 2,000 students, with the peak eventually expected to reach 25,000. This school was described by some Florida officials as the first of its kind, but there already was an upper-division college and graduate school at Flint, Michigan, and the Lutherans had a two-year senior college at Fort Wayne, Indiana, for graduates of their several junior colleges.

Other states and cities have climbed aboard the junior college bandwagon. Those most active, in addition to the ones mentioned, are Illinois, Maryland, Oregon, Washington and Michigan. New York State established 13 junior colleges in the 12 years after 1950, reaching a total of 24, and expects to expand this number considerably by 1970. In 1963 Arizona opened its first new public institution of higher learning in more than 40 years with the dedication of Arizona Western College, a junior college. St. Louis and Cleveland have community college programs well under way.

Edmund J. Gleazer Jr., executive director of the American Association of Junior Colleges, reports that junior college enrollments are increasing faster than those of any other institutions offering education beyond high school. He says there are more than 700 junior colleges of all kinds—175 church-related, 90 independent private and 425 public. The church-related schools charge relatively low tuitions, but the private institutions cost as much as $3,000 a year for boarding students. Many public junior colleges, particularly those in California, charge no tuition. Those that do levy tuition and fees ask for an average of $147 a year for full-time students. Publicly supported four-year colleges and universities charge somewhat more, and room and board add further to the expense.

Various surveys have indicated that a sizable proportion of the junior college students who go on to senior colleges have followed this path because it is the least expensive. And nearly half of those who go to junior college for this reason need financial assistance to continue as transfer students at regular four-year schools where they earn bachelors' degrees.

"Most educational authorities figure that anywhere from a quarter to a third of the high school graduates qualified to do so do not go on to college for financial reasons," Gleazer says. "We think the mere presence of a junior college in a community makes it financially possible for many of these students to carry on their education and encourages a good many others to do so who actually make out quite well in the senior institution once they receive proper preparation in the junior college."

Although its most spectacular growth has come in recent years, the junior college movement actually began in the late 1880's in what some educators regard as the only truly American educational innovation. It sprang from a belief on the part of educators that the first two years of higher learning might better be offered in special institutions. By 1900 there were eight such schools, all private, with a total of about 100 students. What is believed to be the first public junior college was opened in Joliet, Illinois, in 1901, and within 30 years there were 400 others. The number of junior colleges has increased at a faster rate than that of the four-year schools. When the first data on college enrollment were accumulated by the government in 1870, there were 563 institutions with 52,000 students, most of them undergraduates. All the junior colleges now in existence enroll a total of more than 10 times that number. The first government figures on junior colleges were compiled for 1917–18, when there were 46 schools with about 4,500 students.

Junior colleges are now accepted as institutions that are extending and equalizing educational opportunities and serving their communities in several ways beyond providing at low cost the first two years of a collegiate program. They also offer technical training of a "subprofessional" nature, short courses to upgrade or retrain persons already working, adult or continuing education courses, community facilities for the creative and performing arts, and a center for civic activities.

Junior colleges are particularly useful in training individuals for occupations that require considerable background but not a four-year degree course. That is what is meant by "subprofessional." The occupations so listed include agriculture, business, building trades, dental laboratory work, home economics, secretarial work, music, physical education, drafting, printing, physical therapy, cosmetology, data processing, nursing and auto repair. Being a community institution, a junior college may offer courses in technical subjects tailored to the needs of a local industry. A school in Florida may provide training in the management of citrus groves, while in New York students may be prepared for work in the fashion and printing trades. Medical-secretarial work is taught in Rochester, Minnesota, home of the Mayo Clinic, while petroleum technology is on the curriculum of a Texas junior college. In the Los Angeles Junior College District, which covers 826 square miles, the Harbor Junior College, in an oil field area, teaches petroleum refining technology; Pierce Junior College, in a cattle-farming area, teaches beef production; the East Los Angeles Junior College, near major hospitals, teaches nursing, and the Los Angeles Junior College, in the downtown business area, has a special course in merchandising.

Students who complete these "terminal" courses, as contrasted with "transfer" courses, usually get the degree of Associate in Science, while those who plan to go on to senior college—or at least prepare for it—generally receive the degree of Associate in Arts.

In addition to the occupational benefits, another positive element favoring the junior colleges is their effect on the motivation levels of high-school students. The secondary schools' dropout rate has proved to be smaller in areas that have junior colleges making advanced education available to all who want it. Also, the number going on for further education is higher. This was discovered in Chipola, Florida, where, before the construction of a junior college there, only 7 per cent of the county's high school graduates went on to college. Twelve years after the junior college opened, 52 per cent were in college, most of them at Chipola. Florida counties with easily accessible junior colleges reported a total of 55 per cent of all high school graduates matriculating. Counties without junior colleges reported a rate of 36 per cent.

Research in California supported this. The communities with the highest ratio of high school graduates who took advanced training were those with junior colleges.

Now we come to the transfer student. Several questions often are raised in this regard:

1. *Can a junior college graduate win acceptance at an accredited university or college?*

The answer is that it depends on the student, the junior college he attends and the senior college to which he applies. Most four-year schools that accept junior college transfers—and I have yet to hear of any institution of higher learning that would not accept a good student if there was room for him—require that all transfer applicants, whether from junior colleges or other four-year schools, take examinations, which often are tough. They also must have fulfilled course requirements. Vassar accepts transfers from junior colleges provided they come from accredited schools, have taken required courses and have high enough grades. But then Vassar maintains the same policy toward would-be transfers from any schools. Harvard has a limited number of openings for upper-class transfers and does not bar junior college students who are qualified.

One-third of all junior college students make transfers, and several senior colleges and universities, including Amherst, Occidental, MacMurray, Kenyon, Marietta and Northwestern, actively seek these students to help fill the vacancies left by lower classmen who drop out. Transfers of students from junior colleges in California to the University of California, which maintains high standards, have long been accepted. It is difficult, if not impossible, for a junior college transfer student to get a scholarship for his final two years at any school, but jobs and government-backed loans are available to him.

Among the transfer students there often are some who were turned down as freshmen applicants because of poor grades. The University of California, which encourages students to take their first two years in junior colleges, found that of 2,300 transfers who had been accepted as third-year students, 1,200 had not qualified when they sought admission as freshmen two years before. Junior college thus has been found to be an ideal solution for the "late bloomer" who does not do well in high school but can be awakened intellectually in college. It is a good place also for the person who has not yet decided on a career.

Unlike many top-flight institutions of higher learning, California is able to recognize full credits of a sizable number of students who transfer from junior colleges because the two-year schools in that state offer a high-quality education. A number of big schools will accept transfers from some junior colleges—and also from less highly rated four-year schools—at only partial credit. This depends largely on the quality of the junior college involved and whether the transferring student took the lower-class courses required by the senior college. It would be wise for students entering junior college to try to take courses that will permit them to transfer to a senior college. In order to do this, one should write to the senior college he is aiming for and ask for a list of required lower-class courses. It also would be wise for students hoping to transfer to check on the rating of the junior colleges they plan to attend to make sure they meet the highest standards.

There was a time when prestige schools almost automatically reduced credits of transfer students to limit the number who bought "cheap" Harvard or Vassar degrees by going to free schools for the first two years. This attitude is on the wane, partly because of the large number of dropouts in the first two years, partly because of the new search for the less affluent or so-called "culturally deprived" students and partly because of an upgrading of the quality of junior college curricula.

2. *Is the kind of education offered in junior colleges of high enough quality to rank with that of accredited four-year schools?*

Here, again, it depends, this time mainly on the school. Not all four-year accredited colleges and universities are of equal quality, nor are all junior colleges. While the California junior college system has been tried and found to be of generally good quality, the Florida system is not yet old enough to have passed all the tests. New York's junior college graduates have fared well on transferring to senior colleges.

The quality of some junior colleges may be too low to provide an education that can be recognized by senior colleges of first rank, but other less demanding schools may accept students transferring from these institutions. There can be no generalization on this score, but there is great need for emphasis on one point: Many people are going to have to change their thinking about junior colleges. Too many tend to look down their noses without bothering to find out what the junior colleges really do and how they operate. Most of the graduates do not go on to degrees elsewhere, nor do they intend to. Yet they have the advantage of study beyond high school that equips them better for their livelihoods and also gives them a feeling of educational attainment.

3. *Are junior colleges more extensions of high schools than introductions to higher education?*

For those taking a course that will lead them to transfers to senior colleges, junior college is actually what its name implies, constituting the two lower-class years of study toward a baccalaureate. For those taking terminal courses, it might be possible to regard junior college as an extension of high school, but it would seem more appropriate to look upon this aspect of the junior college as a trade school or technical school opportunity. Students do go on from junior colleges to engineering, law and medical schools. They go on to Ph.D.'s and become professors at four-year universities as well as at junior colleges. And they also go out to become hairdressers, electricians and movie technicians. But in the cases of all of these graduates, they have received training that was not available to them in high school.

This leads to the conclusion that many of the critics of junior colleges do not understand their twofold function: serving the serious student who will transfer to a senior college and, at the same time, serving the high school graduate who is preparing for a job. One is academic, the other technical, and critics should take both into consideration.

The benefits of junior colleges are many, not only to their students but to the communities in which they are built. Junior colleges attract business and industry; increased real estate values and an influx of new money for the community generally result. The junior college structures themselves cost less than some university facilities; the fact that they are commuter schools makes it unnecessary to build expensive living and eating facilities.

Some educators believe that with the rapid growth of junior colleges there may be an evolution of the entire higher educational system into something quite different from its present form in which one studies four years for a baccalaureate and then goes on to advanced degrees. Perhaps most students eventually will take their first two years in junior college and then go on to four years in senior college to earn a master's degree. Or perhaps junior colleges will become three-year, no-tuition or low-tuition schools and the senior colleges will shrink to three years, with an advanced degree awarded after a total of six years.

Without defining exactly what he thinks will take place, Francis Keppel, United States Commissioner of Education, agrees that "today, with the spread of junior colleges, we may be on the brink of another educational revolution, one which brings appropriate educational opportunities within the financial and geographic reach of the many at the same time that it supplements and strengthens the programs of four-year institutions and advanced professional schools. The spread of such a zest for learning can contribute to consistently rising standards of excellence, in society as well as in schools."

Other bargains to look for

While the junior college is one of the biggest educational bargains in the country, colleges and universities generally are trying to ease the financial burdens. Dollar-short students would do well to look into some of these measures, to see how they might benefit from them:

Academic speed-ups. A number of schools have launched speed-up programs through advanced placement, qualifying examinations, the introduction of three semesters a year in place of the traditional two and accelerated studies in which two degrees (a bachelor's and a master's or a doctor's) can be obtained for the same price and in the same time as one.

Advanced placement involves the acceptance of freshman students at a time when in ordinary course they would be starting their senior year in high school. These students must take examinations to prove their proficiency, and the fact that they are unusually bright often brings financial aid if they need it.

Qualifying examinations also benefit the brighter students, making is possible for them to win credits for courses without enrolling in them if they make high test scores. Independent study, such as that discussed in the next chapter, is encouraged widely. In New York State, for example, students can earn up to two years of college credits by passing proficiency examinations that are recognized by nearly 100 colleges and universities.

The trimester system (three semesters a year) is being used increasingly, possibly most extensively in Florida, where the entire State University system is operating on a year-round basis that fully utilizes buildings and equipment and adds a month to the annual teaching time of the faculty. Year-round programs are in force elsewhere, including the University of Pittsburgh, which is credited with pioneering a trimester system that makes it possible to take a four-year course in three years.

Yale University recently adopted a program to encourage a limited number of exceptional undergraduates to earn bachelors' and masters' degrees simultaneously in four years. Tulane and Harvard Universities also have plans for producing doctoral candidates in greatly reduced time. This requires harder work on the part of the students, but it speeds them on the road to Ph.D.'s, of which there is a growing shortage as institutions of higher learning grow and multiply.

College cooperatives. Streamlining efforts of other kinds are being made by colleges and universities. The Western Interstate Commission for Higher Education, with headquarters in Boulder, Colorado, has arranged for more than 50 public colleges and universities in 13 states to exchange a variety of services, the most important of which is filling classroom vacancies by exchanging students at resident rates instead of charging the higher out-of-state fees. In this way a Colorado student could attend U.C.L.A. for an annual fee of $148 instead of the nonresident charge of $648. Under this arrangement, students can shift from state universities in an area extending from Hawaii and Alaska to New Mexico, so that classes in various specialties can be filled without added cost to the students and without wasted space at the schools.

Economy measures of more indirect benefit have been in effect for several years in the Philadelphia area, where Bryn Mawr, Haverford and Swarthmore have been trading faculty members and students. Amherst, Mount Holyoke and Smith have joined with the University of Massachusetts to carry on a cooperative doctoral program and to develop a joint astronomy department and an FM radio station.

The College Center of the Finger Lakes at Corning, New York, has brought together several western New York schools for cooperative faculty research and the sharing of touring lecturers. Vassar, Bard, Bennett and Briarcliff have formed an association to cooperate in similar ventures, while nine colleges in the Rochester, New York, area are working toward an interchange of faculties, establishment of joint courses, elimination of duplications, sharing of libraries and other facilities, and development of a common closed-circuit TV station for simultaneous instruction on all the campuses. They hope eventually to have a central accounting and records department, to coordinate their alumni fund drives and to make combined purchases of supplies—all to save money and keep tuition down.

While junior colleges offer many obvious financial advantages, some of the economy measures effected by four-year schools may not be so apparent to students. However, as more schools introduce streamlining techniques, some degree of control of inflation on the campus may result. It is heartening to know that the officials of some schools are at least trying to protect the pocketbooks of students and their families instead of contenting themselves with one round after another of tuition increases.

For further information on junior colleges

Refer to:

American Junior Colleges, a complete directory, Council on Education, Washington, D.C. ($9).

Facing Facts About the Two-Year College, Prudential Insurance Company of America, Prudential Plaza, Newark, New Jersey.

Junior Colleges, an Introduction, American Association of Junior Colleges, 1777 Massachusetts Avenue, N.W., Washington, D.C. 20036.

The Junior College Journal, American Association of Junior Colleges ($4 a year).

Universal Opportunities for Education Beyond the High School, Educational Policies Commission, National Education Association, 1201 16th Street, N.W., Washington, D.C. 20036.

15

BENEFITS ON THE FRINGES OF ACADEME

... evening, correspondence and television study

The high cost of college cannot always be measured in terms of money. For many highly motivated but dollar-short individuals, the largest price is paid in *time*, for they find they must engage in their study by mail, through extension courses at night schools or with the help of television. Hundreds of thousands of people, old and young, hale and infirm, get all or part of their higher education by these means, which can take at least twice as long as resident study and frequently cannot lead to a degree even then. A full four-year college course, for example, usually requires seven to nine years when taken at night. Correspondence study also brings results so slowly as to require the utmost in patience and diligence.

It is possible to win a college degree entirely through attendance at an evening school at an accredited college or university. Many persons do just this. The most one can expect from study by correspondence, extension and television, however, is enough credits to cover two years of work toward a baccalaureate. Meanwhile, the person who must work for a living often is able to put aside enough money in two years of full-time work and part-time study to finish college as a full-time student.

Teaching by television

One of the most exciting developments in education, from the elementary grades through college, has been the growth of educational television. By far the most extensive use of this medium has been made in closed-circuit instruction in regular degree courses on campuses. This has helped ease the teacher shortage by putting classrooms over widely scattered areas within the range of a single televised instructor. It has been used to make the knowledge of a famous professor available to many more students than could be reached in a single classroom. Since this form of educational television benefits only the full-time student, we shall consider mainly the open-circuit form, which is most often made available by commercial stations but is also provided in several areas over private, nonprofit channels, some of them on university campuses.

Through the televised classroom program that is "attended" at home, the campus can be extended to any person with a working TV set within receiving range of the station. The student who wishes grades and credits combines viewing with correspondence study in most cases. Some schools also schedule discussion periods and consultations for television students who live within a reasonable distance of the campus.

One of the earliest successful TV teaching programs was begun in 1957 by New York University on the local C.B.S. station. The "Sunrise Semester" program expanded to the national network, with two courses given each term. The opening bell often is the ring of the alarm clock, for classes start at 6:30 A.M. every day except Sunday. One subject is offered on Mondays, Wednesdays and Fridays, and another on Tuesdays, Thursdays and Saturdays. The fees are set by the individual colleges in the student-viewers' home areas. They may range from a few dollars to N.Y.U's high price of $150 a course. College credits are awarded to enrolled students who pass examinations.

Probably the most extensive and meaningful of all the educational TV opportunities is offered by the Chicago City Junior College, which has spread its campus over a 75-mile radius through video instruction. With a sizable grant from the Ford Fund for the Advancement of Education, Chicago's "TV College" was launched in 1956 on a three-year experimental basis. Credit courses in English composition, biology, social science and national government were offered on Station WTTW, and the North Central Association agreed to recognize courses if they were based on the same standards that prevailed on the campus. Actually, the instructors demanded more of their TV students than of those in the classroom, with the result that the homebound scholars were found to have achieved at least as much as the regular students, and in some cases more. Chicago area residents now can earn the junior college degree of Associate in Arts almost entirely by television. During each semester the remote-control undergraduates are invited to visit branches of the junior college, and they may telephone their instructors with questions at specified times. In the interim they mail their assignments and quizzes. The Chicago program grew to 50 periods of instruction a week, available for credit to any student who met entrance requirements and enrolled in one of its seven branches. Fees have ranged from $5 for eight semester-hours and $10 for nine or more taken by a resident of Chicago to $19.50 per semester-hour plus fees for legal residents of other states. TV students residing in Illinois but outside Chicago pay $11.50 plus fees per semester-hour.

The widest possible audiences are reached by offering courses on a rerun basis, in both afternoon and evening, to fit the schedules of housewives and workers; two educational sessions are carried also during the regular school lunch hour for any teachers who care to watch. Of those who register for a course, eight out of 10 finish it. In the first three years more than 42,000 courses had been taken for credit by some 27,000 students, including quite a few who were engaged in on-campus study, too. A special program was added for inmates of the Illinois Penitentiary at Stateville and the Women's Reformatory at Dwight, Illinois.

What is generally accepted as the first educational TV station, KUHT, went on the air in Houston, Texas, in 1953. Since then the medium has grown almost as fast as commercial television, which seems truly remarkable when one considers the fact that radio was never fully exploited for educational purposes in all the years it was the nation's principal communications facility. Today there is scarcely a course offered by schools and colleges that is not being taught somewhere on TV.

So acceptable has such a means of study become that the College Entrance Examination Board offers advanced placement examinations for some courses, enabling students who can qualify in certain subjects to take more advanced classes in senior colleges that do not give credit for TV study. One of the first programs so recognized was the summer session conducted on WNDT, an educational channel in New York. This course covered a full year of work in calculus and United States history in eight weeks of daily lessons, including an hour and a half of mathematics and two hours of history. Each lesson was given in the morning and then repeated in the afternoon and evening, with instructional materials and grading for both courses costing the student $70. About 60 colleges indicated that they would consider the test grades of students for advanced placement or straight credit. This program also was underwritten by the Ford Fund for the Advancement of Education, which in the 10 years from 1953 to 1963 gave $76.5 million for the development of television as a teaching and cultural instrument. The National Defense Education Act of 1958 provided other major funds for experimentation by schools and colleges in improving television teaching facilities.

Opportunities for televised study exist in nearly every part of the country. The University of North Carolina has been developing a TV correspondence program offering one full academic year of instruction over a two-year period. The University of Detroit uses both closed- and open-circuit TV to reach a maximum audience. It presents two 45-minute lectures weekly over a closed circuit to day students on the campus, then repeats the classes in the evening over a closed circuit to evening-division students on campus and over an open-circuit station to off-campus extension students. All the students attend one 55-minute discussion period in a classroom each week.

Floridians, in their effort to put some kind of higher education within reach of every person in the state, have launched a network of educational stations under the supervision of the State University of Florida. Six states in the upper Midwest have joined to form one network, while others have been launched by Michigan and states along the east coast from the Chesapeake Bay to Maine.

Advantages of TV study

One major advantage of TV study, beyond the economics and the convenience of scheduling, is that it makes it possible for a person to work at his own pace, with examination results the basis of his grade. Many top-ranking colleges and universities have on-campus programs of independent study, and study by television differs little from them as far as results are concerned. Some courses seem to be more adaptable than others to television presentation, among them such vocational subjects as bookkeeping, shorthand and accounting, and such college courses as astronomy, languages, mathematics and science. It has been estimated that by 1971 about half of all degree programs will be available for credit on television. This form of presentation can become an important part of correspondence study, which appeared in the 1870's and has grown into an educational force to be reckoned with throughout the world.

Correspondence courses

Study by mail has been regarded with disdain in some academic circles since the first courses were posted. But the attitude is changing, largely as a result of the developing partnership with television study sponsored by colleges and universities for degree credit and the extensive study-by-mail courses encouraged by the armed forces (which will be discussed at length in the next chapter). Correspondence study is a serious business to those engaged in it, whether they are full-time jobholders who pore over lessons at night or G.I.'s in remote posts cramming for examinations. More students now enroll in home-study courses every year than enter colleges and universities. Most concentrate on vocational training, but a growing proportion take courses for college credit. At least a fourth of all certified public accountants get their training by mail, and it is estimated that 10 to 15 per cent of all professional engineers do at least part of their preparation this way.

Eventually, most correspondence study is likely to become associated with television instruction, just as nearly all TV study now includes some correspondence. While this sort of course is not always the least expensive way to study, it usually is the *only* way available to those who enroll. The person who has financial obligations can work and study through correspondence courses. So can a woman tied down at home or a disabled person. A worker hoping to advance in his job may get the added knowledge he needs through study by mail.

What now is a major factor in American education began in 1873, when Illinois Wesleyan University launched mail courses for degree credit. This was about 20 years after the correspondence study movement began in Germany with a language course. In 1871 Cambridge University, in England, had adopted some correspondence techniques, and in 1887 the University of London developed a course. The famous Chautauqua organization in New York State provided collegiate instruction by mail and conferred diplomas and degrees for a number of years beginning in the 1880's. The granting of degrees for correspondence study has now been almost entirely abandoned except by a few nonaccredited, unrecognized schools.

It is estimated that three and a half million people were engaged in home study in 1962 in private, public, military, religious and business courses. More than 1,175,000 of the total were students of accredited private schools and more than a million and a half were involved in federal and military programs. The major universities offering correspondence instruction enrolled about 200,000, some 130,000 of them for college credits. About 300,000 were involved in study opportunities offered by nonaccredited private correspondence schools, many of which engage in practices that have been questioned through the years.

Since no college or university degrees recognized in academic circles are granted by correspondence study alone, a student usually undertakes the first two years of study by mail and completes the final two years in full-time attendance. A few schools permit three years of study at home and some limit such a practice to only one semester or a year, but most follow the half-and-half pattern.

The National University Extension Association, organized in 1916 at the University of Wisconsin, now has a membership of nearly 100 universities that offer instruction in extension classes, on radio or television, and through institutes and correspondence. Sixty of the members also belong to the association's division of correspondence study. Each sets its own policies on credits and fees.

Generally university correspondence courses cost the student from $5 to about $20 per semester-hour. Books usually are provided for the courses with higher fees. The University of California charges $17 per course for students residing in the state and $20 for out-of-state residents.

It would be impractical to list every college and university offering correspondence study. However, a few examples may serve as a guide to the general types of programs and the range of fees. The University of California sets a 24-month limit for completion of a course, with fees varying according to subject. The English Bible as Literature costs $2.25 for 31 lessons and three semester-hours of credit, while 16 lessons in Elementary Modern Icelandic, with four credits, costs $14.50. The History of Music, in 13 lessons, provides two credits toward a degree at the University of Illinois at a cost of $30.50.

Loyola University of Chicago grants a flat three credits for every course, with each consisting of 40 lessons costing $7 plus the price of textbooks. The State University of Iowa grants a maximum of 30 credit-hours toward a degree, while Pennsylvania State University and Southern Methodist University allow only 12 semester-hours toward graduation. The best way to ascertain the courses, credits and fees for an individual school is to write to its extension division and ask for a catalogue.

The Extension Association frequently warns students to investigate mail-order programs carefully. One should avoid any curriculum that guarantees a degree entirely by correspondence study. The accredited universities in turn scrutinize the would-be correspondence student, discouraging indiscriminate enrollment and rejecting students who are not adequately prepared or who do not have realistic goals. A student must be highly motivated, able to express himself well on paper and possessed of a considerable amount of self-discipline and orderliness.

As is the case with TV study, some schools sponsoring correspondence courses provide group discussions periodically for students who can get to the campus or some central location near their homes. Arrangements are made also in some schools for regular meetings of instructors and students. It is possible on several campuses for students to combine correspondence and class study.

Private correspondence schooling

Almost as old as the university correspondence movement is the private study-by-mail institution, the best known and largest of these being the International Correspondence Schools, known as I.C.S., with headquarters in Scranton, Pennsylvania. Some of its students find they can apply their correspondence credits toward college degrees; others win advanced standing in university classes. The degree of acceptance, as we have noted, is up to the individual institution. Stanford University, for example, grants credits for study completed through I.C.S. if a student passes examinations in the courses he has taken. The Wisconsin Institute of Technology, in Platteville, allows one credit for each six I.C.S. instruction units that have been completed successfully. In most cases, however, examinations are required before credits are given.

(It is advisable for a would-be correspondence student, regardless of what school he wishes eventually to attend, to inquire of the extension division of his state university or the National University Extension Association at the University of Minnesota about his chances of receiving university credit for his efforts.)

The International Correspondence Schools charges $15 for a course in solid geometry, $28.50 for general science, $13 for blueprint reading and $39 for French. There is an extra $10 matriculation fee for the first course in which one enrolls; the school pays all postage and provides all textbooks.

Founded in 1890, I.C.S. had as its original goal the training of miners who wanted to pass examinations enabling them to qualify as foremen. By 1907 the millionth student had enrolled in courses as varied as those offered in a large university. As of the early 1960's, the total number of participants had reached about seven million, and their ranks had included Capt. Eddie Rickenbacker, the aviator and airline pioneer; Senator W. Stuart Symington of Missouri; Arthur Godfrey, the radio personality; industrialists Charles E. Wilson and Robert G. Le Tourneau, and the late Philip Murray, president of the C.I.O. More than 60,000 persons enroll each year in the school, which has come to be known as "the Harvard of home-study institutions." I.C.S., in turn, helped to found the National Home Study Council, which since 1926 has promoted sound educational standards and ethical business practices in the field.

A mark of the esteem in which correspondence study is held is found in the recognition accorded it by business and industry. The Chamber of Commerce of the United States reports that 7,000 concerns have used correspondence study to teach and upgrade at least 10 million workers. One young man went to work as a laborer in a large industry upon graduation from high school. Soon he began taking correspondence courses in business and won a place in the stockroom. He continued to study and was promoted to inventory clerk. Correspondence study of mathematics was interrupted by Army service, during which he took a course in accounting. After returning to his job as inventory clerk he was upgraded again and still continued to study, this time taking English and business at an evening school. Work and study became his life and he continued to rise in the corporation until he achieved a key position.

Companies generally encourage study by their employees, particularly if the courses improve their value on the job. Many concerns have refund plans under which employees pay their tuition and training costs for home study and then get all or part of the money back after completing courses satisfactorily. Correspondence courses often are expensive—up to $200 to $300 a unit for engineering—but the students work throughout their study programs and not only are better off economically than if they were full-time students but also manage to win promotions as a result of their scholarship.

Evidence of the effectiveness of correspondence study was found in a University of Wisconsin investigation, which showed that correspondence students did just as well in examinations as full-time students. A University of Michigan survey also found no significant difference between the two methods of studying. The principal ingredient that makes for a good student is motivation, and the place in which one studies apparently has little or no bearing on that.

What to some would be a shortcoming of TV-correspondence study is the lack of group discussions and exchanges of ideas. Some students do better in organized group work, of course. But independent study is being encouraged increasingly at such quality schools as Vassar and Yale for students who can benefit most from it. The correspondence or TV student progresses at his own speed instead of having to stick to the pace of a group, and he is not slowed down by the distractions of the conventional classroom. It may be frustrating for the home student who wants to ask a question, but if he is patient, he can get his answers by mail or telephone.

One bit of evidence indicating that independent study may not be enough is the aforementioned fact that no accredited institution of higher learning will give a degree based solely on correspondence work, and that most schools try to arrange for consultations between students and teachers and for group discussions whenever possible. However, a 100 per cent increase in the number of correspondence students is expected by 1974, with the number of universities offering courses increasing and the programs already in force expanding. It seems certain that correspondence study will attain higher status and wider acceptance, although it may never be possible for one to earn a college degree solely this way.

Extension programs

Students who must work at full-time day jobs can study at night in college and university extension programs if they work and live near enough to a campus. Since most extension courses are in the evening, they offer a partial solution to the problem of college expenses by enabling a student to work full time. Night courses often cost more than day classes, however, and many universities do not provide four-year programs in their evening sessions, particularly in those conducted in libraries and public schools. Those that do have a complete curriculum at night are in urban centers and attract the largest number of extension students. These schools also supply a taste of academic life and include evening students in university activities. As a result, the rate of growth of extension student bodies in recent years has kept slightly ahead of that of the general daytime campus population.

Night school scholarships are almost nonexistent, but it is possible for students at some larger schools to get loans on easy terms. Colleges and universities offering evening courses are represented by the National University Extension Association and the Association of University Evening Colleges. All of these schools are involved in full-time higher education and include junior, community and state colleges as well as universities.

There are about 750 to 800 institutions of higher learning offering extension courses and some are involved also in correspondence study. Far more students are engaged in university night school pursuits, however, than in correspondence work for degree credits. The Association of University Evening Colleges estimates that 400,000 students are enrolled in fully accredited college and university evening classes. It seems unlikely that many students were engaging in this kind of part-time academic work from choice. Social and economic pressures are usually responsible.

Evening attendance, like TV and correspondence study, attracts mainly the highly motivated students who are making a real sacrifice to get an education. Some seldom see their families during the week because of the demands of jobs and school. They may be supporting several persons while at the same time financing school and fighting for time to study.

"We detect many instances where the outcomes of evening college work are more meaningful than what is frequently observed among full-time day students," observes Edwin H. Spengler, executive secretary of the Evening College Association.

The university extension movement as we know it started in England, and only since 1920 has it been an educational force of importance in the United States. The first real development of university evening instruction occurred in the Midwest. Now extension is a major effort of most of the leading colleges and universities in the country, with nearly a million and a half active participants.

In discussions of how to beat the high cost of college, one seldom hears anyone mention the three study programs we have just considered—television, correspondence and extension study. Yet all three provide real opportunities for those who cannot get a higher education any other way. The drawbacks have been described: It takes much longer to complete a course of study by correspondence than in the classroom and most of the human contacts so valuable in campus life are absent. The evening school student has the distractions of job and family and often pays a higher tuition than the under-graduate who attends by day. Being a full-fledged undergraduate offers the richest academic experience. What we have been consider-ing here are substitutes one can try if a conventional college course is beyond reach.

For further information on evening, correspondence and TV study

Refer to:

Chicago's TV College, by Clifford G. Erickson and Hymen M. Chausow, Chicago City Junior College, 3400 North Austin Avenue, Chicago, Illinois 60634.

Compendium of Televised Education, Michigan State University, Lan-sing, Michigan.

Directory of Accredited Private Home Study Schools, National Home Study Council, 1601 18th Street, N.W., Washington, D.C. 20009 ($3 a year).

Educational Television, the Next 10 Years, Stanford University Press, Stanford, California.

Teaching by Television, the Ford Foundation, 477 Madison Avenue, New York, New York 10022.

The Home Study Review, National Home Study Council.

Write to:

Association of Evening Colleges, Brooklyn College, Bedford Avenue and Avenue H, Brooklyn, New York, New York 11210.

Chicago City Junior College.

Fund for the Advancement of Education, 477 Madison Avenue, New York, New York 10022.

International Correspondence Schools, Scranton, Pennsylvania 18515.

Learning Resources Institute, 10 Columbus Circle, New York, New York 10019.

National Home Study Council.

National University Extension Association, 122 Social Science Tower, University of Minnesota, Minneapolis, Minnesota 55455.

16

JOIN THE NAVY AND SEE THE ACADEMIC WORLD

... educational opportunities in the armed forces

Opportunities for college study are so extensive in the United States today that young men are attending Harvard-sponsored classes under water. Part-time undergraduates in dungarees—7,500 of them—are working for Harvard degree credits in their spare time aboard missile-carrying, nuclear-powered submarines and at shore stations through the Polaris University Extension Program, which was developed jointly by the United States Navy and the Commission on Extension Courses at Harvard.

The curriculum includes history, computer mathematics, chemistry, physics, English composition and various electives, with the credits earned applicable toward an eventual Harvard degree if studies are completed on the campus. While cruising in the deep the men attend classes conducted by teachers who talk to them from movie screens. Reading time is devoted to textbooks and lessons, and discussion periods and laboratory work are reserved for tours of duty ashore. The cost of such a course is nominal. It is unlikely that participants can complete more than the equivalent of three months' study in a calendar year, but the program gives them a chance to begin or continue college work and provides a useful and intellectually stimulating activity that is suitable to the confined life aboard a submarine.

There probably is no opportunity more unusual in higher education than that afforded by the Polaris University, but it is only one of a number of programs offered by the armed forces to millions of part-time students in uniform. A young man, whether enlisted or drafted, can find a wide variety of ways in which to increase his knowledge and improve his skills at little or no expense to himself, while at the same time serving Uncle Sam—*if he really wants to*. The opportunities range from mail-order courses to full four-year programs at universities and even medical and other graduate work. They are open to civilian undergraduates who enroll in Reserve Officers Training Corps (R.O.T.C.) courses leading to commissions on graduation or to privates who have never been on a university campus. Except for the R.O.T.C. programs and the four-year highly selective and intensive programs provided by the service academies, nearly all the courses now being taken by servicemen and women have been developed since World War II.

The biggest "college" in the world

The largest single educational operation in the world is that of the U.S. Armed Forces Institute (U.S.A.F.I.), established during World War II to help fulfill the desire of men and women to continue their educations while in uniform. It began as the Army Institute on April 1, 1942, in a building on the University of Wisconsin campus. The first catalogue offered 64 courses provided under contract by the International Correspondence Schools (discussed in the preceding chapter). Hundreds of courses at the high school and college level also were provided under contract by 70 colleges and universities. As the program grew, it became increasingly independent, with the eventual development of correspondence courses and self-study texts by the institute's own editorial staff and with the purchase of more courses from universities.

By 1943 correspondence courses were being offered to personnel in every branch of the armed forces, and the program was given its present name. It was decided after the war to make the institute a permanent educational facility offering courses comparable to those in civilian institutions and also filling the needs of the various branches for specialist training apart from a college curriculum.

The institute provides opportunities for continued education during active duty anywhere, whether near a large city college or on Greenland's icy wastes, and in any branch of the armed forces. Its headquarters is still at the University of Wisconsin, which has been a leader in correspondence education for more than 50 years. Much of the course material and tests used by the institute is written and graded by members of the university faculty. In addition, more than 40 colleges and universities cooperate with the institute by offering correspondence courses through their extension divisions. A student enrolls in a university course through the institute, but after that he corresponds directly with the school, which may grant credits toward a degree.

As is the case with all correspondence and extension study, neither the institute nor the cooperating colleges and universities grant degrees for study completed by mail. The most one can hope to earn toward a degree is two years of credit. The rest of the courses must be taken on campus. Some schools give more credit than others for the same courses; many will give full credit if a student passes a special examination covering a specific subject. But *any* academic recognition for study while in the service is of major importance when one considers the cost and the circumstances under which the courses are taken. An Armed Forces Institute student pays $5 to enroll in his first course when it is one provided through the institute itself. If he completes it satisfactorily, he is entitled to take other courses at no further cost, so it would be possible for him to obtain the equivalent of two years' college instruction for a mere $5.

Subjects offered under contract by colleges are more expensive—usually around $15 or $20 per course and sometimes a little more. It takes much longer to complete the equivalent of two years in college by mail than in full-time campus study, because one is limited to one or two courses at a time; but for the person who is in service for several years and who wants to try eventually for a degree, he will be just that much farther along the academic road if he puts his free time to constructive educational use.

More than 6,000 courses are now offered by the participating schools, and the institute provides more than 200 courses, from elementary school subjects through those of college level, and including language and technical subjects. The most popular subjects offered by the institute are English composition, college algebra, psychology, accounting, German, United States history and sociology. The favorite technical courses are electronics, mechanical drawing and the use of the slide rule.

In its first 20 years the institute enrolled a total of more than five million students and distributed more than 44 million textbooks. Worldwide enrollments in 1963 alone totaled more than 320,000, with the students engaged in either group or correspondence study. When possible, students on active duty form groups to study a subject together. At some installations they use filmed classroom lectures or discussions and have seminar periods of their own. When camps or other posts are near institutions of higher learning, it is possible to arrange for experts in various subjects to lead discussions.

Many civilian schools and agencies recognize institute courses, tests and examinations for accreditation purposes, but the institute does not regulate this. Each accrediting body decides whether to give official recognition to armed forces correspondence work. In some cases, the American Council on Education, through its Commission on Accreditation of Service Experiences, recommends that credits be granted for successful completion of institute tests.

It is up to the student to apply to a school or civilian agency for credit after he has satisfactorily taken a course or passed an end-of-course examination without actually having enrolled. Such an application can be made while a person is on active duty or after he leaves the service. Anyone wishing to study by mail for college credit while in the service (or even in civilian life) should check with the schools in which he is interested to determine the requirements and costs. The fees charged for military students are the standard prices charged all correspondence students (see preceding chapter).

There are many interesting stories in the Armed Forces Institute's files. One concerns a chief warrant officer in the Army who took most of the history courses offered as well as other undergraduate subjects. Eventually he won a bachelor's degree in history with honors from Roosevelt University in Chicago and a master's degree in history from Denver University. (While on active duty in those areas, he was able to spend enough time on the campuses to establish residence requirements for degrees.) Later he received a certificate qualifying him to teach social studies in high schools in Colorado, thus having assured himself a career on retirement after 20 years in uniform.

An airman first class who took institute studies that gave him two years of college credit finished as a full-time student after leaving the service and later became a social worker. A naval destroyer became a floating school during a six-month Mediterranean cruise. Most of the crew became involved in some sort of study, either in groups or solitary education by mail.

There are many testimonials of former students in the institute's files, of which the following from a former seaman is typical:

"Today I was thinking of U.S.A.F.I., and wanted to share my thoughts with you. Eight years ago when I began a four-year term in the Navy I had given up education 'forever.' Today I am working on a Ph.D. in psychology. U.S.A.F.I. was responsible for this. The interest and concern demonstrated by the U.S.A.F.I. teachers helped instill a continuing interest in education. It is difficult for your teachers to go on correcting papers and never see the pupils, often to have them just quit after a few lessons. It is for this reason that

I would like to remind them that there are permanently grateful persons like myself whom they have never seen."

On-campus military training

While the biggest opportunity for education in the armed forces is on military installations, probably the best-known one offers military training on campuses. The R.O.T.C. programs are conducted by the Army and Navy for regularly enrolled students and involve obligations for service upon graduation. Air Force programs offered to students are conducted off-campus in the senior year.

The naval program, although open to relatively few, is the more generous of the three in the financial support it gives. Actually, there are two N.R.O.T.C. programs, one a four-year commitment, the other of shorter duration.

In the first, a student takes college courses in naval science along with his regular academic work and is commissioned a regular officer in either the Navy or the Marine Corps upon graduation. He undergoes six to eight weeks of training each summer and participates in training cruises during his first and third summer vacations. To be accepted for this course a student must pass a Navy college aptitude test and must meet the entrance requirements of the school he wants to attend. During the four years in college, the N.R.O.T.C. student receives a retainer of $50 a month or a maximum of $500 a year. He becomes a midshipman, Naval Reserve, and the cost of his travel between home and school is paid.

The second N.R.O.T.C. service-study opportunity is known as the contract program. This is for students who already have been admitted to a school and then are chosen by the commanding officer of the campus unit for naval training. These students are civilians who sign contracts agreeing to take naval science courses, participate in drills and sail on one summer training cruise. In return they receive uniforms, allowances of $27 a month during their final two years in college, draft deferments and reserve commissions. The Navy maintains N.R.O.T.C. units, contract and four-year, at more than 50 schools, plus one élite contract unit at the Massachusetts Institute of Technology, where a corps of highly skilled technical officers is trained.

Of much greater scope is the Army R.O.T.C. program, with general military science being offered at more than 200 schools and specialized programs in artillery, armor, infantry or other branches at nearly 50. The program entails a minimum of 360 hours of classes in four years of college plus additional time in training camp each summer. R.O.T.C. graduates, who are commissioned as second lieutenants in the Army Reserve, are subject to two years of active service, three years in the Ready Reserve and one on a Stand-by Reserve basis. Those who receive flight training in their senior year are required to sign for three years' active duty in the Air Force.

Men who enroll in advanced R.O.T.C. training in the last two years of college receive a total of $535 for the two-year course plus $117 for attending a six-week summer training session between the junior and senior years and a five-cent-a-mile allowance for travel between home and camp. Uniforms and textbooks for military courses are provided by the government. Between 1946 and 1950 some 18,500 college-trained reserve officers were graduated from college; the current enrollment is approaching 200,000 at nearly 250 schools.

Other armed forces programs

Several other training programs are provided by the armed forces. Here are some of the ways military personnel may take college and university courses for credit toward degrees:

Residence courses taught on posts by qualified instructors from nearby institutions of higher learning.

Campus courses taught at the facilities of schools near military posts by members of the faculties.

Overseas residence courses for personnel serving outside the United States. Several universities maintain centers abroad at which servicemen and women study. The University of Maryland has such installations in Britain, France, West Germany, North Africa, Newfoundland, Greenland, Iceland, Japan, Okinawa, Korea and Guam. Florida State University operates in the Caribbean area, the University of Hawaii in the central Pacific and the University of the Philippines in the south Pacific. An American International College is maintained in the Azores. Regular classroom instruction is provided by teachers from the staffs of the participating colleges and universities at only nominal fees and sometimes with partial payment of tuition by the government.

Group study at a military or naval installation with civilian instructors or, if they are not available, qualified military personnel being employed to conduct classes. Whether credits are recognized for this study is determined on an individual basis by colleges and universities. The Armed Forces Institute's texts and tests are used in group study.

Tuition aid opportunities, through which the services will pay up to 75 per cent (to a maximum of $35 per semester-hour) of the tuition of personnel enrolled in college-level classes conducted by civilian schools. The student is expected to pay the rest of the tuition plus fees and the cost of books. Also, of course, the student must meet the entrance requirements, and in cases where he is studying on a campus, it must be near the home base. It is through this program that the various branches of the armed forces have arranged for classes at overseas bases conducted by teachers from schools sponsoring the courses. This is not a correspondence program.

Armed forces extension courses to give training in specialties in the services and thus better equip personnel for their assignments and for promotions. These are not college-level courses. Nearly 300 technical and specialty training schools operated by the armed forces offer more than 1,000 courses to more than 300,000 graduates a year. Personnel are selected by competitive aptitude examinations.

Degree-completion programs for personnel who wish to finish their formal college educations. The Air Force has three of these plans, called "boot-strap programs." One provides a final semester of on-campus, full-time study toward a degree and another provides an entire year of study. The third is a short-term course at a technical school or college to equip a man better in his job or career field in the service. In all three cases the student must have been on active duty as an airman for at least a year. He receives full pay and food-and-quarters allowances but must meet his tuition and other college expenses. In the two boot-strap programs, the student is obligated for two additional years of service. In the short-term program, he must serve one more year in exchange for a course of up to 10 weeks and two more years for any course of more than 10 weeks.

The Marine Corps college degree program is available to all regular and reserve officers from warrant officer through lieutenant colonel who can complete their baccalaureate requirements in a maximum of two semesters. While they are full-time students they receive all regular pay and allowances but foot their educational bills. They must remain on active duty for two years after completing their programs.

The Army degree-completion program is open to all active personnel with three years' service who can earn a baccalaureate in 12 months or a graduate degree in six months of full-time attendance. They pay all of their expenses out of their normal income and allowances and must serve two years after receiving a baccalaureate and four years after receiving a graduate degree.

The Navy enlisted scientific education program, which is for men and women between the ages of 21 and 25 who are on active duty. It provides four years of uninterrupted college attendance leading to a degree in engineering, science or mathematics. Applications are judged by a selection board. Upon being chosen, a student takes a nine-week summer refresher course in mathematics, physics and English and is oriented in college requirements. After acceptance at a college or university, he obligates himself for six years' service in the regular Navy, keeping his pay grade and rating. He maintains his enlisted status and is eligible for advancement as it is due. The student receives full pay and allowances while in college. The Navy pays tuition and fees and finances books, while the student pays his own board and room bills.

Upon graduation and completion of Officer Candidate School or the Naval Preflight School, he becomes an ensign in the unrestricted line of the regular Navy provided he passes a physical examination. If he does not measure up to the rigorous physical standards, he is considered for the restricted line, or staff corps. Every person commissioned must serve at least nine months on active duty for every six months of education, with a minimum of four years.

The Army enlisted college training program, in which selected personnel receive full-time schooling in civilian schools of their choice in technical subjects, science and managerial fields. The Army pays all the tuition costs and the student enjoys full duty and pay status.

Armed forces work-study programs, which provide Civil Service cooperative training opportunities in science and engineering. The students must be high school graduates and pass Civil Service examinations. They also must live in the areas where work plans are offered. These work-study programs, usually lasting five years, lead to Bachelor of Science degrees. A student receives a salary from the Army, Navy or Air Force during periods of employment under Civil Service ratings and also may get some financial assistance toward school costs. The Air Force, for example, offers a program at its Command and Control Development Division. For acceptance, the applicant must have completed two years in engineering or science and must be screened by a selection committee. He then takes a three-year course leading to a master's degree.

College equivalence provisions, which enable students to qualify for up to 24 semester-hours of college work by taking General Educational Development tests for admission to colleges. It is up to the college to decide whether the student will be accepted and what number of credits he will receive.

Specialized programs are available to help finance medical educa-

tion and study toward becoming nurses, dieticians, occupational therapists and physical therapists. The Navy nursing program, for example,
is open to single women of any rating who are high school graduates
and who have been on active duty at least a year. They draw $99.37
a month plus tuition, books, room, board and uniforms for up to
four years toward a nursing degree in any accredited school. In return
they must serve one year on active duty for each year they have been
in school.

The biggest scholarship bonanza of all

Undoubtedly the most generous scholarship opportunities in the
nation are those provided by the service academies—West Point,
Annapolis and the Air Academy—and the United States Merchant
Marine Academy. A total of more than 13,000 men are enrolled at
any one time in the academies that train officers for the country's
armed forces. About 1,000 attend the Merchant Marine Academy at
Kings Point, New York. The grand total of students studying full
time for four years, at *no* cost for tuition, room, board, books and
medical fees, is far larger than the sum of the two largest civilian
scholarship programs—the National Merit and General Motors
awards. In addition to getting a first-class college education free, the
men at the three service academies are given allowances covering
their transportation between home and school and $111.15 a month
for personal expenses. The Merchant Marine students receive $300
a year for uniforms and books but pay their personal expenses.

Competition is keen for admission to all these institutions, which,
in a sense, are work-study schools since they combine academic
study and career experience. The entire sophomore year at the
Merchant Marine Academy is spent at sea, in service aboard United
States merchant ships. During this period, the cadets are paid $111.15
a month for working eight hours a day. They also are required to
study a given number of hours a day. On graduation they are licensed
as officers in the Merchant Marine and may become active-duty naval

officers if they wish. The three service academies require a certain amount of active duty during the four years, and all graduates who pass the requirements are commissioned to serve in the armed forces for four years.

Nominations by senators and congressmen constitute the single largest source of candidates for admission to the service academies. Other would-be students are named by the President, are drawn from regular and reserve components of the respective services, are sons of deceased veterans, have attended special military or naval schools or have been sent by foreign governments. The nominees are required to pass stiff medical and physical tests and to show high academic aptitude. Each student admitted to the Merchant Marine Academy must be nominated by a member of Congress, must have completed a full college preparatory course and must qualify in a national competitive examination. Each is also required to pass a naval officer's physical examination.

As you can see, opportunities for learning while serving are unlimited, whether a person is studying for a college degree or a specialty that may eventually lead him to a useful and well-paying position in civilian life. Anyone who comes out of the service without having improved the content of his mind has only been cheating himself.

For further information on educational opportunities in the armed forces

Refer to:

Catalogue of U.S. Armed Forces Institute, Madison, Wisconsin 53703.

High School News Service Report, Department of Defense, Washington, D.C., 20025 (free to high schools).

The Student's Guide to Military Service, Michael Harwood, Channel Press, Manhasset, New York.

You and the Army R.O.T.C., Department of the Army, Washington, D.C. 20025.

Your Life Plans and the Armed Forces, National Association of Secondary School Principals, 1201 16th Street, N.W., Washington, D.C. 20036.

Write to:

Armed Forces Institute, Washington, D.C. 20025.
Department of the Army, Washington, D.C. 20025.
Department of the Navy, Washington, D.C. 20025.
R.O.T.C. Division of the Army, Washington, D.C. 20025.

For further information about the service academies

Write to:

Admissions Office, United States Military Academy, West Point, New York.
Registrar, Air Force Academy, Colorado Springs, Colorado.
United States Naval Academy, Annapolis, Maryland.
Superintendent, United States Merchant Marine Academy, Kings Point, New York.

Also write to the schools on your list to determine whether they have any of the military educational programs.

17

WHAT ELSE IS NEW?

... some ideas and experiments

The American college student and his family have friends everywhere. Legislators want to help them finance a higher education. So do bankers, businessmen and industrialists. Labor leaders are doing everything they can to provide cushions for college costs. Regardless of where one turns, he hears expressions of concern about inflation on the campus and suggestions of what can be done about it. New ideas crop up constantly, some of them doomed to failure, of course, but others holding out fresh hopes.

Tax relief efforts

One lost cause so far has been federal tax relief for the parent supporting a student in college. Legislators sensitive to the sentiments of voters (particularly the swelling number of college students and their parents) have been trying for several years to obtain passage of laws that would reduce the taxes of parents and others financing college. Two pieces of legislation along these lines were defeated early in 1964, and they were among well over 100 similar measures suggested in only slightly more than a year. One bill would have allowed a maximum credit of $325 to be subtracted each year from the tax of a college student's parent. The other would have granted a special deduction for young taxpayers working their way through college.

The first was a major proposal while the second would have helped only a fraction of all students. Strong opposition to the tax credit was mustered by the Democratic administration, which maintained that the $750 million it would cost at that time (and the eventual $1 billion a year) was more than the government could afford. President Johnson felt that federal aid to education should be provided instead through grants and loans, which, his aides argued, are more efficient and equitable and, in the long run, would be less costly to the taxpayers. The Treasury Department opposed the relief on the ground that the tax system should not be required to meet expenses that could be dealt with in other ways. Many taxpayers were against it because the childless taxpayer would be subsidizing other people's children. Educators were in disagreement among themselves. The Association of State Universities and Land-Grant Colleges said no; the Association of American Colleges, representing nearly 840 liberal arts schools, said yes, and the American Council on Education, the largest of the three, representing 1,100 colleges and universities, was divided.

A new savings idea

Rexford Moon, director of the College Scholarship Service and a leader in efforts to smooth the financial path to college, has offered what could prove to be a most workable plan for saving ahead for college. Moon proposes that the nation's employers join in the development and support of voluntary, contributory college savings plans, with the total funds accumulated to be pooled and invested in growth securities.

His idea would be to establish a national, nonprofit College Assurance Savings House to service the accounts of unions and employers. It would function in much the same way as the Teachers Insurance and Annuity Association and other nonprofit savings-investment groups do in the areas of retirement and medical benefits.

"Certainly it is not improper to think of preparing for a child's education as one does now for retirement or continued good health," Moon says. "If we can increase personal financial preparation, we can use more of our scholarship dollars in the future to support the deprived rather than those who simply come unprepared."

The guaranteed plan

A promising program for college planning has been adopted experimentally by a handful of schools. Known as the "guaranteed plan for tuition payments," it offers assurance that an individual student's costs will not increase during his four years in college even though the school may be forced to raise its charges to students who register later.

The College of Idaho, at Caldwell, for example, introduced a program in the fall of 1963 under which every freshman would be guaranteed the same tuition charges for his four years. Students enrolling as transfers with advanced standing were promised comparable guarantees. An entering freshman in 1963, paying $1,000 in tuition and fees, was able to project a four-year budget without any increases.

Coe College, in Cedar Rapids, Iowa, started an optional guaranteed-cost plan in 1963. It works a little differently from the Idaho program, involving varying rates for each year but a guaranteed average. Coe promises to each student accepting the plan a specific charge for each of the four years; for example, the average tuition set for a freshman entering in the fall of 1963 was $1,950 a year, at the rate of $2,050 in the first, $1,975 in the second, $1,925 in the third and $1,850 in the fourth. Students who were in the sophomore class or above when the plan became effective were promised an annual average of $1,900 for the rest of their stay. The declining scale is based on the fact that most dropouts occur in the early months of college and on the hope that reductions in later years might prove an incentive to stay.

A plan similar to that at Coe is in operation at St. Olaf College, Northfield, Minnesota, and other schools are watching all of them with interest.

Advanced placement

A policy that first appeared before World War II but that did not achieve real dimensions until 1953 is advanced placement. In that year the College Entrance Examination Board instituted a testing plan, unrelated to previous provisions for compressing a degree program by taking extra courses, under which students who can pass qualifying examinations in required courses are given credit for these courses without having to take them.

A battery of examinations is given each spring to the brightest high school seniors in the country to determine whether they qualify to receive credit for certain college courses without taking them. More than 30,000 young people—10,000 more than in the previous year—took such tests in 1964, with about two-thirds of them getting credit from the colleges of their choice for satisfactory completion of each three-hour examination they undertook. Some of the students did so well that they were allowed to skip the freshman year of college in 1964. Research on the program during its first 10 years showed that the students who won such advanced placement did better in college on the whole than those who enrolled in four-year curricula.

Advanced placement provides a good way to cut down on college costs by enabling a student to earn a degree in three years instead of four. However, most students who have availed themselves of the program thus far have not been looking for short cuts to education; rather they have sought the advantage of taking courses in subjects they did not know rather than coasting through "cinch" courses. In the future, as the advanced placement program grows, increasing numbers of students may very well decide to use it as an economy measure.

Volunteer work for credit

Among other proposals advanced to help students has been that of Dr. Max F. Baer, director of the B'nai B'rith Youth Organization, who suggested the establishment of a federal-state program under which young people would earn college tuition through volunteer service to the community. Such a program would be financed by the federal government and administered by the states. Volunteers would work for certified public and private agencies, earning tuition credits in proportion to the amount of time they put in. Baer envisages this as a way for youngsters to help meet the cost of college and, at the same time, provide a partial and temporary alleviation of the chronic manpower shortage in social service agencies. It also would emphasize the importance of service to the community and might even encourage more persons to choose careers in social service.

Study abroad

The junior-year-abroad programs of a number of colleges and universities have given a big impetus to study in foreign countries, particularly in Europe. Through these programs American schools have formed liaisons with European schools whereby substantial groups of students transfer abroad for a year of study for credit and then return home for their senior year and graduation. As a result, an increasing number of individual students are going abroad in search of educational bargains. Many foreign universities charge no tuition, and when there are fees they are modest. Room and board are relatively inexpensive in most foreign university towns. The major financial stumbling block to study abroad is the cost of getting there; to paraphrase the slogan of the Cunard Line: Getting there can be half the cost.

The problem of the high cost of getting there has been solved for students participating in the junior-year programs. The schools either charter airplanes, which enables one to travel at far less than commercial rates, or send their students on ships chartered by the Council on Student Travel, which carries youngsters across the Atlantic for as little as $162.50 each, a price somewhat lower than the minimum freighter fares. The lone student setting out on his own can take a freighter if he cannot find a way to join a student group on a charter flight or ship. Freighter fares from New York to British ports start at around $200, and to German ports at about $230. Otherwise, his journey will not be a bargain, for the transportation companies that ply the Atlantic have not yet established special student rates, even though most student travel to and from Europe either could or actually does occur in off seasons. Once in Europe, a student has the financial advantage of special rates for surface travel, reduced prices for the theater and the opera, and inexpensive hostels when touring.

More than 100,000 American students apply for passports every year, many of them, of course, with no intention of studying abroad. At least 15,000 of them—and possibly more—actually registered in foreign institutions, most of them in Europe, in 1962 and 1963. Although a good number of American "students" enrolled in foreign schools are teachers seeking advanced training or graduate students with generous fellowships, the number of undergraduates going abroad to study increases every year. It seems certain that the number will go higher, although in all likelihood it will never be significant in terms of the total United States college population. Foreign study may seem appealing on paper when one notes that in Denmark, for example, universities charge only nominal fees and room and board cost a mere $60 a month. In Italy, the catalogues say, tuition and fees may run to around $100 to $125 a year, with room and board at a *pensione* costing a mere $4 to $6 a week. Tuition in Portugal is likely to be $50 a year, with the rock-bottom living costs $30 a month. University fees in Spain are $2 per course, while living costs may total $100 a month. (Oxford and Cambridge, in England, on the other hand, are comparable to American universities, costing up to $2,000 a year, not including the price of getting there.)

Yes, in general, the picture does look good on paper, but—

While it *can* be a bargain and should be investigated by those *qualified* to study abroad, there are considerations that must be taken into account before one devotes too much time and thought to pursuing such a program:

First, even though the total cost, including transportation, is less than that of attending college near home, it is advisable to have all the anticipated funds at hand or assured before departing. Americans, especially students under 21, have a difficult time getting jobs in foreign countries.

Second, there are few scholarships for foreign study at the undergraduate level. Most grants are fellowships, which means they are almost entirely for graduate work.

Third, an American should bear in mind that the European university, excellent though it may be, does not always offer a program that is acceptable to employers and academic institutions in this country. A student pursuing languages or history in Europe may encounter few academic hurdles when he returns, but technical courses often are not recognized except as supplementary work. The junior-year programs, on the other hand, are set up with American requirements and standards in mind. A student going abroad on his own would be wise to look into the possibility of participating in a course with which an American university is associated.

Fourth, the decision to go abroad to study should not be made in haste. This kind of education takes a good deal of careful planning, financial resources, linguistic abilities and general knowledge of the chosen country. It takes a long time to learn a language fluently enough to use it in making classroom notes, reading textbooks and taking examinations. This kind of training should begin no later than the first year of high school, and earlier if possible.

The young person planning to attend a foreign college should consult educational advisers about which school to attend for the training he wants. He should inquire if the school of his choice gives degrees recognized in the United States. He should also look into the costs of housing and job possibilities so thoroughly that there will be no major unpleasant surprises for him when he unpacks his suitcase in a strange land.

Jobs abroad

It is much more difficult for a student to earn money in Europe than in the United States, but there are *some* opportunities. Princeton University has succeeded in placing undergraduates in summer jobs with banks, hotels and business concerns in Europe, and the International Association of Students in Economics and Commerce helps a number of students obtain employment in foreign countries every year. So there are jobs, if one can find them.

Antioch College, in its work-study program (see Chapter 15), includes an optional year abroad involving jobs and classes. The work experience, although not meant primarily as economic aid, does help hold down the cost. Some Antioch students work during nine or 10 months of their year and go to school only briefly. By doing this they can finance their year and build up enough cooperative work credits toward graduation so they can spend more time studying when they get back to Yellow Springs. The students work as teachers or in offices of such organizations as UNESCO. The International Rescue Committee, the Red Cross and the YMCA and YWCA also offer opportunities. Some students work on farms, in homes or in factories. Governmental services, businesses, tourist organizations and libraries provide many opportunities. These openings suggest to other students what they might expect to find abroad. However, one should bear in mind that Antioch sends "scouts" to track down work assignments. The young person on his own might not have so easy a time finding a job for himself.

If, despite the warnings and difficulties, a young person still is intent on going abroad for a degree and has made the necessary plans and investigated the possibility thoroughly, there is no reason why he should not *try* to take undergraduate training overseas. Perhaps as more students become involved in such study, the way will become smoother. Meanwhile, a young person should bear in mind that he will be a long way from home and help. He needs to be sure he knows what he is doing.

Some suggestions

Here are some things to do to try to earn money while studying abroad—and you will note that most of them entail making the search *before you leave home:*

1. Get in touch with a consul general of the country to which you plan to go or the cultural attaché at that country's embassy and inquire about job possibilities and regulations.

2. Consult the country's tourist bureau and information service.

3. Write to American hotel organizations with establishments abroad.

4. Check with the local chamber of commerce and the United States Chamber of Commerce, the YWCA, the YMCA, the United Nations, UNESCO, American Express, banks with branches abroad, export companies and businesses with foreign branches.

5. Get in touch with the United States embassy in the country to which you are going. You might also check the State Department, the United States Information Agency, the Voice of America, Radio Free Europe and the military services to find out what they have to offer. Remember that to get a job with the United States government one usually must be over 21.

For further information on study abroad

Refer to:

A *Guide to Study Abroad*, by John A. Garraty and Walter Adams, Channel Press, Manhasset, New York.

Educational and Cultural Exchange Opportunities, Department of State, Washington, D.C.

Employment Abroad, Facts and Fallacies, Chamber of Commerce of the United States, 1615 H Street, N.W., Washington, D.C. 20066.

Handbook on International Study for U.S. Nationals, Institute of International Education, 800 Second Avenue, New York, New York 10017.

If You'd Like to Study Abroad, Science Research Associates, Inc., 259 Erie Street, Chicago, Illinois 60611.

New Horizons in Education: the Benefits of Study Abroad, Pan American World Airways, New York, New York (available in book stores).

Study Abroad, 1964–65, UNESCO Publications Center, New York, New York.

Work, Study, Travel Abroad, National Student Association, 265 Madison Avenue, New York, New York 10017, and 2161 Shattuck Avenue, Berkeley, California 94704.

Write to:

Chamber of Commerce of the United States, 1615 H Street, N.W., Washington, D.C. 20006.

Experiment in International Living, Putney, Vermont.

Institute of International Education.

National Student Association.

Pan American Union, Washington, D.C. 20006.

18

HELPING HANDS

... the guidance counselor

The "bread and butter" avenues of help offered students and families in college financing are many. Most of those discussed in the preceding pages have emphasized actual dollars-and-cents planning, but there is still another kind of help that should be sought whenever it is available. That is the advice offered by the school guidance counselor, who can exert an influence on the lives of students second only to that of parents as far as looking ahead to college is concerned.

This new educational specialty—or at least new variation of the older profession of vocational counseling—has been developed in the recent national rush for college. Although the personal and psychological needs of youngsters and their families take up an enormous amount of counseling time, an important part of the work is the practical matter of financial and career planning for college or other post-high-school training. The counselor can be of considerable service in awakening a youngster and his family to the realization that *it is never too early to start planning for college—* but it can be too late.

A *counseling schedule*

While most counseling for college is offered in high schools, the elementary grades or junior high school are considered by many guidance experts to be the ideal time to begin consultations on the college question. The seventh or eighth grade seems to be the best time for a student to seek out an adviser—if an adviser has not already made an appointment with him—to evaluate his talents and determine whether he should be nurtured as college material. The counselor begins by testing the student's scholastic aptitudes to find where he stands and to discover any latent capabilities that need development. If the answers warrant it, the counselor helps the student plan for college, keeping his interests and aptitudes in mind.

In the ninth grade the college-minded student enrolls in the basic science, mathematics, English and foreign language courses he will need for admission to almost any college. Counselor and parents encourage him to apply himself so he will earn good marks. Aiming scholastically for the top colleges is likely to assure one of acceptance at others.

It is not too early to start learning in the ninth grade about the colleges themselves. A youngster should undertake his search for the *right* college by scanning catalogues provided by the counselor or sent for by mail, and he should keep this up in the tenth grade while also taking additional college preparatory courses and branching out to engage in extracurricular activities of potential help in developing his talents.

All college possibilities should be investigated as thoroughly as possible. When one considers the investment involved and the future career years that are at stake, it is clearly unwise to buy a college education without shopping for it. Consumers often seem to give more consideration to the purchase of a $2,500 automobile than to four years of college costing four times that or more. The automobile is replaceable but the college course can never be bought again.

By the time a student is in the junior year, he ought to have a fair idea of what various schools have to offer him. He and his counselor now draw up a list of half a dozen or so to visit. When he and his family go to a school, they are making a mistake if they limit the call to a scenic tour of the campus. A youngster properly advised by a counselor will have been in correspondence with the admissions director and will try to stop in and speak with him. If possible the campus visit should coincide with a conference for prospective students. Colleges usually keep counselors apprised of such events, which often are posted on high-school bulletin boards.

Get to know old grads

It sometimes helps to become acquainted with a graduate of a school in which one is interested. The alumnus can give advice and much information that is not in the catalogue. He also may line up a scholarship or other sources of aid. The school counselor sometimes can direct a student to a graduate of a particular college or university for an informal chat; if he does not know any graduates of a particular school, he may advise the student to write to its alumni office and ask for names. Students who live in large cities can get in touch with the local alumni chapter or consult a fraternity or sorority.

Scouting for students

There are few if any high schools of any standing that are not visited by college recruiting experts at least once a year. Alert counselors maintain a number of such contacts and arrange for college orientation days at which students and representatives of colleges and universities sit down and exchange views. The scouts sent out by institutions of higher learning are looking for the best scholars, of course, but they can be of assistance to the average students, too.

As part of such orientation programs, a number of colleges and universities arrange for the circulation of film strips and recordings about their programs through an organization such as Guidance Associates of Pleasantville, New York. These often give a more graphic idea of what campus life is about than could ever be gleaned from a catalogue.

Time for tests and applications

While all these explorations and investigations are under way, the counselor will have started the college aspirant on the examination trail with a Preliminary Scholastic Aptitude Test (better known as PSAT) in his junior year. In the latter half of the year, the student also will take a National Merit Qualifying Test. In the senior year the student will begin applying to colleges and will take the College Entrance Examination Board examinations. His parents will start filling out the financial forms they must submit if they want to be considered for financial aid—one for the National Merit program, one for the local branch of the Fall River Dollars for Scholars plan and one for the College Scholarship Service.

The student will then send application forms to the colleges in which he is interested and for which he and his counselor feel he is eligible. Hopefully, through the counselor's encouragement, the student's family will have been setting aside money since at least the eighth grade, if not before.

If he has been well advised by his counselor, a student will apply to a wide variety of colleges, not just the Ivy League schools or other prestige institutions. There are good schools across the nation and the counselor, in making recommendations, should give consideration to the geographic situation of his students as well as their financial status.

In helping a student shop for a college, the well-equipped counselor will invite him to study some of the freshman class profiles prepared by the College Scholarship Service and will show him the handbook compiled for counselors of college-bound students by the Association of College Admissions Counselors. The counselor's files should also be well stocked with current lists of scholarships being offered locally as well as nationally, including descriptions of how to go about applying for them.

The complexities of counseling

Clearly, college counseling can be an exacting task. The adviser should start by gathering material about scholarships and data on the individuals who want them, then should pass out information about grants to deserving pupils, trying to suggest the right grant for each. To do this effectively the counselor will need information about the tests and qualifications required, application forms and filing dates. The various forms used in applying for financial need also should be on hand. All of this material must be kept up to date, which is a staggering job of research, collation and dissemination. Just how large it is becomes clear when one considers that thousands of scholarships are awarded each year, many of them locally, and that 2,000 colleges and universities publish materials. The countless vocational possibilities compound the complexities of counseling.

"Counseling, as it is seen in the secondary schools today, has evolved rapidly in the past 10 or 15 years," says Loren L. Benson, chairman of the counseling department in a Hopkins, Minnesota, high school and former president of the American School Counselor Association. "It is basically a postwar development, although guidance programs have been present for a number of years and the idea of vocational guidance dates back to almost 1910.

"You will find that there are many differences in programs and in the amount of training of counselors in various parts of the country, as well as ratio problems. You might find some schools with as small a load as 185 students per counselor and some schools with no counseling programs at all or a fantastic ratio of 1,500 or

1,600 to 1, in which a counselor can do little more than meet the crisis needs of those people demanding the most attention."

Benson emphasizes that the field of counseling involves far more than merely planning ahead for college. Counselors are expected to give personal, psychological and vocational advice as well as information about higher education. However, Benson points out that high schools need extensive files of information and many reference sources that can be used by students in finding college opportunities. Some school counselors issue periodic bulletins listing scholarships and deadlines for applying for them. They also guide students in finding ways to get information for themselves.

There is today an estimated total of 33,000 full-time, trained guidance counselors in the nation's secondary schools. To achieve a national minimum of a counselor for every 300 high school students set by the American School Counselor Association, there should be more than 50,000 counselors. The federal government has recognized the need for more and better counseling with a $65 million grant under the National Defense Education Act to support and expand local guidance programs. Federal money also pays for the administering of millions of scholastic aptitude and achievement tests.

A matter of parental concern

A discussion of counseling inevitably leads to consideration of the need for parents to learn more about the real talents and capabilities of their children and to become better informed about opportunities for training beyond high school but apart from academic colleges. The parents of low-aptitude students must learn to accept the fact that their youngsters simply are not college material. A wish for college is a natural outgrowth of an unrealistic insistence on college for everyone as a "right." Parents of students with lower aptitudes were found in a recent survey to be more likely to want college degrees for their children than did the children themselves. Instead of the youngsters being "under-achievers," their parents were "overaspirers." At the same time, parents of youths with high ability seemed to under-aspire for them, educationally speaking.

Some people regard a higher education as the *right* of every person in the country. Perhaps it would be better to say that every person with the capability and desire for a higher education is entitled to seek it. Better dissemination of information about vocational training opportunities and increased efforts to give the vocationally trained person a status more equal to that of the college graduate might help overcome the idea that college attendance is either a necessity or a right. This is an area in which guidance counselors can and often do render a real service.

For further information on guidance counseling

Refer to:

A *Handbook for the Counselors of College Bound Students*, Association of College Admissions Counselors, 610 Church Street, Evanston, Illinois.

Counselor Education . . . a Progress Report on Standards, American Personnel and Guidance Association, 1605 New Hampshire Avenue, N.W., Washington, D.C. 20009.

Financing a College Education, a Guide for Counselors, College Entrance Examination Board, 475 Riverside Drive, New York, New York 10027.

The Counselor in a Changing World, by C. Gilbert Wrenn, American Personnel and Guidance Association.

The Personnel and Guidance Journal, American Personnel and Guidance Association ($10 a year).

Write to:

American School Counselor Association of the American Personnel and Guidance Association, 1605 New Hampshire Avenue, N.W., Washington, D.C. 20009.

Guidance Associates, Pleasantville, New York.

19

WHAT ARE YOU DOING?

... a checklist for the college-bound

If you are a parent, now is the time to ask yourself, "What am I doing to help my children get a college education?" If you are a student, you might wonder, "What am I doing to help myself and my parents get me through college?" If you are a parent, are you planning ahead financially or leaving the matter to chance and the *hope* that your children are going to be smart enough (and poor enough) to win scholarships? If you are a student, are you working and saving to help pay for college? If you foresee financial difficulties, are you thinking about alternatives that might prove less costly?

Is service in the Army, Navy or Air Force going to help solve your problem? Perhaps going to night school and working days will be the answer. Don't forget about the opportunities of junior colleges. And by all means do not leave work-study institutions off your list just because their administrations play down the earning aspects of the programs; you may find a course and job that not only will be educationally beneficial but also will keep you going financially. There is, as you have seen, a wide range of choice before you. The important thing is that you *do something*, whether you are a student job-hunting or a parent counting pennies or trying to help start a Dollars for Scholars chapter or some other scholarship movement.

Hopefully, you have found some answers in the preceding pages. If you have, *now* is the time to put what you have learned to work. As was stated at the outset, right now is the right time to begin preparing—tomorrow may be too late. What are you going to do about it *today*?

To help you decide how you are going to approach the matter of college financing, the following checklist is provided for your guidance. The sources of specific information and aid listed at the end of each chapter will help you decide what to do after you have checked off the list. You will find that you can outline *your own plan* for financing college.

If you are a student . . .

1. Have you had a conference with your school guidance counselor on opportunities available for scholarships and what you can do to plan for college?

2. Have you decided upon a career or profession?

3. Have you drawn up a list of your six favorite colleges and written to them for catalogues, scholarship information and data on student aid?

4. Have you started saving money to help pay for your education?

5. Have you arranged for a weekend or part-time job?

6. Have you started learning a skill that will help you get a job in college—typing, shorthand, library work and the like?

7. Have you been concentrating on getting good grades so you will have an easier time getting aid if you need it?

8. Have you investigated application or test times for the National Merit Scholarship Awards, the College Entrance Examination Board, the Fall River Dollars for Scholars stipends and other awards?

9. Have you checked with local clubs, churches, businesses and fraternal organizations to find out whether they have scholarships?

10. Have you looked up the alumni of the colleges in which you are interested to learn about campus life in detail and perhaps enlist support in obtaining a scholarship and a job?

11. Have you sent for information on government aid programs, mainly loans that benefit students?

12. Have you sought information on government training programs and on opportunities in the armed forces?

If you are a parent . . .

1. Have you started a realistic program to plan for college?
Savings?
Investments?
Insurance?
Bonds?

2. Have you computed your present assets under the formulas of the College Scholarship Service and the National Merit Corporation to see if you could pay for college today?

3. Have you computed college costs, based on your child's list of schools, for the time he will enroll in college, using the projection of a 5 per cent yearly increase in tuition?

4. Have you talked with your child's guidance counselor to find out how you can help and what you can do to encourage him to work toward college?

5. Have you sent for information and started studying the various loan programs so that when the time for college comes you can make an educated choice and not rush headlong into a high-cost program?

6. Have you arranged to take your child on a tour of his favorite colleges so all of you will know what you are planning for?

7. Have you helped your child plan a college preparatory course and encouraged him to work for good grades so he will have a chance for a scholarship?

8. Have you discussed your child's career goals in detail so you can help guide him to the right choice?

9. Have you made sure whether your child is of college caliber or better equipped for a vocational school?

10. Have you written to the department of education in your state capital for information on your state's college aid program?

11. Have you sought to join or start a Dollars for Scholars chapter in your community?

12. Have you joined a credit union, if one is available where you work, on the chance you might want to borrow from it for college?

These are some of the important things you can do to plan ahead. Some concentrated thinking will surely suggest other questions and courses of action that arise from your particular situation. If you, the student, and you, the parent, have taken none of the steps listed, you may be headed for difficulty when college enrollment time comes. The best advice for you is to get started now, *today*, on a program. If you have done some of the things on the list, you have taken the first steps in the right direction. If, however, you are among the minority that has done something about all of the things listed, it would be surprising indeed if you encountered any real college financial problems. You will have arrived at your own program for beating the high cost of college—with or without a scholarship. Good luck!

ACKNOWLEDGMENTS

Every person and organization mentioned in this book had a role, directly or indirectly, in its creation. Obviously it is not possible to single out each of them for a word of thanks here, but the gratitude is no less heartfelt.

As is to be expected in the preparation of a book of this type, however, there have been some individuals and groups that have been so generous in sharing information and advice that I would be remiss were I not to express a special "thank you" to them.

First, then, a word of appreciation to the Reverend David R. Wilkerson, director of Teen Challenge, for introducing me to Bernard Geis, the publisher of this book. Second, to Faye Henle, who makes sense out of dollars on radio station WOR in New York, for generously sharing with me many of the fruits of her research on the subject of college financing.

Help came from many other sources as well. Dr. Irving Fradkin, founder and president of the Citizens' Scholarship Foundation, was a continuous source of assistance and encouragement, as was William R. Young, director of public relations of the National Merit Scholarship Corporation. Rexford G. Moon Jr., director of the College Scholarship Service, and David S. Owen, assistant director, provided extensively of their expert knowledge in the presentation of the need analysis discussions. Murray Frankel, a top salesman of the Prudential Insurance Company of America, took considerable time from his busy schedule to discuss financing college through insurance and to draw up sample programs. Joe Jefferson, director of the College Admissions Center, and Ellen M. McCune, assistant director, cleared up a number of questions about college admissions procedures. The Credit Union National Association and several of its officials were equally helpful with financial information.

A major source of information was, of course, the United States Office of Education of the Department of Health, Education and Welfare, largely through Dr. Martin Mayes, acting director of information, and Dr. J. Harold Goldthorpe, specialist for financial assistance of the division of higher education. Richard H. Grant, director of public information of the Investment Company Institute, rounded up considerable data on mutual funds, and Dudley Harmon, executive director of the Massachusetts Higher Education Assistance Corporation, explained the administration of state college loans to the author.

The story of correspondence study was told with a great deal of assistance from Hal V. Kelly, director of information of the National Home Study Council, while Graydon De Land, general manager of the college division of Stanley Home Products, was his usual helpful self in preparation of the discussion of the role of direct selling in working one's way through college.

Special contributions were made also by the public relations staff of the American Association of Junior Colleges and by Ed Wieland, director of the education and scholarship programs of the American Legion. Each of a number of appeals for information made to Stephen B. Friedheim, director of public relations of the American Personnel and Guidance Association, brought an immediate response.

On the college level, those who were unusually cooperative in-

cluded: Mrs. Jessie Cambron Treichler, public relations director of
Antioch College; Janet L. Dunkelbarger, news director of Vassar
College; James Z. Zigerell, administrative assistant of Chicago City
Junior College; Sheldon Garber, of the information staff of the
University of Chicago; John P. De Camp, public relations director
of the University of Cincinnati; G. H. Baughman Jr., program di-
rector of the Drexel Institute of Technology; Dustin M. Burke, direc-
tor of student employment at Harvard University; Dr. Sharvey
Umbeck, president of Knox College; Lt. Cmdr. Harry P. Hart of the
U.S. Merchant Marine Academy; Gil Goodwin, director of the news
service of the University of Michigan; John S. Bailey, director of
public relations of Northeastern University; Robert Beyers, of the
Stanford University news office; George Sweeney, news director of
Pomona College; and Dr. Elwood P. Kastner, dean of financial aid,
John M. Buckey, director of placement services, and William A.
Spencer, director of information at New York University.

I wish to say a special word of appreciation to W. Clement Stone,
president of the Combined Insurance Company of America, and
William H. Meyers, director of advertising and public relations of
that company, for their moral support and their many helpful suggestions about the book when it was in the preparation stages.

The "most special" word is for my husband, Max L. Lowenthal Jr.
Few writers have the advantage of professional editorial advice at
the breakfast table or the high standards set by this particular family
editor. He never complains about my cooking but when it comes to
hashing up verb forms—well. . . .

CLAIRE COX

INDEX